2004

PSYCHOLOGY OF ADOLESCENTS

PSYCHOLOGY OF ADOLESCENTS

THOMAS A. PRESTER
EDITOR

Nova Science Publishers, Inc.
New York

Senior Editors: Susan Boriotti and Donna Dennis
Coordinating Editor: Tatiana Shohov
Office Manager: Annette Hellinger
Graphics: Wanda Serrano
Editorial Production: Vladimir Klestov, Matthew Kozlowski, Tom Moceri,
      Anthony T. Sovik, Alexandra Columbus and Maya Columbus
Circulation: Ave Maria Gonzalez, Vera Popovic, Luis Aviles, Raymond Davis,
      Melissa Diaz, Marlene Nunez and Jeannie Pappas
Communications and Acquisitions: Serge P. Shohov
Marketing: Cathy DeGregory

Library of Congress Cataloging-in-Publication Data
Available upon request

ISBN 1-59033-727-1

CONTENTS

PREFACE

In an age of duct tape dilemmas when the head of the Department of Home Security prepares emergency kits for his dogs, terrorists reportedly lurking under every bed, and family life unraveling, is it any wonder that adolescents seem to have a difficult time coping? This new book gathers important research in adolescent psychology that helps shed light on some of the problems and responses of our youth.

Chapter 1

ADOLESCENT ADDICTION AND RECOVERY: A STUDY IN EXTREMES

Courtney Vaughn
University of Oklahoma
Norman, Oklahoma
Wesley Long
Family and Adolescent Support Systems
Oklahoma City, Oklahoma

FABLED THINKING VERSUS RATIONAL THOUGHT

It is almost impossible to describe the despondence and hope that we observed and felt during and after our work with adolescent addiction, truly a study of extremes. Just being an adolescent is not easy. Such youngsters are prone to "fabled thinking," such as: "I am invincible and will never become addicted, get pregnant, or die prematurely. Logical 'consequences ... do not apply to me'" (Mitchell, 1998, 31). As we listened to the stories of 14 participants who attempted recovery from substance addiction during adolescence, we observed how fabled thought catapulted them into the abyss of addiction. Temporarily, they were totally unable to deal with turbulent emotions and conflicts, often related to their desires for intimacy and identity (Golden and Schwarts, cited in Polcin, 1992; Irwin, 1993; Moore & Rosenthal, 1993).

Miraculously, 11, and perhaps 12 of the 14 rose out of the ashes to become clean and sober. Gradually they learned, formally, to reason, by following the Twelve Steps of Alcoholics Anonymous (AA) or Narcotics Anonymous (NA), involving surrender to a "higher power," the practice of a Golden Rule, rigorous self-assessment, and atonement for past and continuing unacceptable acts (Appendix A; Mitchell, 1998; Overton, 1991). As a result, each made strides toward establishing a strong identity, becoming "a whole ... person, ... connected with others and yet true to oneself" (Hewitt, cited in Mitchell, 1998).

Thus, for each of those in recovery, adolescent addiction had been the best and worst of times. Highly vulnerable, these youngsters were susceptible to addiction; yet they were also driven to "find themselves" and graced with the faculties to do so. We came to understand why researchers such as Bauer (1994) noted that adolescence may be "an optimal time for healing" (i).

FOCUSING ON FOURTEEN LIVED EXPERIENCES

Striving for an in-depth look at the phenomena of adolescent addiction and recovery, ours was an existential phenomenological study, focusing on the individual perceptions of those who had experienced both (Denzin, 1993; Moustakes, 1994; Swadi, 1992; Tesch, 1990). At the suggestion of teachers, counselors, and administrators from a nationally recognized school/treatment center for young people, we selected seven teenagers: Anthony, an African- and Ali, a Jordanian-American; Melinda, a mixed Native; and Lisa, Jessica, John, and Mick, all Euro-Americans. Ali's family was upper middle class, while the remainder came from lower-middle to underclass homes. Each of these participants were at least six months into the recovery process and projected to have success. The program centered on the Twelve Steps.

The seven adult participants, Linda, Karlie, Jesse, David, Tom, Clint, and Noah had begun recovery as teens. They ranged in age from 21 to 32 and claimed five to fifteen years without drugs or alcohol. We obtained their names through extensive interviews with prominent AA and NA members who sponsored or were well-acquainted with them. All white, these participants consisted of two females and five males. Together the 14 families of origin ranged the socioeconomic spectrum, from under-, lower-, middle-, to upper-middle-class. Because each was relatively young and still building a career, none but Noah might be considered affluent, and only David and Karlie were middle-class.

We conducted open-ended interviews with each one, generating a life history and in-depth responses to questions relating to their demise and subsequent efforts to become and remain clean and sober. Addressing trustworthiness of the younger participants' data we employed ethnographic triangulation techniques: over a year period of time we re-interviewed the seven adolescent participants, and, when possible, questioned selected family members, counselors, and teachers to verify important points. Because the older participants had been active in Twelve Step programs for a number of years, the stress on "rigorous honesty," a linchpin of sobriety, was an excellent portent for a forthright interview (Marshall et al., 1994). After transcribing the data, we individually identified meaning units and resulting themes that described the phenomena of addiction and recovery. Understanding the former, we discovered, was crucial to comprehending the latter. Then, we compared results, finding no major areas of disagreement (Moustakes, 1994; Tesch, 1990).

MOM AND DAD
WOULD THEY "FLIP OUT" OR "GIVE US CANDY?"

As children none of the participants was cradled by consistency or boundaries. Nor were most of their caretakers able to give them much attention and love because often the adults were addicts and mentally ill. Divorced or dead parents were the norm, while physical, sexual, and emotional abuse was common.

Linda, Melinda, David, and Tom lived in homes with mentally ill mothers. Twenty-one at the time of our study, Linda's parents had been divorced for 13 years. A paranoid-schizophrenic, her mother, Roberta, became profoundly depressed and generally abdicated her maternal responsibility to Linda and her older sister. Melinda's parents never wed, but when the child was ten her mother married a recovering alcoholic, a union that produced a son. The couple divorced when Melinda was ten, and her mother became profoundly depressed. Like Linda's mother, Melinda's, almost totally withdrew.

She said she couldn't handle us kids, ... and her solution was just to go to her room and not to look at it. ... [I] wanted them [mother and step-father] back together because it really hurt and everything because I missed my dad, and it wasn't the same.

David's mother and father divorced when he was five. Later diagnosed as schizophrenic, his mother used drugs and alcohol openly and moved her three children from place to place. Tom's parents were recovering alcoholics, but his father relapsed twice, and his mother was clinically depressed. Tom remembered:

That could be pretty disruptive to a household--scary. She'd get weird. We'd be out on a vacation, and she would be kind of silent and moody, and obviously in a space where we couldn't ever really reach her--just be real weepy. And so we'd be out on this vacation, and we'd have to go home all of a sudden. [I was] 13, 14 when I realized this was going on. And I blamed myself.

Anthony's and John's mothers failed them in different ways. When Anthony was ten his parents broke up and his mother, Anthony, and the other children in the family moved into a government housing project. She became an addict making her a normal fixture in the drug infested community. John, on the other hand, longed for any kind of mother because his died when he was six. Having no participating father, John went to live with his grandfather who also died. Eventually, Jake, a neighbor, adopted him.

Karlie and Lisa were victims of physical and sexual abuse. Karlie was the second of two daughters, whose middle-class parents were alcoholics and drug users. The family's finances were always precarious, and Karlie's life was turbulent. Her father beat and molested her. For a time, Karlie's mother did not stop him. She did, eventually, file for a divorce and quit using drugs and alcohol, attending AA frequently. However, gone much of the time, the woman thoughtlessly kept a loaded gun in a house wherein lived a profoundly disturbed child. "I wanted to die. ... I would put [the gun] to my head. I would watch commercials on TV, and at the end of the commercial think that it could all be over in about thirty seconds," Karlie recalled. Lisa's parents were heroine addicts. They ultimately divorced, but only after spending several years in a physically violent relationship. Her father regularly bludgeoned her mother. One night, after an orgy of drug use, he lay comatose while one of his male friends raped Lisa, throwing $40 on her bed before leaving. During the next few years Lisa and her older sister lived in one foster home after another.

Male children were sexually and physically abused, as well. Twenty-two year old Jesse's incompatible parents divorced when he was a year old. Four years later, one of his father's male friends molested him. Mick's father used drugs and alcohol and battered his sons, sandwiched between boughts of excessive kindness. "We didn't know what he was going to be like when he came in, ... if he was going to flip out about what happened at work today, or if he was going to bring some candy to us." When Mick was 12 his parents divorced. Clint spoke for many of the battered, declaring, "I was a pissed-off little kid. I carried a knife and a gun to school in the second grade, and we used to steal mail out of other people's mail boxes on the way to school." Most of his hostility arose from the regular beatings he received from his alcoholic father, a career military man. He stated firmly, "I had seen the 'Brady Bunch,' and I knew that we did not have a normal family life."

Several older siblings also abused various participants. Jessica's parents divorced when she was quite young. Eventually, her father served time in a penitentiary for alcohol-related offenses and died a few years after his release. When Jessica was 11 her mother re-married, and Jessica's new step brother began to terrorize her. Once he pointed a gun to her "head and pulled the trigger, and there weren't any bullets in it." When Jesse was ten, an older brother began regularly attacking him. This lasted two years, ending when "I could finally kick his ass." Needless to say, Jesse felt alone and isolated.

NUMBING THE PAIN
"IT WAS THE ONLY RELIEF I COULD FIND"

Given the heartbreaking turbulence of their early lives, all of the participants became poly-drug users. Marijuana, acid, cocaine, crank, crystal methane, crack cocaine, ecstasy, PCP, and alcohol headed the list. With the exception of Ali, parents kept alcohol if not drugs in their homes, making them readily available to children. Usually initiated into the world of drugs and alcohol by parents and older siblings, the participants were young--ranging from age 6 to 14. Thus, the inevitable downward spiral was set in motion early.

It seemed to the participants that educators in all of their schools, public and private, either denied their problems or were unable to help them. Anthony explained, "I went to school one day and the principal told me in his office that he felt I was causing problems for students and staff." Anthony received a one-half time suspension until further notice. But notification never came, and his mother never followed up.

If some adults tried to ignore the problem, others used drugs and alcohol with the youngsters. Jessica confided, "I never paid for it [drugs]. The only thing I've ever bought was a six-pack of beer." Tom concurred, recalling, "We would ride our bicycles up to the 7-11 and wait for somebody [an adult] to come along and buy us beer." Even after Tom returned from treatment he found it hard to stay clean and had to drop out of an alternative school because a teacher smoked marijuana with the students. When Linda was eight and her sister twelve, the older girl dated a man in his twenties who obtained drugs and alcohol for both girls. At 14 David's alcoholic parents sent him to treatment; he had been using since the age of eight. After 30 days they picked him up, took him to a party on their yacht, and, along with all of their friends, got roaring drunk. David added that, later, in military school, "Mom came to the rescue by sending me grass [marijuana] in the mail."

Associations with drug abusing siblings also engendered a sense of false intimacy, and brought on intense situations in which the teenagers were unable to differentiate themselves from those with whom they formed "close" bonds. The result was promiscuity, violence, and completely diffused identities. Like soldiers in a foxhole, siblings were drawn to escape together. Speaking for both daughters, Linda stated, "It was the only relief I could find ... to live and not feel my life." At 12, Mick also began using with his brother, obtaining their first marijuana from their father's "stash." By the time Mick was 16 he was addicted to crack cocaine. At seven, Jesse's brothers introduced him to alcohol and later to marijuana. "I liked the feeling that [drugs] gave me. I didn't feel like crap all of the time, because they [parents] were always telling me what a piece of crap I was." However, by 14, his life revolved around using--drugs, alcohol, and women. Jesse had sex with two and three girls a day, was violent toward male and female friends, sold drugs, used various substances intravenously, and attended one party after another.

As Jesse's case illustrated, lost and alienated siblings found like-minded peers. Elaborating on these relationships, David described his military school experience:

> The one thing everybody ought to know about military schools is everybody puts their troubled children in them to straighten us all up together, and really what it does is give us a place to sit down and compare notes--how to be better deviants. There were some seriously disturbed people there. I became an exceptional liar.

Also trying to isolate the "problem child," Noah's divorced parents sent him to boarding schools that were filled with other troubled but wealthy youth. This was a tremendous mistake, because drugs and alcohol were constantly smuggled in and, as a result, Noah's substance use increased. He did graduate and enrolled in college, but after his best friend died in an automobile accident, he lapsed into a profound depression: "I drank from the time I got up until the time I went to bed."

Clint's use was so bad that "It got to the point that I didn't know who I was, didn't care who I was, knew I was doing myself wrong, but just didn't care." But really, he did, desperately seeking the unconditional approval and love of a girl. She regularly gave him money for drugs, but, testing her further, Clint insisted she have sex with him in a school bathroom. He described getting caught by teachers. "It made no sense whatsoever. They saw us, and I tried to deny it. 'You didn't see what you saw!'" When their relationship ended Clint began an affair with an older married woman and her daughter. At 17, he was hopelessly addicted.

Other participants' claimed that they began using explicitly to be accepted by peers. Tom hungered to "fit in [with friends], so I tried it [marijuana], and I loved it." Like Clint, when Tom discovered sex, he immediately fell in love, but "she left, and that was devastating. All I had left at that time were [drugs and alcohol]. There was a period of time where I just didn't care if I died or not. I would just go out and drink [and] got in a legal scrape or two." Soon, going for 24 hours without a drink became impossible. At 13 Melinda was even "afraid to use, but they started teasing me and calling me names, and I felt I had to. ... I thought they would stop being my friends." A few years later, Melinda's mother banished her from the house, and her step-father insisted that she be put in treatment.

Six of the seven adolescent participants were in gangs. As a preteen, John began using marijuana, and at 13 he was participating in gang-related felonious acts. According to him, gang membership gave young people a "sense of security that is involved in it and the sense of love that they feel from other people. They probably haven't gotten it in any of their life." Eventually, like many of the other participants, John was arrested. His list of crimes included destruction of property, assault and battery, theft, and petty larceny. He was tried, convicted, and sentenced to a drug treatment program.

Racial antagonisms also helped lead to gang involvement that further alienated participants from the dominant society. The non-white youngsters recounted painful rejections that encouraged their drug abuse. When noticed at all, Ali was called "camel jockey" and "sand nigger." He explained:

> I was a good wrestler and didn't get any attention from that. Our school was big on wrestling, and I thought this would make me more popular. When a guy who was kicked off the wrestling team invited me to his house I thought this was the beginning for me. All they did was get high, and before long I was getting high with them, buying drugs, and giving them away so that students would like me.

Sadly, Melinda was rejected by both non-white and white youth. Reared "like a Caucasian" she could not find acceptance with Native students who practiced various tribal traditions. Nor were the Euro-American students very accommodating. Melinda lamented, "It was hard making and keeping friends, and I thought and still do that a lot of it had to do with my race."

USING BEATS LIVING "I'LL NEVER MAKE IT"

Initially, Melinda, Anthony, and Ali used before the one-year anniversary of their sobriety. This occurred for several of the older participants, who eventually could claim numerous years of clean living (DeJong, 1994; Friedman et al., 1986; Rush, 1979; Swadi, 1992). Currently, Ali is sober again, but he continues to struggle with racially- and ethnically-oriented issues. According to ethnic identity development models and the lives of noted Americans such as Malcolm X, a young person of color may feel self-hatred due to dominant cultural stereotypes. Such insecurities are often overcome by insulating oneself in a separatist setting, surrounded by positive supporters and role models (Bennett, 1999; X & Haley, 1966). Melinda, Anthony, and to some extent Ali did not experience that while using or in sobriety.

After spending some time in treatment, Anthony's prognosis was positive. He worked on a GED, and his counselors observed him successfully managing his emotions. But after his release, the old frustrations surfaced when dealing with the white world. He told us, "When you're not high white people think you are; when you're not stealing, white people think you are; when you're looking for work, white people think you ain't." Reflecting on Anthony's words, he may have been saying, "I'll never make it."

Ali left treatment as a star. He had shown leadership abilities and considerable emotional and academic growth. But racial issues encouraged Ali's relapse as well. After attending an AA meeting, two attractive white (blond) women approached him for a ride home. Ali complied. Flattered by the attention, he became an easy target. Like other pretenders who attend Twelve Step meetings, these women were only there to prey on unsuspecting youngsters like Ali, who had transportation and could help them sell drugs. Soon Ali was smoking and selling crack; he was arrested and ultimately sent to prison. While incarcerated he told us, "I feel so stupid. I should have known that a woman in her thirties wouldn't want a man not even 20. She needed someone with a car, access to money, and crazy enough to supply her needs."

Neither were Ali's, Melinda's, or Anthony's families and communities very supportive. While in treatment, Melinda wanted "her [mother] to know how I was doing, and how I was working on trying to get home. ... She came once during my stay and only stayed thirty minutes. Me and my father pleaded with her to stay, and she wouldn't." Melinda's stepfather refused to let her live with her brother and him after her release. She called her brother a few times but then disappeared, and, eventually was presumed dead.

As in John's case Anthony's family and friends threw a party for him, but it was not a church social. At the least, alcohol was served, and his brother and mother encouraged him to partake. Once again, Anthony faced the pressure to be the "man of the house" and provide financially for his entire family. Combined with his own addictive tendencies and the desperate desire to appear successful, Anthony was soon selling drugs. Arrested, convicted, and sentenced to prison, at the time of this writing, Anthony is alone, locked in a cell contemplating his fate.

In other ways, Ali's family never showed consistent support. Filled with shame, his father spoke openly in a treatment center family meeting, "it is uncommon for a person from Jordan to involve him-self with drugs, and Ali has shamed the family." That was one of the family's first and last visits. But following Ali's treatment center stint, his parents gave him an expensive car. It was as if they could only show him love when he appeared to be "normal." At this writing, Ali has been released from prison, declared his sobriety, and claimed a newfound sense of self. He is working, beginning to feel more unconditional acceptance from his family, and attempting to embrace his ethnic self (Garrod et al., 1992). If Ali's family can remain supportive, rather than enabling, and Ali adheres to the structure and advice of the Twelve Steps and their sincere followers, he has a chance (Craig, 1993; Marshall & Marshall, 1993; Walfish et al., 1990).

CRISIS, SURRENDER, SPIRITUALITY, AND REASON
"GOD, DON'T EVER LET ME LOSE THIS FEELING"

Each of the survivors talked about what Twelve Steppers call a "bottom," which, hopefully, Ali has attained. It is a crisis when the user realizes that all human assistance seems futile and only a spiritual commitment can save her/him. Many of the participants first experienced such a "surrender" while in 30-day-treatment or living in a half-way house afterwards (Hall, 1985; Nowinski, 1990; Prezioso, 1986; Reinert et al., 1995; Tiebout, 1944, 1953, 1954). At the tender age of 14, Linda went out one night with a carload of friends, drinking and taking a handful of pills. When she became violent and out of control, the group drove her home and pushed her out of the car on to Bev's (the neighbor's) front lawn. She dragged Linda, barely conscious, into her house and called Roberta, Linda's mother. Linda adored Bev who had, months earlier, banned the troubled girl from her home. Being poured back into that house must have been cathartic because, at that moment, Linda thought:

I just couldn't do it anymore. I knew I needed some help. I could hear them, but I couldn't see them. I was lying on the floor, and my best friend's mom [Bev] was the only person I would listen to, because I thought she was the greatest person in the world. Even though she had said that I wasn't allowed in her house anymore, I felt like that was the best thing that she could have done for her daughter, and I respected her for that, because I knew what I was.

That night, with Linda's consent, Roberta put her daughter in a 30-day treatment program. There, Linda was introduced to the Twelve Steps, but for her just getting through a day without using was about all she could muster. At the suggestion of her counselors, Linda moved into a halfway house after her time expired at the treatment center. At 14, she was the youngest resident, giving her a modicum of special attention. When a 13 year-old checked in, Linda reacted badly, psychologically mistreating the youngster. At a group counseling session other residents confronted Linda, pointing out the pettiness in her behavior. Linda ran out of the session and into her room. What followed was a surrender experience:

> I sat in this big red chair, and I'm like, 'OK, damn it, I'm going to try this thing,' And I can't remember what I said, but it wasn't a long prayer, because I wasn't sure how to pray anyway. I just said a simple little prayer, and I instantly felt better. I was crying hysterically, and I instantly quit crying. I just felt a little peace. And that's when I started believing in God, and that's when I knew that this deal (Twelve Steps) was going to work for me. I just gave some part of me over to Him.

Jesse's mother also sent him to treatment after he almost killed one of his best friends, but Jesse faked his first few months in recovery. While living in a halfway house, Jesse's NA sponsor Jack, another recovering addict, introduced him to Melissa. It was through this relationship that Jesse finally broke through his own facade. One day, Melissa

> got in my face, yelling at me. I didn't want to listen to what she was telling me. 'It's not your fault that you got molested, that your dad didn't want any part of your life, that your brother beat you up.' It took everything I had to keep that stuff in. And that was the first realization that came to me, that it wasn't my fault. ... She had to get back to work, and I went to the only place I felt comfortable, Wino Park, where I had slept strung out on crank. And I just said [to God]. 'Help!' And right at that moment, the crying stopped. I knew I was going to be OK. And I went to a meeting and cried--in front of a bunch of people.

Early in treatment, Tom was skeptical, but, eventually, he started believing, "I wasn't a bad person. I had a disease. There was a reason I did all of these crazy things." One evening, alone and quiet, Tom remembered thinking:

> In the Big Book [the AA manual] it says, 'who are you to say there is no God?' At that moment I felt like God loved me. Everything was forgiven, but there is nothing to forgive. God is not your enemy after all. I was laughing, crying. At some point I got on my knees and I thanked God. I said, 'God, don't ever let me lose this feeling.' I remember going to bed that night and sleeping peacefully and waking up the next morning, ... and God was still there.

Clint had a similar experience:

> When I went into treatment, I remember looking in the mirror when someone told me that [my] behavior was alcoholic. I remember looking at myself and thinking about the things I had done and knowing that I was out of control due to alcohol. I knew that my life was bad due to alcohol--not due to my mom, not due to my dad, not due to not doing well in school, not due to being dumb. I sat there crying, saying, 'I am an alcoholic.'

One night Jessica overdosed and was taken to a hospital. She had been found in a hotel room with eight adult men, who were arrested for drinking and having sex with a minor. She did not remember much of what happened, but the humiliation brought her to her knees. "When I finally decided to stop I asked God to help me with my drug problem, and He did. I [continue to] pray because without Him I know I would be using again and back to my old ways."

At his older brother's insistence, David began attending AA meetings; he recognized the ensuing months as a period of surrender,

> ...because there was nothing left to do. I weighed 150 pounds and I'm six foot. I looked bad. My face was sunken in. My left eye was wide open all the time--bugged out--and my right eye was almost closed. I was desperate for some answers. How in the world did my life get so fucked up? I thought I was going to die. AA offered instructions. Some genuinely nice people who wanted to help me live told me to ask God for help in the morning and thank Him at night. And I did. And it worked. Just belonging--to know that people understood my insane thinking--I found myself believing that God was going to help me. I could see it working in my life and other people's lives.

Amid the depth of a depressive drinking bout, Noah remembers praying to God, "'If you really do exist, and you are paying attention to me, and if you want the best for me, show me how I can live.' That was the first time I had prayed since I was seven years old, when I asked for my parents not to get divorced."

LIFE GOES ON
"I JUST FIGURED IF I WAS SOBER, THAT WAS ENOUGH"

Buttressed by faith and fear, the 12 sober participants used the Twelve Steps, sponsors, other NA and AA members, and some family members to help them overcome grief, alienation, and shame and to deal rationally with perplexing emotions, conflicts and identity issues (Cavaiola et al., 1990; Olmstead et al., 1991). Several problems involved the disintegration of love relationships (Polcin, 1992). Linda's boyfriend returned to drugs and alcohol, but she did not use, realizing that she would have to start all over again. When Jesse's girlfriend, Melissa, left him he persevered. Sitting by his telephone for a long period, initially, he debated whether to call his drug dealer or Jake, his NA sponsor. Praying for the strength to make the right choice, he called Jake. Jesse also turned to his mother, the loss of whose love he was really grieving. Today the two are good friends. While attending classes at a community college, John met and fell in love with a woman. Just before they were to marry, she became pregnant by another man. John was crushed but continued to work and cope with his pain through faith. Two years earlier, most certainly he would have used to numb the pain.

The participants developed the ability to foresee the potentially negative consequences of certain behaviors. After a year or two of sobriety, Tom began to feel estranged from AA. Realizing the first step in the relapse process, often, is to quit attending AA meetings, Tom went back into treatment and, after his release continued to attend AA meetings. This has helped him face his own marriage and divorce, augmented by the pain of living apart from his son. He has received a bachelor's degree and is now working on a master's. Like several of the other participants, Tom is employed in an adolescent treatment facility. The oldest participant, Tom was disturbed by the younger recovering addicts who "seem to have so many more problems than I had, such as sexual abuse, and a greater variety of drugs at their disposal." Tom persisted anyway.

Clint's initial struggle as a sober youth was to develop a moral code. For example, during the first year he continued to shoplift. "I just figured that if I was sober, that was enough." Following the Twelve Steps forced him to put himself in the shopkeepers' place. He changed his ways, finished a GED, and obtained a job counseling adolescent addicts.

At 14 Karlie began attending AA meetings. "At about two weeks into AA, I knew I was an alcoholic, and I hated it, [but] I stayed sober." Befriended by recovering adults and a strong sponsor, who listened and asked Socratic questions but did not preach, Karlie slowly began to reason through her problems (Gazzini, 1993; Myers, 1991). She finished high school and college and found a responsible job. She sang and played the guitar for entertainment, but when Karlie experienced real stress, she prayed and meditated, reassuring herself that "this too shall pass." Tracing the events in her life, Karlie summarized for herself and many of the others, "I was a kid from a war-zone home who managed to stumble into AA and be safe enough, long enough, for the steps to heal me. I built a family there" (Blume, 1994; Craig, 1993; Johnson & Pandian, 1991; Marshall & Marshall, 1993; Slagle, 1992; Stewart & Brown, 1993; Vik et al., 1992; Walfish et al., 1990).

Like Karlie, Mick found help from recovering adults. In a halfway house he was encouraged by a few older men, serious about recovery. As a result, Mick diligently worked the Twelve Steps and eventually found employment. Following a suggestion from his parole officer, Mick enrolled in a local junior college. Proud of himself, he told us,

> I get pumped about going to school. I love that, man. I love being able to say, 'hey, I'm going to college. ... I got to work,' ... makes me feel good to be productive and have an organized lifestyle. ... I pray everyday that I won't ever use again. I no longer crave drugs or alcohol. There was a time if I smelled drugs it took all I had to stop from trying to get some. Prayer has taken that away from me. I think I've beat my addiction but I got to keep going to meetings.

The families of other recovering participants played crucial roles (Stewart & Brown, 1993). Jessica's mother provided her child with the support necessary to enable Jessica's sobriety. The older woman insisted to school officials that Jessica be readmitted, and she attended support group meetings because "I want to continue to learn about addiction and how I can continue to help Jessica. When I think I have all the answers, I might quit coming." She also drove her daughter 50 miles to attend AA and NA sessions. Jessica confessed:

> I don't know what I would do without my mother. We used to have so many fights and problems. She told me she loved me, and she wanted me to stop using drugs. ... My mother works at the bank and everyone in town knows her. She told my teacher that I would be glad to talk about drugs and how they almost ruined my life. It's kind of funny that I speak to students every two weeks about staying away from drugs.

Proud that she was asked to provide drug education for her school, Jessica reasoned, "I think my assisting in the drug groups helped me. Even if I wanted to get high...I don't. I would disappoint so many people. People look up to me, and I couldn't do that to them."

John went to treatment twice but his guardian, Jake, never abandoned him. He attended family meetings, even after John turned, primarily, to Christianity not Twelve Step programs for support. John saw Jake as an angel. "I was involved with gangs, guns, and drugs all while I'm staying in his home, and he was patient with me, never pressuring me. He asked me if I wanted help with my drug use. If needed he would get me into treatment or counseling."

Lisa's once crippled family members also gave her support. "For the first time in my life I actually love myself, ... and no one is ever going to use me again. I won't let them." She confronted her father, and he was able to take it without striking back.

'Your drug addiction almost killed you and Momma. You never considered me and Jill [her sister]. We went from foster home to foster home, and you never tried to change and come get us. I forgive you but I would never do my kids like you done us.'

Lisa, Mick and other participants even frequented NA and AA meetings with their parents. Mick observed, "I used to get high with my brother, steal drugs from my father's 'stash,' and get drunk with my mother. Now that we're all sober I don't have anybody to get high with; plus we would all know if somebody slipped [relapsed]."

REFLECTIONS

If love and trust can grow where anger and confusion once reigned, then the hope and healing presented in our report is authentic. For anyone who has ever experienced the innocence of youth, it is almost impossible to comprehend what the participants' childhoods were like. The adults who joined and contributed to the youngsters' destructive and illegal lives, were despicable. And yet, in all likelihood, they, too, were addicts who had grown up similarly. It is, therefore, crucial that more efforts be made to reach adolescent addicts. Such programs and procedures should not only deal with the individual but attack the social breeding grounds for adolescent addiction such as racism, sexism, social and economic causes for family dysfunction, and formal education's all too often denial (Ginzberg, et al., 1988).

Contrary to some research, from an addiction point-of-view, for the recovering participants severe tragedy and poly-drug use had negative but also positive effects (Rush, 1979; Friedman et al., 1986; Swadi, 1992; & DeJong, 1994). Reaching an early bottom catapulted them into a state of surrender, and in sobriety they had few years of irrational thinking to reverse. Painful as it is, only when crushed by defeat, will an adolescent addict be forced to abandon fabled thinking and learn to contemplate the possible consequences for all types of prospective decisions. Knowing this, when addressing young audiences Jesse always answers one question the same way. "If you could, what would you change about your life?" "Nothing," Jesse flatly states, "everything I did got me to where I am today, and that's a good place."

APPENDIX

The Twelve Steps of Alcoholics Anonymous

1. We admitted we were powerless over alcohol--that our lives had become unmanageable.
2. Came to believe that a Power greater than ourselves could restore us to sanity.
3. Made a decision to turn our will and our lives over to the care of God as we understood Him.
4. Made a searching and fearless moral inventory of ourselves.
5. Admitted to God, to ourselves and to another human being the exact nature of our wrongs.
6. Were entirely ready to have God remove all these defects of character.
7. Humbly asked Him to remove our shortcomings.
8. Made a list of all persons we had harmed, and became willing to made amends to them all.
9. Made direct amends to such people wherever possible, except when to do so would injure them or others.
10. Continued to take personal inventory and when we were wrong promptly admitted it.
11. Sought through prayer and meditation to improve our conscious contact with God, as we understood Him, praying only for knowledge of His will for us and the power to carry that out.
12. Having had a spiritual awakening as the result of these steps, we tried to carry this message to alcoholics who still suffer, and to practice these principles in all our affairs.

REFERENCES

Bauer, A. M. (1994). Supportive counseling for students recovering from substance abuse. Paper presented at the annual meeting of the National Association of School Psychologists, Seattle, WA.

Bennett, C. I. (1999). *Comprehensive multicultural education: Theory and practice*. Boston: Allyn and Bacon.

Blume, T. W., Green, S., Joanning, H., & Quinn, W. S. (1994). Social role negotiation skills for substance-abusing adolescents: A group model. *Journal of Substance Abuse Treatment, 11*, 197-204.

Cavaiola, A. A., Schiff, M. & Kane-Cavaiola, C. (1990). Continuing care for the chemically dependent adolescent: Aftercare or afterthought: *Journal of Adolescent Chemical Dependency, 1*, 77-93.

Craig, B. J. (1993). Addicted student: Classroom behavior, teacher response. Paper presented at the annual meeting of the Conference on College Composition and Communication, San Diego, CA.

DeJong, W. (1994). Relapse prevention: An emerging technology for promoting long-term drug abstinence. *The International Journal of the Addictions, 29*, 681-705.

Denzin, N. K. (1993). *The alcoholic society: Addiction and recovery of the self*. New Brunswick, NJ: Transaction Publishers.

Friedman, A. S., Glickman, N. W., & Morrissey, M. R. (1986). Prediction of successful treatment outcome by client characteristics and retention in treatment in adolescent drug treatment programs. A large-scale cross-validation study. *Journal of Drug Education, 6*, 149-165.

Garrod, A., Smulyan, L., Powers, S. I, & Kilkenny, R. (1992). *Adolescent portraits: Identity, relationships, and challenges*. Boston: Allyn and Bacon.

Gazzini, J. C. (1993). Adolescent substance recovery: A preliminary investigation of peer and family influences. Doctoral dissertation, Union Institute Graduate School.

Ginzberg, E., Berliner, H. S., & Ostow, M. (1988). *Young people at Risk: Is prevention possible?* London: Westview Press.

Hall, H. A. (1985). The role of faith in the process of recovering from alcoholism. Doctoral dissertation, Drew University.

Irwin, C. E. (1993). Adolescence and risk taking: How are they related? In *Adolescent risk taking.* (pp. 7-28) N. J. Bell, & R. W. Bell (Eds.). Newbury Park, CA: Sage.

Johnson, V. & Pandian, R. J. (1991). Effects of the family environment on adolescent substance use, delinquency, and coping styles. *American Journal of Drug and Alcohol Abuse, 17*, 71-88.

Marshall, M. J., Marshall, S., & Heer, M. J. (1994). Characteristics of abstinent substance abusers who first sought treatment in adolescence. *Journal of Drug Education, 24*, 151-162.

Mitchell, J. J. (1998). *The natural limitations of Youth: The predispositions that shape the adolescent character*. London: Ablex Publishing Corporation.

Moore, S. & Rosenthal, D. (1993). *Sexuality in adolescence*. London: Routledge.

Moustakes, C. (1994). *Phenomenological research methods*. Thousand Oaks, CA: Sage Publications.

Myers, P. L. (1991). Cult and cult-like pathways out of adolescent addiction. *Journal of Child and Adolescent Substance Abuse, 1*, 115-137.

Nowinski, J. (1993). *Substance abuse in adolescents and young adults: A guide to treatment*. New York: Norton and Company.

Olmstead, R. E., Guy S. M., O'Malley, P. M., & Bentler, P. M. (1991). Longitudinal assessment of the relationship between self-esteem, fatalism, loneliness, and substance use. *Journal of Social Behavior and Personality, 6*, 749-770.

Overton, W. F. (1991) Reasoning in the adolescent. In *Encyclopedia of adolescence, Vol II.* (pp. 912-925). R. M. Lerner, A. C. Petersen, & J. Brooks-Gunn (Eds.). New York: Garland.

Polcin, D. L. (1991). A comprehensive model for adolescent chemical dependency treatment. *Journal of Counseling and Development, 70*, 376-382.

Prezioso, F. A. (1986). *Spirituality and the treatment of substance abuse*. Washington, DC: U. S. Department of Education.

Reinert, D. F., Estadt, B. K. Fenzel, L. M. Allen, J. P., & Gilroy, F. D. (1995). Relationship of surrender and narcissism to involvement in alcohol recovery. *Alcoholism Treatment Quarterly, 12*, 49-58.

Rush, R. V. (1979). Predicting treatment outcomes for juvenile and young-adult clients in the Pennsylvania substance abuse system. In *Youth drug abuse: Problems, issues and treatments.* (pp. 649-667). Lexington, MA: Lexington Books.

Slagle, R. A. (1992). The semiotic boundaries of human experience. Paper presented at the annual meeting of SCA, Chicago IL.

Stewart, M. A., & Brown, S. A. (1993). Family functioning following adolescent substance abuse treatment. *Journal of Substance Abuse, 5*, 327-339.

Swadi, H. (1992). A longitudinal perspective on adolescent substance abuse. *European Child and Adolescent Psychiatry, 1*, 156-170.

Tesch, R. (1990). *Qualitative research: Analysis type and software tool.* New York: Falmer Press.

Tiebout, H. M. (1944). Therapeutic mechanisms of Alcoholics Anonymous. *American Journal of Psychiatry, 100*, 468-473.

Tiebout, H. M. (1953). Surrender versus compliance in therapy with special reference to alcoholism. *Quarterly Journal on Studies of Alcohol, 14*, 58-68.

Tiebout, H. M. (1954). The ego factors in surrender in alcoholism. *Quarterly Journal of studies on Alcohol, 15*, 610-621.

Vik, P. W., Grizzle, K. L., & Brown, S. A. (1992). Social resource characteristics and adolescent substance abuse relapse. *Journal of Adolescent Chemical Dependency, 2*, 59-74.

Walfish, S., Massey, R., & Krone, A. (1990). Interpersonal relationships of adolescent substance abusers. *Journal of Adolescent Chemical Dependency, 1*, 5-13.

X, Malcolm, & Haley, A. (1966). *The autobiography of Malcolm X.* New York: Grove Press, Inc.

Chapter 2

FAMILY FUNCTIONING AND PSYCHOLOGICAL WELL-BEING, SCHOOL ADJUSTMENT AND SUBSTANCE ABUSE IN CHINESE ADOLESCENTS: ARE FINDINGS BASED ON MULTIPLE STUDIES CONSISTENT?

Daniel T.L. Shek
Department of Social Work
The Chinese University of Hong Kong

The influence of the family environment, including the related dynamics, interaction patterns and functioning on the adjustment of individual family members is emphasized in different family theories (Jacob, 1987). Specifically, family therapists and clinicians have suggested that a family with poor functioning is conducive to the development of psychopathology in childhood and adolescence (Beavers & Hampson, 1990; Papero, 1990). For example, Munichin (1974) suggested that malfunctional generational hierarchy would impair the healthy development of children members in a family. Satir and Baldwin (1983) proposed that family communication plays an important role in child and adolescent development.

Family ecological theorists have similarly proposed that key family processes, such as marital discords of the parents (Feldman, Fisher, & Seitel, 1997; Fincham, 1994), family conflict (Robin & Foster, 1989), and parent-adolescent relational problems are conducive to the development of psychological problems in adolescents (Maccoby & Martin, 1983). For example, parenting style has been identified by many researchers to be an important factor contributing to antisocial behavior (Farrington, 1995; Patterson, Crosby, & Vuchinich, 1992).

Empirically, support for the thesis that family functioning or competence is linked to adolescent adjustment is far from conclusive. On the one hand, there is evidence showing that family functioning influences adolescent psychological well-being and problem behavior, including psychopathology (Kaslow, Warner, John & Brown, 1992; Martin, Rozanes, Pearce

& Allison, 1995; Prange, Greenbaum, Silver, Friedman, Kutask, & Duchnowski, 1992), suicide (Garber, Little, Hilsman, & Weaver, 1998; McKenry, Tishler, & Kelley, 1982), identity (Bosma & Gerrits, 1985) and self-esteem (Mandara & Murray, 2000; Shagle & Barber, 1995; Sweeting & West, 1995). There are also findings indicating that poorer family functioning was related to higher levels of substance abuse (McKay, Murphy, Rivinus, & Maisto, 1991; Smart, Chibucos, & Didier, 1990), smoking (Doherty & Allen, 1994), delinquency proneness (Tolan & Lorion, 1988), and poorer academic achievement (Wentzel, 1994).

On the other hand, there are research findings which do not suggest that family functioning is related to adolescent development: Walker, McLaughlin, and Greene (1988) found no support for the relationship between adolescent functional somatic complaints and family functioning; Hundert, Cassie and Johnston (1988) showed that family functioning scores did not differentiate children in intrusive and less intrusive treatment programmes; Alnajjar and Smadi (1998) reported that family functioning in delinquent and non-delinquents did not differ. Obviously, the relationship between family functioning and adolescent adjustment is far from conclusive and further studies need to be carried out.

An examination of the existing studies examining the linkage between family functioning and adolescent development reveals that there are several methodological limitations pertinent to the existing studies. The first limitation is that few studies have employed multiple indicators of family functioning in a single study. The employment of different measures of family functioning in a single study is important if one is interested to look at how different measures of family functioning based on different family functioning models might moderate the link between family functioning and adolescent adjustment (Shek, in press, e). In addition, the employment of similar measures of family functioning and adolescent adjustment in a single study can help researchers to triangulate the findings.

The second limitation is that there are few studies in which a wide range of adolescent developmental outcome variables were included. The inclusion of multiple measures of adolescent adjustment would give us a wider perspective on the problem area. In addition, it can help us understand the relative contribution of family functioning on different aspects of adolescent development. This question is important because the general conjecture that poor family functioning results in a deterioration of the development of adolescents is an assumption only.

The third methodological limitation of the existing studies is that the related sample sizes, particularly those in the longitudinal studies, are generally small: Varni, Katz, Colegrove, and Dolgin (1996) recruited 77 school-aged children in their prospective study of family functioning predictors of adjustment in children with newly diagnosed cancer; Cumsille and Epstein (1994) examined the links between family cohesion and family social support and adolescent depression in 93 families; Ohannessian, Lerner, Lerner, and von Eye (1995) investigated the relationship between discrepancies in perceptions of family functioning and adolescent psychological symptoms in 74 sixth- and seventh-grade students and their parents. Obviously, one basic problem associated with such small sample studies is the problem of power (Kraemer & Thieman, 1987). In particular, the use of multivariate statistical tests (such as multiple regression analyses that have been widely used) in small samples increases the possibility that the obtained data are due to chance effect (Tabachnick & Fidell, 1989).

The fourth methodological limitation is that few attempts have been carried out to replicate the existing studies. In the broader context of science, there are views arguing that replication is an important criteria that should be used to evaluate scientific findings. For example, in an attempt to highlight the misinterpretations associated with statistical tests of significance, Cohen (1994) argued that social scientists "must finally rely, as has been done in all the older sciences, on replication" (p.997). Similar view was held by Shaver (1993) who suggested that "the notion of reproducibility leads directly to replication, widely agreed upon as a crucial element of science, but largely missing from reports of social science" (p.312). Shaver (1993) further argued that "editors should not only actively encourage the reporting of replications, but in many instances demand replication before results can be published" (p.312). Obviously, the scientific value of a study of the relationship between family functioning and adolescent adjustment can be substantially enhanced if we can produce evidence to show that the related findings can be generalized to different adolescent samples.

The fifth limitation is that in most of the related studies, psychological well-being was defined in terms of adolescent psychiatric morbidity and distress where indicators such as anxiety and depression symptoms were employed (e.g., Martin et al., 1995; Varni et al., 1996). In contrast, there are few studies examining the link between family functioning and adolescent positive mental health. Conceptually, psychological well-being can be defined in terms of the absence of manifested psychiatric symptoms, or presence of positive mental health or existential attributes (Bradburn, 1969; Diener, 1984; Ryff & Singer, 1996). According to the latter view, indicators such as life satisfaction, existential well-being, self-worth, or sense of mastery, should be focussed upon. Therefore, it would be theoretically illuminating if measures of psychiatric morbidity and positive mental health can be included in a single study. Furthermore, the focus on measures of positive mental health is important for there are views suggesting that the family environment might influence adolescent adjustment via the existential functioning of a person (Shek, 1997, 1998a).

A survey of the literature in this area shows that most of the existing studies have been conducted in Western societies. With a few exceptions (Shek, 1997, 1998a), no scientific study has to date been done to examine how family functioning is related to adolescent adjustment in the Chinese culture. From a cross-cultural perspective, the lack of related research findings in the Chinese context would motivate one to ask whether family functioning is related to the adjustment of Chinese adolescents, and whether such influences would be different from those phenomena observed in the Western culture. These questions are legitimate for cross-cultural differences in family processes would lead to the emergence of different phenomena.

As far as the family is concerned, there are views suggesting that Chinese people place a strong emphasis on the family and they have a strong affective involvement within the family (Yang, 1981). In addition, children and adolescents are expected to carry out their filial responsibilities and family duties. Under the Confucian emphasis of the importance of harmonious social order, expression of self and emotion was de-emphasized in the traditional Chinese culture. As Wright (1964) pointed out, family members must be "forebearing and restrained in order to avoid disturbing the peace of the group" (p.33). Shon and Ja (1982) also pointed out that "because harmonious interpersonal relationships are so highly valued, direct confrontation is avoided whenever possible (p.216)" In fact, the use of forbearance ("bai ban ren nai" - to use all forbearance) and self-suppression in dealing with family issues were emphasized in the traditional Chinese culture (Yang, 1981).

It can be conjectured that traditional emphases on the importance of the family over an individual might fuel the negative impact of family functioning on adolescent psychological well-being. Because there have been to date few studies to examine this issue in the Chinese culture, it is important to accumulate more empirical evidence in this area. However, before we can accomplish the task in a satisfactory manner, we must be able to assess family functioning objectively.

There are two ways by which family functioning can be assessed. The first way is to translate the existing measures of family functioning. Although clinical practitioners and researchers have attempted to translate the existing Western measures of family functioning and use them in different Chinese contexts, Phillips, West, Shen, and Zheng (1998) remarked that "unfortunately, few clinicians or researchers go to the trouble of rigorously assessing the psychometric properties of the translated instruments in the target culture" (p.105). Second, because Chinese people may have different views of the family, it would be important to develop culturally sensitive measures to assess family functioning. Unfortunately, as pointed out by Shek (2001a & b), few researchers have developed such measures in the Chinese culture.

Against the above background, the findings based on a series of studies are reported in this paper to examine the relationship between family functioning and adolescent adjustment. There are several features of these studies. First, multiple measures of family functioning, including translated Western measures and an indigenous measure, were used in these studies. Second, multiple measures of adolescent development, including psychological well-being, school adjustment and substance abuse, were employed. Third, with respect to adolescent psychological well-being, measures based on psychological symptoms and positive mental health were used. Fourth, different adolescent samples, including adolescents with low academic achievement, adolescents with individual and family problems, and adolescents in the community, were employed.

The findings based on three studies are reported in this paper. In Study 1, the relationships between family functioning and adolescent adjustment were examined in a sample of adolescents with low academic achievement. In Study 2, the findings based on clinical and nonclinical participants were used to examine the relationship between the two domains. In Study 3, the findings based on adolescents in a community sample were examined.

STUDY 1

Sample and Procedures

The study is based upon the responses of 361 secondary school students (240 boys and 121 girls; mean age=14). They were all Secondary 1 and Secondary 2 students in a Band 5 school. In Hong Kong, a Band 5 school is a school with students whose academic performance are in the lowest range in the Secondary School Placement Allocation exercise. The purpose of the study was mentioned and confidentiality of the data collected was repeatedly emphasized to all students in attendance on the day of testing. The students were asked to indicate their wish if they did not want to participate in the study (i.e., "passive" informed consent were obtained from the students). All participants responded en masse to all instrument scales in the questionnaire in a self-administration format. Adequate time was provided for the participants to complete the questionnaire. A trained research assistant was present throughout the test administration session.

Instruments

Measures of Family Functioning

- *Chinese Self-Report Family Inventory (SFI)*: The Self-Report Family Inventory is a 36-item scale which assesses family functioning or competence (Beavers, Hampson, & Hulgus, 1990). Beavers and Hampson (1990) found that the SFI was able to distinguish competent families from dysfunctional ones. The Chinese SFI was developed by Shek (1998b). Research findings on the reliability, validity and factor structure of the SFI have been reported (Shek, 1998b, 2001a & b; Shek & Lai, 2001).
- *Chinese Family Assessment Device*: The FAD is a 60-item measure assessing family functioning based on the McMaster model (Epstein et al., 1983). According to Kabacoff, Miller, Bishop, Epstein, and Keitner (1990), the General Functioning Scale of the FAD (GF) can be used as an indicator reflecting global family functioning. The Chinese version of the FAD was translated by a team comprising two psychologists (including the author) and a social worker. Every effort was made to ensure that the meaning embedded in the original English items is present in the translated version. The translated items were then back-translated by a translator fluent in both English and Chinese languages. The team then discussed any discrepancies between the translated and back-translated items until a consensus was reached. There are research findings suggesting that the Chinese FAD possesses good reliability and validity status (Shek, in press, a & b).
- *Chinese Family Awareness Scale (FAS)*: The Family Awareness Scale is a 14-item scale designed to measure family competence outlined in the Beavers-Timberlawn Model of Family Competence. Research findings on its internal consistency, concurrent validity, and construct validity have been reported (Green, 1987). The Chinese version of the scale was translated by a team comprising two psychologists (including the author) and a social worker. Vigorous procedures were carried out to ensure that the meaning embedded in the original English items is present in the translated version. There are research findings suggesting that this scale is valid and reliable (Shek, in press, c).
- *Chinese Family Assessment Instrument (FAI)*: Based on an extensive review of the existing family functioning measures and research findings on the perceptions of Chinese people on the characteristics of happy families (Shek, in press, d), a 33-item Chinese Family Assessment Instrument was developed to assess different aspects of family functioning, including mutuality, communication, conflict and harmony, parental concern, and parental control. Shek (in press, e) showed that the FAI is temporally stable and internally consistent and there is support for the concurrent and construct validities of the test.

Measures of Psychological Well-Being

- *Trait Anxiety Scale of the Chinese State-Trait Anxiety Inventory (A-TRAIT)*. The Trait Anxiety Scale (A-Trait) of the State-Trait Anxiety Inventory was constructed to measure trait anxiety (Spielberger, Gorsuch, & Lushene, 1970). It was translated by Tsoi, Ho and Mak (1986) who found that pregnant women who had stillbirth or the birth of a handicapped child had higher trait anxiety than those pregnant women who already had given birth to a normal child. Shek (1988a, 1991) showed that this scale is reliable and valid.

- *Existential Well-Being Scale (EXIST)*. The Existential Well-Being Scale, which formed a part of the Spiritual Well-Being Scale, was constructed by Paloutzian and Ellison (1982) to assess life direction and satisfaction. The Chinese version of the Existential Well-Being Scale was translated by the author and adequate reliability and validity of this scale has been reported (Shek, 1992).

- *Life Satisfaction Scale (LIFE)*. The Satisfaction with Life Scale was designed by Diener, Emmons, Larsen, and Griffin (1985) to assess an individual's own global judgment of his or her quality of life. The Chinese version of this scale was translated by the author and adequate reliability of this scale has been reported (Shek, 1992).

- *Mastery Scale (MAS)*. Modelled after the Mastery Scale of Pearlin and Schooler (1978), the 7-item Chinese Mastery Scale was constructed by the author which attempts to measure a person's sense of control of his or her life. Shek (1992) showed that this scale possesses acceptable psychometric properties.

Assessment of School Adjustment

One item was constructed to assess a respondent's perception of his or her academic performance when compared with schoolmates in the same grade (APC). The respondents were asked to rate "Best", "Better than usual", "Ordinary", "Worse than usual", or "Worst" in this item. Besides, another item was constructed to assess the respondent's satisfaction of his or her academic performance (APS). The respondents were asked to rate "Very satisfied", "Satisfied", "Average", "Dissatisfied", or "Very Dissatisfied" in this item. Finally, one item was constructed to assess the respondent's perception of his or her conduct (CONDUCT). The respondents were asked to rate "Very good", "Good", "Average", "Poor", or "Very Poor" in this item. Shek (1997) showed that these three items were temporally stable.

Assessment of Drug Abuse

One item was constructed to assess whether the respondent had ever smoked (SMOKE). The respondents were asked to respond "Frequently", "Sometimes", "Rarely", or "Never" to this item. Shek (1997) showed that this item was temporally reliable. A higher SMOKE score indicates a lower level of smoking behavior in this study.

Another item was constructed to assess whether the subject had ever abused opiate-related drugs (HDRUG). The respondents were asked to rate "Frequently", "Sometimes", "Rarely", or "Never" to this item. Shek (2001a & b) showed that this item was temporally stable. Besides, another item was used to assess the extent of consumption of psychotropic substances (SDRUG). The respondents were asked to rate "Frequently", "Sometimes", "Rarely", or "Never" to this item. Shek (2001a & b) showed that this item was temporally stable. Higher SMOKE, HDRUG or SDRUG scores indicate lower levels of psychotropic drug abuse in this study.

On the basis of the above discussion, it was predicted that, if there is a relationship between the family functioning and adjustment in Chinese adolescents, family functioning variables would be significantly associated with the various sets of variables related to psychological well-being, school adjustment, and drug abuse. Specifically, it would be expected that those with better family functioning (lower SFI, GF, FAI scores and higher FAS scores) would have better mental health (lower A-TRAIT scores and higher EXIST, MAS and LIFE scores), better school adjustment (lower APC, APS and CONDUCT scores), and lower levels of drug abuse behavior (higher SMOKE, HDRUG, and SDRUG scores).

Results and Discussion

In view of the large number of correlations between the family functioning scores and measures of adolescent adjustment, the multistage Bonferroni procedure was carried out to determine those significant correlations which are not attributable to Type 1 error. All correlations (i.e., 52 correlations) were initially included in the evaluation and the analysis stopped when there were no more significant correlations at a particular step (Larzelere & Mulaik, 1977). Several observations can be highlighted from the findings presented in Table 1. First, irrespective of which family functioning measure was used, the related correlation coefficients on the relationship between family functioning and adolescent psychological well-being were statistically significant. Second, the findings provide some support for the thesis that adolescents with better family functioning had better school adjustment. Finally, the findings suggest that there is some linkage between family functioning and drug abuse indexed by SMOKE and SDRUG. Following the suggestions by Cohen (1992), the magnitude of the differences obtained could be regarded as having low to medium effect sizes.

To look at the relationship between family functioning and adolescent adjustment in a more condensed manner, a principal components analysis was performed on the adolescent adjustment measures, yielding three factors with eigenvalues exceeding unity, accounting for 60.1% of the variance. To avoid overfactoring, further analyses using the scree test (Cattell, 1966) showed that three factors could be meaningfully extracted. The three-factor solution, which could be considered as adequate representations of the data, was rotated to a varimax criterion for interpretation. The first factor, which could be labelled as Mental Health (MH) which included A-TRAIT, EXIST, MAS and LIFE, explained 32.1% of the variance. Factor II explained 16.4% of the total variance, which included APC, APS and CONDUCT. Because these items are concerned with school adjustment, this factor could hence be labelled School Adjustment (SA). The final factor included SMOKE, HDRUG and SDRUG, which could be labelled as a DRUG factor, accounting for 11.6% of the variance. Table 2 shows the varimax rotated factor structure of the measures of adolescent adjustment.

Table 1. Correlation Coefficients on the Relationships between Different Measures of Family Functioning and Indicators of Adolescent Adjustment (Study 1)

	SFI	GF	FAS	FAI
A-TRAIT	.40*	.43*	-.41*	.35*
EXIST	-.51*	-.51*	.56*	-.50*
MAS	-.30*	-.39*	.36*	-.27*
LIFE	-.49*	-.43*	.43*	-.42*
APC	.23*	.15[a]	-.18*	.19*
APS	.13[a]	.17*	-.21*	.18*
CONDUCT	.20*	.17*	-.18*	.17*
SMOKE	-.28*	-.21*	.18*	-.19*
HDRUG	-.07ns	-.03ns	.04ns	-.08ns
SDRUG	-.17*	-.15[a]	.06ns	-.13[a]
MH	-.55*	-.57*	.54*	-.51*
SA	.12[a]	.07ns	-.15[a]	.10ns
DRUG	-.19*	-.12[a]	.08ns	-.13[a]

Note. SFI: Chinese Self-Report Family Inventory. GF: General Functioning Scale of the Family Assessment Device. FAS: Chinese Family Awareness Scale. FAI: Chinese Family Assessment Instrument. A-TRAIT: Trait Anxiety Scale of the State-Trait Anxiety Inventory. EXIST: Existential Well-Being Scale. MAS: Mastery Scale. LIFE: Life Satisfaction Scale. APC: Academic performance when compared with others. APS: Satisfaction with academic performance. CONDUCT: School conduct. SMOKE: Smoking behavior. HDRUG: Abuse of opiate-related drugs. SDRUG: Abuse of psychotropic drugs. MH: Mental Health factor. SA: School Adjustment factor. DRUG: Drug Abuse factor.

A two-tailed multistage Bonferroni procedure was used to evaluate the correlations between different measures of family functioning and indicators of adolescent adjustment for inflated Type 1 error. pFW is based on the familywise Type 1 error rate.

[a] Border significance; $pT < .05$

* $pFW < .10; pT < .004$

Correlation analyses show that while family functioning based on all measures of family functioning was significantly related to adolescent mental health, family functioning indexed by SFI and FAI were significantly related to DRUG and there was weak support for the linkage between family functioning and school adjustment. Following the procedures recommended by Steiger (1980), further analyses showed that the correlations between Mental Health and measures of family functioning were substantially higher than the related correlations between SA and measures of family functioning (p < .01 in all cases). Results also showed that different measures of family functioning were more strongly related to MH than to DRUG (p <.01 in all cases). This finding suggests that different family functioning measures used in this study are more sensitive to measures of psychological well-being than to measures of school adjustment and substance abuse.

**Table 2. Rotated Varimax Solutions of the Different Measures
of Adolescent Adjustment in the Different Samples**

	Study 1			Study 2			Study 3		
GHQ	-	-	-	-	-	-	-.73	.20	-.04
A-TRAIT	-.78	.12	-.06	-.80	-.06	.10	-	-	-
EXIST	.80	-.20	.04	.82	.06	-.13	.86	-.09	.09
MAS	.75	-.23	-.02	.76	-.01	-.14	.80	-.07	.05
LIFE	.67	-.01	.14	.73	.08	-.08	.77	-.13	.03
APC	-.14	.81	-.07	-.12	.04	.81	-.16	.83	.03
APS	-.18	.85	-.01	-.18	.16	.80	-.12	.80	.05
CONDUCT	-.14	.55	-.33	-.08	-.33	.58	-.11	.62	-.14
SMOKE	.18	-.23	.68	.13	.76	-.06	.10	-.17	.63
HDRUG	-.03	-.01	.68	-.09	.58	.05	-.01	.08	.81
SDRUG	.05	-.08	.87	.15	.83	-.02	.06	.02	.85
Variance Explained	32.1	16.4	11.6	29.8	17.0	13.2	30.6	17.8	13.9

Note. GHQ: General Health Questionnaire. A-TRAIT: Trait Anxiety Scale of the State-Trait Anxiety Inventory. EXIST: Existential Well-Being Scale. MAS: Mastery Scale. LIFE: Life Satisfaction Scale. APC: Academic performance when compared with others. APS: Satisfaction with academic performance. CONDUCT: School conduct. SMOKE: Smoking behavior. HDRUG: Abuse of opiate-related drugs. SDRUG: Abuse of psychotropic drugs. For each variable, the highest loading among the factors is underlined.

STUDY 2

To examine the replicability of the findings based on Study 1, the relationship between family functioning and adjustment of adolescents was examined in a clinical group (160 boys and 121 girls) and a non-clinical group (269 boys and 182 girls).

Sample and Procedures

A "clinical" group (with individuals from families which are clinically presenting) and a "nonclinical" group (with individuals from families which are not dysfunctional) are usually employed in a typical study which is intended to validate family functioning instruments and there are different ways by which subjects in such groups could be recruited. For the clinical subjects, researchers have recruited psychiatric patients (e.g., Green, 1987, 1989) and members from families receiving family therapy (e.g., Hampson, Beavers, & Hulgus, 1989) as subjects. In contrast, families that are not currently receiving any counseling service (e.g., Hampson, Beavers, & Hulgus, 1989) and ordinary college students (e.g., Epstein, Baldwin, & Bishop, 1983) have been employed to represent non-clinical participants.

Four different samples of clinical subjects were included in the present study. The first sample consisted of 114 subjects (98 boys and 16 girls) attending schools admitting adolescents with behavioral and emotional problems. The second sample consisted of 123 subjects (51 boys and 72 girls) whose families were currently receiving family counselling from family service centres because of family problems (such as marital problems, relationship problems among the family members and/or adjustment problems of the children). The third sample consisted of 22 female students who were receiving counseling service from school social workers because of family problems. The final sample consisted of 22 female adolescents who were out-patient psychiatric patients with non-psychotic disturbances. The combination of subjects in these four samples forms the Clinical Group (N=281). In terms of external behavioral criterion, all the subjects were currently receiving counselling service because of family problems, which included marital problems of the parents, relationship problems among the family members and/or individual problems of adolescent members in the family.

In contrast, 451 participants from two schools (269 boys and 182 girls) were recruited to form the Non-Clinical Group. For each participant, the participant and his or her family had not sought professional help because of family problems. In terms of external behavioral criterion, subjects in this group have not received counselling because of family problems, which included marital problems of the parents, relationship problems among the family members and/or behavioral and emotional problems of adolescent members in the family.

All participants responded en masse to all the instrument scales in the questionnaire in a self-administration format. Adequate time was provided for the subjects to complete the questionnaire. Informed consent was obtained for all participants. Except for those questionnaires collected via family service centres, a trained research assistant was present throughout the test administration session.

Instruments

The participants responded to the same measures of family functioning and individual adjustment used in Study 1.

Results and Discussion

With the exception of the family functioning scores, results showed that the two groups did not differ in the background demographic and socio-economic characteristics, including age (mean age=15 and 15 in the Clinical Group and Non-Clinical Group, respectively), educational attainment (percentage of respondents studying Secondary Two (i.e., Grade 8 in the American system) and below=46% and 55% in the Clinical Group and Non-Clinical Group, respectively), sex ratio (percentage of male respondents in the Clinical Group and Non-Clinical Group=57% and 60%, respectively), family monthly income (mean family income=HK$20,429 and HK$18,680 in the Clinical Group and Non-Clinical Group respectively, which are roughly equivalent to US$2619.1 and US$2,394.9, respectively), and number of persons in a household (mean number of persons=4.4 and 4.5 in the Clinical Group and Non-Clinical Group, respectively).

Because the correlation patterns were highly similar in the two groups, the data of the two groups were combined for analyses. The findings based on the bivariate correlations are presented in Table 3. Based on the multi-stage Bonferroni correction procedure, several observations can be highlighted. First, all measures of family functioning were significantly related to measures of psychological well-being. Second, there was some support for the linkage between family functioning and school adjustment. Finally, there was some support for the hypothesis that poor family functioning was related to higher levels of substance abuse. Following the suggestions by Cohen (1992), the magnitude of the differences obtained could be regarded as having low to medium effect sizes.

Table 3. Correlation Coefficients on the Relationships between Different Measures of Family Functioning and Indicators of Adolescent Adjustment (Study 2)

	SFI	GF	FAS	FAI
A-TRAIT	.44*	.46*	-.47*	.43*
EXIST	-.49*	-.50*	.49*	-.52*
MAS	-.41*	-.45*	.43*	-.39*
LIFE	-.47*	-.47*	.50*	-.46*
APC	.19*	.14*	-.14*	.17*
APS	.11^a	.11^a	-.16*	.15*
CONDUCT	.17*	.16*	-.16*	.15*
SMOKE	-.21*	-.20*	.15*	-.19*
HDRUG	-.04ns	-.02ns	-.01ns	-.01ns
SDRUG	-.14*	-.18*	.07ns	-.13*
MH	-.56*	-.60*	.59*	-.57*
SA	.11^a	.09^a	-.12*	.09ns
DRUG	-.13*	-.14*	.06ns	-.12*

Note. SFI: Chinese Self-Report Family Inventory. GF: General Functioning Scale of the Family Assessment Device. FAS: Chinese Family Awareness Scale. FAI: Chinese Family Assessment Instrument. A-TRAIT: Trait Anxiety Scale of the State-Trait Anxiety Inventory. EXIST: Existential Well-Being Scale. MAS: Mastery Scale. LIFE: Life Satisfaction Scale. APC: Academic performance when compared with others. APS: Satisfaction with academic performance. CONDUCT: School conduct. SMOKE: Smoking behavior. HDRUG: Abuse of opiate-related drugs. SDRUG: Abuse of psychotropic drugs. MH: Mental Health factor. SA: School Adjustment factor. DRUG: Drug Abuse factor.
A two-tailed multistage Bonferroni procedure was used to evaluate the correlations between different measures of family functioning and indicators of adolescent adjustment for inflated Type 1 error. *pFW* is based on the familywise Type 1 error rate.
^{a} Border significance; *pT* < .05
* *pFW* < .10; *pT* < .008

To reduce the data volume, factor analysis based on identical factor analytic procedures used in Study 1 was performed on the adolescent adjustmental variables. Results showed that three factors could be replicated, accounting for 59.9% of the variance (29.8%, 17% and

13.2% for the first, second and third factors, respectively). An examination of the content of these factors suggest that the factors could be termed "Mental Health (MH)", "Drug Abuse (DRUG)" and "School Adjustment (SA)", respectively. Analyses based on coefficients of congruence show that the factors extracted are higher similar to those obtained in study 1 (coefficients of congruence=.99, .98, and .98 for Mental Health, Drug Abuse, and School Adjustment, respectively). The varimax rotated factor structure can be seen in Table 2.

Correlation analyses show that all measures of family functioning were significantly related to Mental Health. The findings also gave support to the relationships between family functioning and school adjustment as well as substance abuse. Analyses based on Steiger's (1980) recommended procedures showed that the correlations between family functioning and Mental Health were significantly higher than the corresponding correlations between a) family functioning and SA and b) family functioning and DRUG (p < .01 in all cases).

In short, similar to the findings of Study 1, results showed that perceived family functioning as assessed by different family measures was generally related to adolescent psychological well-being, school adjustment and substance abuse in the clinical and non-clinical samples.

STUDY 3

One of the limitations of the previous studies of the relationship between family functioning and adolescent adjustment is that convenient samples have been commonly employed. To tackle this problem and to further replicate the findings based on Study 1 and Study 2, a community survey based on adolescent students was carried out.

Participants and Procedures

The participants were 3,649 adolescents in Hong Kong. The participants were Secondary 1 (N=880), Secondary 2 (N=898), Secondary 3 (N=930) and Secondary 4 (N=941) students. They were selected from secondary schools in Hong Kong by the multiple stage stratified random sampling method, with school banding (i.e., ability of the students) as the stratifying factor (Moser & Kalton, 1980). A total of 26 schools from different parts of Hong Kong participated in this study. The participants could be considered as heterogeneous for they came from different areas and socio-economic classes in Hong Kong. The mean age of the participants was 14 years.

During the data collection process, the purpose of the study was mentioned and confidentiality of the data collected was repeatedly emphasized to all students in attendance on the day of testing. The students were asked to indicate their wish if they did not want to participate in the study (i.e., "passive" informed consent was obtained from the students). All participants responded en masse to all instrument scales in the questionnaire in a self-administration format. Adequate time was provided for the subjects to complete the questionnaire. A trained research assistant was present throughout the administration procedure.

Instruments

As far as the assessment of family functioning is concerned, the GF, SFI, and FAI used in Study 1 and Study 2 were employed. Concerning the assessment of adolescent adjustment, the Existential Well-Being Scale, Mastery Scale and Life Satisfaction Scale used in Study 1 and Study 2 were employed. In addition, the Chinese version of the 30-item General Health Questionnaire (GHQ) was employed. The General Health Questionnaire has been developed to measure current non-psychotic disturbances (Goldberg, 1972). Chan (1985) found that the Chinese GHQ compared favourably with the English version at the scale level, and there was further evidence suggesting that this scale possesses acceptable psychometric properties (Shek, 1989, 1993).

Results and Discussion

Results showed that all measures of family functioning were significantly correlated with measures of adolescent adjustment (except HDRUG) and the significant results were not due to inflated Type 1 error (Table 4).

Similar to Study 1 and Study 2, factor analyses were performed to examine the dimensions of the measures of adolescent adjustment. Results showed that three factors identified in Study 1 and Study 2 could be replicated, accounting for 62.3% of the variance (30.6%, 17.8% and 13.9% for the first, second and third factor respectively). An examination of the factor solution suggests that the factors could be termed "Mental Health (MH)", "School Adjustment (SA)" and "Drug Abuse (DRUG)", respectively. Analyses based on coefficients of congruence show that the factors extracted are higher similar to those obtained in study 1 (coefficients of congruence=.99, .98, and .98 for Mental Health, School Adjustment, and Drug Abuse, respectively) and Study 2 (coefficients of congruence=.99, .98, and .98 for Mental Health, School Adjustment, and Drug Abuse, respectively). The varimax rotated factor structure is presented in Table 2.

The findings on the correlation between the factor scores and the family functioning measures show that all the related correlation coefficients are statistically significant. Further analyses showed that the correlations between family functioning and measures of adolescent adjustment were substantially higher than the related correlations between family functioning scales and measures of school adjustment and substance abuse (p < .01 in all cases). This finding suggests that family functioning is more intimately related to individual psychological well-being than to school adjustment and substance abuse in this community sample of adolescents.

Table 4. Correlation Coefficients on the Relationships between Different Measures of Family Functioning and Indicators of Adolescent Adjustment (Study 3)

	SFI	GF	FAI
GHQ	.39*	.40*	.39*
EXIST	-.57*	-.59*	-.58*
MAS	-.47*	-.51*	-.54*
LIFE	-.52*	-.53*	-.46*
APC	.19*	.16*	.18*
APS	.18*	.15*	.17*
CONDUCT	.18*	.18*	.19*
SMOKE	-.18*	-.17*	-.18*
HDRUG	-.02ns	-.05*	-.02ns
SDRUG	-.10*	-.09*	-.08*
MH	-.59*	-.63*	-.60*
SA	.14*	.11*	.14*
DRUG	-.07*	-.07*	-.06*

Note. SFI: Chinese Self-Report Family Inventory. GF: General Functioning Scale of the Family Assessment Device. FAS: Chinese Family Awareness Scale. FAI: Chinese Family Assessment Instrument. A-TRAIT: Trait Anxiety Scale of the State-Trait Anxiety Inventory. EXIST: Existential Well-Being Scale. MAS: Mastery Scale. LIFE: Life Satisfaction Scale. APC: Academic performance when compared with others. APS: Satisfaction with academic performance. CONDUCT: School conduct. SMOKE: Smoking behavior. HDRUG: Abuse of opiate-related drugs. SDRUG: Abuse of psychotropic drugs. MH: Mental Health factor. SA: School Adjustment factor. DRUG: Drug Abuse factor.

A two-tailed multistage Bonferroni procedure was used to evaluate the correlations between different measures of family functioning and indicators of adolescent adjustment for inflated Type 1 error. pFW is based on the familywise Type 1 error rate.

[a] Border significance; $pT < .05$

* $pFW < .05$; $pT < .001$

GENERAL DISCUSSION

The primary objective of this paper was to examine the relationship between adolescents' perceived family functioning and their adolescent psychological well-being, school adjustment, and problem behavior. Based on the existing family models (e.g., Walsh, 1993) and empirical evidence (e.g., Shek, 1997, 1998a), it was expected that adolescents who have a more favourable perception of family functioning would have better mental health and school adjustment and a lower level of substance abuse.

To examine the relationship between family functioning and adolescent adjustment, three studies based on different adolescent samples are reported in this paper. Results generally showed that higher levels of perceived family functioning were significantly related to better adolescent psychological well-being (including psychological symptoms and positive mental health), better school adjustment (perceived academic performance and school conduct) and lower levels of substance abuse (smoking and illicit drug use). One salient observation across these studies is that the relationship between perceived family functioning and adolescent adjustment could be replicated in different adolescent samples using both translated and indigenous measures of family functioning.

With reference to the relationship between family functioning and adolescent well-being, it was found that those who experienced better family functioning (as indexed by translated and indigenous measures) generally had a lower level of psychological symptoms. This observation is basically consistent with the previous research findings that a lower level of family competence was related to a higher level of adolescent psychopathology (Martin et al., 1995; McFarlane et al., 1995; Shek, 1997, 1998a).

Besides psychological distress symptoms, the present study also shows that family functioning is associated with adolescent positive mental health, including life satisfaction, sense of mastery and existential well-being. This finding is consistent with Shek (1997, 1998a) who found that family functioning was related to purpose in life, self-esteem and life satisfaction in Chinese adolescents. Because there are few studies addressing the relationship between family functioning and positive mental health, the present findings can be regarded as encouraging.

There are at least four possible explanations of the above findings. The first interpretation is that family functioning exerts a direct and/or indirect impact on adolescent psychological well-being. This interpretation has indeed been shared by many family theorists (Papero, 1990) and data arising from previous cross-sectional studies have been interpreted in the light of this hypothesis (e.g., Martin et al., 1995; McFarlane et al., 1995; Shek, 1998a). Theoretically, there are at least two ways by which family functioning might influence adolescent adjustment - family functioning can be regarded as a stressor which affects the emotional life of an adolescent, and family functioning would affect the willingness of the child to be socialized by the parents and/or the willingness of the parents to socialize the child (Darling & Steinberg, 1993). Because few attempts have been conducted to examine these possible mediating factors, further research should be carried out along these lines.

The second possible explanation is that those with mental health problems tend to perceive one's family in a more negative manner (i.e., perceptual distortion hypothesis). However, the validity of this possibility is not high for two reasons. First, an examination of the correlation patterns in the clinical and non-clinical groups in Study 2 showed that they are highly similar. In other words, the patterns of correlation coefficients are relatively the same in adolescents with and without individual and/or family problems. Second, because the samples in Study 1 and Study 3 were drawn from normal student population (i.e., not clinical samples), this possible explanation can also be partially dismissed (Shek, 1988b).

Third, the findings can be explained in terms of the concept of spurious correlation (i.e., two variables are correlated because both of them are caused by a third variable). One possible source of spuriousness is response styles, such as social desirability. In the absence of data on social desirability, this possibility remains to be a viable alternative explanation.

Finally, we should be mindful of the possibility that behavior of the adolescent (e.g., distress and lack of life meaning) may be a precursor of poor family functioning. Although several studies have failed to support the thesis that a distressed or dissatisfied person would perform poorly in the family and maintain a poor relationship with the family members (e.g., Dressler, 1991; Mirowsky & Ross, 1989), there are research findings suggesting that individual psychological adjustment influences family functioning. Using children's and parents' reports of family functioning (N=378), Shek (1998a) examined the relationships between family functioning and adolescent psychological well-being. Results showed that family functioning based on ratings obtained from different sources were concurrently related to hopelessness, life satisfaction, self-esteem, purpose in life, and general psychiatric morbidity at Time 1 and Time 2. Longitudinal and prospective analyses (Time 1 predictors predicting Time 2 criterion variables) suggest that the relations between family functioning and adolescent psychological well-being were bidirectional in nature.

Because the research design intrinsic to these three studies is cross-sectional in nature, all of the above four interpretations are plausible. Therefore, interpretation of the present data in terms of causal links amongst the variables should proceed in caution. However, this limitation is also present in the existing cross-sectional studies examining the link between family functioning and adolescent adjustment. In view of the paucity of research data on this topic in the Chinese context, the present findings can be regarded as stimulating and they reinforce the previous findings on the linkage between family functioning and adolescent psychological well-being.

The data also provide some support for the links between family functioning and school adjustment and substance abuse, although the effect sizes were observed to be small for the significant correlations. These data are generally consistent with the previous findings that family functioning was related to academic performance (Wentzel, 1994), conduct problems (Frick, Lahey, Loeber, & Stouthamer-Loeber, 1992), and substance abuse (Doherty & Allen, 1994). Basically, the four interpretations outlined earlier for adolescent psychological well-being are also applicable here. Of course, we should be aware of the limitation of the related findings for only one single item was used to measure each construct related to school adjustment and problem behavior.

The present findings generate a number of issues that deserve our attention. First, besides psychological distress symptoms, the present study shows that family functioning is associated with adolescent positive mental health. This observation is important for there have been few previous attempts in investigating the relationship between these two domains. In particular, because life meaning and existential well-being (Frankl, 1963) have been regarded as basic motivational forces governing human behavior, one may hypothesize that family functioning might influence different aspects of adolescent adjustment via such motivational factors. This possibility is quite attractive, particularly in view of the fact that not much effort has been made to locate the mechanisms which mediate between the family environment and adolescent developmental outcomes (Darling & Steinberg, 1993).

The second issue is that the findings based on the three studies consistently show that family functioning has a stronger correlation with measures of psychological well-being than with indicators of school adjustment and substance abuse. There are two possible explanations of this observation. The first explanation is that compared with school adjustment and substance abuse, family functioning may have a more direct effect on the psychological well-being of adolescent children. This explanation is reasonable because poor family functioning (such as family conflict) may easily generate stress and frustration (e.g., a sense of lack of control) on adolescent children, which may in turn spill over to school adjustment and substance abuse. One implication of this interpretation is that future studies should take into account the emotional lives of adolescents in relation to family functioning. The second explanation is in terms of the methodological limitation of the present studies.

Because only a few items were used to measure school adjustment and substance abuse, the sensitivity of the measures may be low, thus contributing to the relatively lower correlation coefficients observed in these two domains.

Third, the findings show that family functioning based on different family models (Beavers Systems Model, McMaster Family Functioning Model, and Indigenous Derived Model) are related to adolescent psychological well-being. This observation can be accounted for by at least two explanations - either there is a substantial overlap of the content of the existing models and measures of family functioning or the linkage between family functioning and adolescent adjustment is relatively stable across theories and cultures. If the first possibility is valid, there is a need to refine and integrate the content of the existing models of family functioning. If the latter explanation holds, there is a need to further explore what are the common mechanisms involved in the relationship between the family environment and adolescent adjustment across cultures. There are two possible directions for future research in connection with these explanations. First, effort should be made to examine the relationships between discrete dimensions of family functioning (such as communication, problem solving, emotional expressiveness) and adolescent adjustment across cultures. Second, qualitative studies should be carried out to examine the experiences of adolescents in families with different levels of family functioning so that the related mechanisms can be explored.

Finally, because the patterns of correlations between the Family Assessment Instrument (FAI) and measures of adolescent adjustment are highly similar to the patterns of correlations between other translated measures of family functioning and adolescent adjustment, one might question whether there is a need to construct local tools. In the area of family assessment, there are views suggesting that Western measures may not be applicable in non-Western contexts. For example, in an attempt to evaluate the application of the Family Assessment Device to two non-Anglo ethnic groups, Morris (1990) concluded that "this study provides some warning signals for family practitioners using the FAD, or any other standardized family assessment device, with an ethnically varied population" (p.115). However, the findings generated from the studies reported in this paper appear to be not consistent with the conclusions reached by Morris (1990). The reported studies generally suggest that the findings based on the translated scales and the locally developed scale are relatively similar.

There are several possible explanations of this observation. First, it may be possible that the ingredients of healthy family functioning across cultures are relatively universal. While there are views arguing that the conceptions of family functioning may differ for different cultures (Walsh, 1993), there are also views suggesting that certain psychological constructs appear to be universally applicable. In the area of personality assessment, for example, Yik and Bond (1993) reported that the findings based on imported and indigenous measures of personality perception for Hong Kong Chinese did not differ much and they argued that "imported measures may cut the phenomenal world differently from the imported measures, but still enable scientists to predict behavior just as effectively .... the present results would challenge the investment required to develop local instrumentation on scientific grounds" (p.75).

The second possible explanation is that in view of the rapid pace of westernization in Hong Kong, it is possible that Chinese people are also very Westernized. As a result, the use of translated Western measures would yield findings that are similar to those based on the indigenous measure, which might include items that are relatively Westernized. Finally, the observed results may be due to spuriousness. One possible source of spurious relationship is common method variance because all the measures employed are self-report rating scales. Obviously, these possibilities constitute exciting research hypotheses for the future studies.

There are four limitations of the present study. First, because the research findings reported in the present study are based on adolescents in Hong Kong, there is a need to replicate the findings obtained and to assess the generalizability of the findings in different adolescent samples in different Chinese communities. In particular, whether the present observations can be replicated in Chinese people living in non-Chinese contexts (e.g., Chinese Americans) remains to be explored. Second, the assessment of family functioning was limited to adolescents in these studies. Because there are research findings suggesting that parents and their adolescent children may have different perceptions of their families (Noller & Callan, 1986), assessment based on parents' perspective may enhance our understanding of the problem area. In particular, it would be methodologically desirable if both family functioning and adolescent adjustment can be assessed by multiple informants, including those informants outside the family.

The third limitation is that because all measures employed in these studies are based on the self-report method, it is possible that the significant correlations between the family assessment tools and measures of adolescent adjustment are due to common method variance. It would be illuminating if other methods of assessment (e.g., observational and interview methods) can be included to assess family functioning and adolescent adjustment as well. Finally, because there is only one longitudinal study in this area in the Chinese culture (Shek, 1998a), more longitudinal studies should be carried out to clarify the causal relationship between family functioning and adolescent adjustment. Despite these limitations, the present studies can be regarded as ground breaking and they constitute interesting additions to the literature.

REFERENCES

Alnajjar, A., & Smadi, A. (1998). Delinquents' and non-delinquents' perception of family functioning in the United Arab Emirates. *Social behavior and Personality, 26*, 375-382.

Beavers, W. R., & Hampson, R. B. (1990). *Successful families: Assessment and intervention.* New York: Norton.

Beavers, W. R., Hampson, R. B., & Hulgus, Y. F. (1990). *Beavers systems model manual.* Dallas, Texas: Southwest Family Institute.

Bosma, H. A., & Gerrits, R. S. (1985). Contemporary approaches to the study of families with adolescents. *Journal of Early Adolescence, 5*, 69-80.

Bradburn, N. M. (1969). *The structure of psychological well-being.* Chicago: Aldine.

Cattell, R. B. (1966). The scree test for the number of factors. *Multivariate Behavioral Research, 1*, 245.

Chan, D. W. (1985). The Chinese version of the General Health Questionnaire: Does language make a difference? *Psychological Medicine, 15*, 147-155.

Cohen, J. (1992). A power primer. *Psychological Bulletin, 112*, 155-159.

Cohen, J. (1994). The earth is round (p < .05). *American Psychologist, 49*, 997-1003.

Cumsille, P. E., & Epstein, N. (1994). Family cohesion, family adaptability, social support, and adolescent depressive symptoms in outpatient clinic families. *Journal of Family Psychology, 8*(2), 202-214.

Darling, N., & Steinberg, L. (1993). Parenting style as context: An integrative model. *Psychological Bulletin, 113*(3), 487-496.

Diener, E. (1984). Subjective well-being. *Psychological Bulletin, 95*(3), 542-575.

Diener, E., Emmons, R. A., Larsen, R. J., & Griffin, S. (1985). The Satisfaction with Life Scale. *Journal of Personality Assessment, 49*, 71-75.

Doherty, W. J., & Allen, W. (1994). Family functioning and parental smoking as predictors of adolescent cigarette use: A six-year prospective study. *Journal of Family Psychology, 8*(3), 347-353.

Dressler, W. W. (1991). *Stress and adaptation in the context of culture: Depression in a southern black community.* Albany, NY: State University of New York Press.

Epstein, N. B., Baldwin, L. M., & Bishop, D. S. (1983). The McMaster Family Assessment Device. *Journal of Marital and Family Therapy, 9*, 171-180.

Farrington, D. P. 1995. The development of offending and antisocial behavior from childhood. *Journal of Child Psychology and Psychiatry and Allied Disciplines, 36*(6), 929-964.

Feldman, S. S., Fisher, L., & Seitel, L. (1997). The effect of parents' marital satisfaction on young adults' adaptation: a longitudinal study. *Journal of Research on Adolescence, 7*, 55-80.

Fincham, F. D. (1994). Understanding the association between marital conflict and child adjustment: An overview. *Journal of Family Psychology, 8*, 123-127.

Frankl, V. E. (1963). *Man's search for meaning: An introduction to logotherapy.* New York: Washington Square Press.

Frick, P. J., Lahey, B. B., Loeber, R., & Stouthamer-Loeber, M. (1992). Familial risk factors to oppositional defiant disorder and conduct disorder: Parental psychopathology and maternal parenting. *Journal of Consulting and Clinical Psychology, 60*(1), 49-55.

Garber, J., Little, S., Hilsman, R., & Weaver, K. R. (1998). Family predictors of suicidal symptoms in young adolescents. *Journal of Adolescence, 21*, 445-457.

Goldberg, D. P. (1972). *The detection of psychiatric illness by questionnaire.* Oxford: Oxford University Press.

Green, R. G. (1987). Self-report measures of family competence. *American Journal of Family Therapy, 15*, 163-168.

Green, R. G. (1989). Choosing family measurement devices for practice and research: SFI and FACES III. *Social Service Review, 63*, 304-320.

Hampson, R. B., Beavers, W. R., & Hulgus, Y. F. (1989). Insiders' and outsiders' views of family: The assessment of family competence and style. *Journal of Family Psychology, 3*, 118-136.

Hundert, J., Cassie, J., & Johnston, N. (1988). Characteristics of emotionally disturbed children referred to day-treatment, special-class, outpatient, and assessment services. *Journal of Clinical Child Psychology, 17*(2), 121-130.

Jacob, T. (Ed.). (1987). *Family interaction and psychopathology: Theories, methods and findings.* New York: Plenum.

Kabacoff, R., Miller, I., Bishop, D., Epstein, N., & Keitner, G. (1990). A psychometric study of the McMaster Family Assessment in psychiatric, medical, and nonclinical samples. *Journal of Family Psychology, 3*, 431-439.

Kaslow, N., Warner, V., John, K., & Brown, R. (1992). Intrainformant agreement and family functioning in depressed and nondepressed parents and their children. *American Journal of Family Therapy, 20*(3), 204-217.

Kraemer, H. C., & Thieman, S. (1987). *How many subjects? Statistical power analysis in research*. Newbury Park, CA: Sage.

Larzelere, R. E., & Mulaik, S. A. (1977). Single-sample tests for many correlations. *Psychological Bulletin, 84*(3), 557-569.

Maccoby, E. E., & Martin, J. A. (1983). Socialization in the context of the family: parent-child interaction. In E. Hetheringon (Ed.), *Handbook of child psychology. Volume 4 (p.1-101)*. New York: Wiley.

Mandara, J., & Murray, C. B. (2000). Effects of parental marital status, income, and family functioning on African American adolescent self-esteem. *Journal of Family Psychology, 14*, 475-490.

Martin, G., Rozanes, P., Pearce, C., & Allison, S. (1995). Adolescent suicide, depression and family dysfunction. *Acta Psychiatrica Scandinavica, 92*(5), 336-344.

McFarlane, A. H., Bellissimo, A., & Norman, G. R. (1995). Family structure, family functioning and adolescent well-being: The transcendent influence of parental style. *Journal of Child Psychology and Psychiatry and Allied Disciplines, 36*(5), 847-864.

McKay, J. R., Murphy, R. T., Rivinus, T. R., & Maisto, S. A. (1991). Family dysfunction and alcohol and drug use in adolescent psychiatric inpatients. *Journal of the American Academy of Child and Adolescent Psychiatry, 30*(6), 967-972.

McKenry, P. C., Tishler, C. L., & Kelley, C. (1982). Adolescent suicide: A comparison of attempters and nonattempters in an emergency room population. *Clinical Pediatrics, 21*(5), 266-270.

Mirowsky, J., & Ross, C. E. (1989). *Social causes of psychological distress*. New York: Aldine de Gruyter.

Morris, T. M. (1990). Culturally sensitive family assessment: An evaluation of the Family Assessment Device used with Hawaiian-American and Japanese-American families. *Family Process, 29*, 105-116.

Moser, C. A., & Kalton, G. (1980). *Survey methods in social investigation*. London: Heinemann Educational Books.

Munichin, S. (1974). *Families and family therapy*. Cambridge, MA: Harvard University Press.

Noller, P., & Callan, V. J. (1986). Adolescent and parent perceptions of family cohesion and adaptability. *Journal of Adolescence, 9*, 97-106.

Ohannessian, C. M., Lerner, R. M., Lerner, J. V., & von Eye, A. (1995). Discrepancies in adolescents' and parents' perceptions of family functioning and adolescent emotional adjustment. *Journal of Early Adolescence, 15*(4), 490-516.

Paloutzian, R. F., & Ellison, C. W. (1982). Lonliness, spiritual well-being and the quality of life. In L.A. Peplau and D. Perlman (Eds.), *Lonliness; A sourcebook of current theory, research and therapy (p.224-237)*. New York: Wiley.

Papero, D. V. (1990). *Bowen family systems theory*. Boston: Allyn & Bacon.

Patterson, G. R., Crosby, L., & Vuchinich, S. (1992). Predicting risk for early police arrest. *Journal of Quantitative Criminology, 8*(4), 335-355.

Pearlin, L. I., & Schooler, C. (1978). The structure of coping. *Journal of Health and Social Behavior, 22*, 337-356.

Phillips, M. R., West, C. L., Shen, Q., & Zheng, Y. P. (1998). Comparison of schizophrenic patients' families and normal families in China, using Chinese version of FACES-II and the Family Environment Scales. *Family Process, 37*, 95-106.

Prange, M. E., Greenbaum, P. E., Silver, S. E., Friedman, R., Kutask, K., & Duchnowski, A. J. (1992). Family functioning and psychopathology among adolescents with severe emotional disturbances. *Journal of Abnormal Child Psychology, 20*(1), 83-102.

Robin, A. L., & Foster, S. L. (1989). *Negotiating parent-adolescent conflict.* New York: The Guilford Press.

Ryff, C. D., & Singer, B. (1996). Psychological well-being: Meaning, measurement, and implications for psychotherapy research. *Psychotherapy and Psychosomatics, 65*, 14-23.

Satir, V., & Baldwin, M. (1983). *Satir step by step: A guide to creating change in families.* Palo Alto, CA: Science and Behavior Books.

Shagle, S. C., & Barber, B. K. (1995). A social-ecological analysis of adolescent suicide ideation. *American Journal of Orthopsychiatry, 65*(1), 114-124.

Shaver, J. P. (1993). What statistical significance testing is, and what it is not. *Journal of Experimental Education, 61*, 293-316.

Shek, D. T. L. (1988a). Reliability and factorial structure of the Chinese version of the State-Trait Anxiety Inventory. *Journal of Psychopathology and Behavioral Assessment, 10*(4), 303-317.

Shek, D. T. L. (1988b). Mental health of secondary school students in Hong Kong: An epidemiological study using the General Health Questionnaire. *International Journal of Adolescent Medicine and Health, 3*(3), 191-215.

Shek, D. T. L. (1989). Validity of the Chinese version of the General Health Questionnaire. *Journal of Clinical Psychology, 45*(6), 890-897.

Shek, D. T. L. (1991). The factorial structure of the Chinese version of the State-Trait Anxiety Inventory: A confirmatory factor analysis. *Educational and Psychological Measurement, 51*, 985-997.

Shek, D. T. L. (1992). "Actual-ideal" discrepancies in the representation of self and significant-others and psychological well-being in Chinese adolescents. *International Journal of Psychology, 27*(3 & 4), 229.

Shek, D. T. L. (1993). The factor structure of the Chinese version of the General Health Questionnaire (GHQ-30): A confirmatory factor analysis. *Journal of Clinical Psychology, 49*, 678-684.

Shek, D. T. L. (1997). The relation of family functioning to adolescent psychological well-being, school adjustment, and problem behavior. *Journal of Genetic Psychology, 158*(4), 467-479.

Shek, D. T. L. (1998a). A longitudinal study of the relations of family functioning to adolescent psychological well-being. *Journal of Youth Studies, 1*(2), 195-209.

Shek, D. T. L. (1998b). The Chinese version of the Self-Report Family Inventory: Does culture make a difference? *Research on Social Work Practice, 8*, 315-329.

Shek, D. T. L. (2001a). Reliability and factor structure of the Chinese version of the Self-Report Family Inventory in Chinese adolescents. *Journal of Clinical Psychology, 57*(3), 375-385.

Shek, D. T. L. (2001b). Psychometric properties of the Chinese version of the Self-Report Family Inventory: Findings based on a longitudinal study. *Research on Social Work Practice, 11*(4), 485-502.

Shek, D. T. L. (in press, a). Assessment of Family Functioning in Chinese Adolescents: The Chinese Version of the Family Assessment Device (FAD). *Research on Social Work Practice.*

Shek, D. T. L. (in press, b). The General Functioning Scale of the Family assessment Device: Does it work in the Chinese culture? *Journal of Clinical Psychology.*

Shek, D. T. L. (in press, c). Psychometric properties of the Chinese version of the Family Awareness Scale. *Journal of Social Psychology.*

Shek, D. T. L. (in press, d). Perceptions of happy families among Chinese adolescents and their parents: Implications for family therapy. *Family Therapy.*

Shek, D. T. L. (in press, e). Assessment of family functioning in Chinese adolescents: The Chinese Family Assessment Instrument. In N.N. Singh, T. Ollendick, and A.N. Singh (Eds.), *International perspectives on child and adolescent mental health.* Amsterdam, The Netherlands: Elsevier Science.

Shek, D. T. L. & Lai, K. (2001). The Chinese version of the Self-Report Family Inventory: Reliability and validity. *American Journal of Family Therapy, 29*, 207-220.

Shon, S. P., & Ja, D. Y. (1982). Asian families. In M. McGoldrick, J.K. Pearce, and J. Giordano (Eds.), *Ethnicity and family therapy (pp.208-220).* New York: The Guilford Press.

Smart, L. S., Chibucos, T. R., & Didier, L. A. (1990). Adolescent substance use and perceived family functioning. *Journal of Family Issues, 11*(2), 208-227.

Spielberger, C. D., Gorsuch, R. C., & Lushene, R. F. (1970). *Manual for the State-Trait Anxiety Inventory.* Palo Alto, CA: Consulting Psychologists Press.

Steiger, J. H. (1980). Tests for comparing elements of a correlation matrix. *Psychological Bulletin, 87*, 245-251.

Sweeting, H., & West, P. (1995). Family life and health in adolescence: A role for culture in the health inequalities debate? *Social Science and Medicine, 40*(2), 163-175.

Tabachnick, B. G., & Fidell, L. S. (1989). *Using multivariate statistics.* New York: Harper and Row.

Tolan, P. H., & Lorion, R. P. (1988). Multivariate approaches to the identification of delinquency proneness in adolescent males. *American Journal of Community Psychology, 16*(4), 547-561.

Tsoi, M. M., Ho, E., & Mak, K. C. (1986). Becoming pregnant again after stillbirth or the birth of a handicapped child. In L. Dennerstein & I. Fraser (Eds.), *Hormone and Behavior (pp.310-316).* Holland: Elsevier Science Publisher.

Varni, J. W., Katz, E. R., Colegrove, G., & Dolgin, M. (1996). Family functioning predictors of adjustment in children with newly diagnosed cancer: A prospective analysis. *Journal of Child Psychology and Psychiatry, 37*(3), 321-328.

Walker, L. S., McLaughlin, F., & Greene, J. W. (1988). Functional illness and family functioning: A comparison of healthy and somaticizing adolescents. *Family Process, 27*(3), 317-325.

Walsh, F. (1993). *Normal family processes*. New York: Guilford Press.

Wentzel, K. R. (1994). Family functioning and academic achievement in middle school: A social-emotional perspective. *Journal of Early Adolescence, 14*(2), 268-291.

Wright, B. R. (1964). Social aspects of change in Chinese family pattern in Hong Kong. *Journal of Social Psychology, 63*, 31-39.

Yang, K. S. (1981). The formation and change of Chinese personality: A cultural-ecological perspective. *Acta Psychologica Taiwanica, 23*, 39-56.

Yik, M. S. M., & Bond, M. H. (1993). Exploring the dimensions of Chinese person perception with indigenous and imported constructs: Creating a culturally balanced scale. *International Journal of Psychology, 28*, 75-95.

AUTHOR'S NOTE

The work described in this paper was financially supported by the Research Grants Council of the Hong Kong Special Administrative Region, P.R.C. (Project No. CUHK4012/97H), The Chinese University of Hong Kong, and Madam Tan Jen Chiu Fund. The author wishes to thank Chan Lai-kwan and Danny Yam for their assistance in collecting the data. Address all correspondence to Daniel T.L. Shek, Department of Social Work, The Chinese University of Hong Kong, Shatin, Hong Kong (E-Mail Address: DANIELSHEK@CUHK.EDU.HK).

Chapter 3

Conditional Associations Between Interparental Conflict and Adolescent Problems: A Search for Personality-Environment Interactions

Brian P. O'Connor [*] *and Troy Dvorak*
Lakehead University

Abstract

This chapter examines how the nature and magnitude of adolescent reactions to interparental conflict vary depending on the personality characteristics of the adolescents. Interparental conflict, five-factor model personality characteristics, and internalizing and externalizing disorders were examined in a community sample of 14-21 years olds (N = 376). Three aspects of interparental conflict were assessed, following the recommendations of Grych, Seid, and Fincham (1992, Child Development, vol. 63, pp. 558-572): (1) the occurrence of frequent, intense, and poorly resolved interparental conflict; (2) the degree to which the adolescents felt threatened and unable to cope when interparental conflict occurred; and (3) the frequency of child or adolescent-related conflict and the degree to which the adolescent respondents blamed themselves for the interparental conflict. The research was an extension of previous work by O'Connor and Dvorak (2001, Journal of Research in Personality, vol. 35, pp. 1-26) that focused on parenting styles but not on interparental conflict. A comprehensive sweep of the multivariate space defined by the five factor model revealed conditional effects for interparental conflict in the prediction of problems that varied depending on adolescent personality characteristics. The interactions occurred primarily for males, and for aggression and delinquency. Examinations of the interaction patterns provided answers to

[*] Address correspondence to Brian P. O'Connor, Department of Psychology, Lakehead University, 955 Oliver Road, Thunder Bay, Ontario, Canada, P7B 5E1. e-mail: brian.oconnor@lakeheadu.ca

questions about the relative frequency of adolescent personality resiliency and vulnerability when living in high interparental conflict environments.

Does interparental conflict have an effect on the subsequent development of depression, anxiety and conduct disorders in children and adolescents? Extensive research has repeatedly provided evidence for moderately harmful effects (Buehler, Anthony, Krishnakumar, & Stone, 1997; Cummings & Davies, 2002; Kelly, 2000). However, the magnitudes of the effects vary substantially across studies and there have been growing calls for researchers to switch away from the common focus on main effects to a focus on moderating variables (Cummings, Goeke-Morey, Marcie, & Dukewich, 2001; Davies & Windle, 2001; Emery, 1982; Hetherington, Bridges, & Insabella, 1998; Katz & Gottman, 1997; Kerig, 1998; Margolin, Oliver, & Medina, 2001; Snyder, 1998). The negative effects of interparental conflict may be stronger for some types of children than for others. It is thus important for researchers to discover the factors that increase vulnerability and resiliency among children living in high interparental conflict environments. Personality-environment interactions of this kind have been relatively neglected in empirical research, yet they are often considered important in developmental theories, in diathesis models of psychopathology, and in person-environment fit models of psychological adjustment.

Personality-environment interactions have recently been examined in research on the potentially harmful effects of inadequate parenting styles (O'Connor & Dvorak, 2001). Main effects for inadequate parenting on child and adolescent psychopathology often occur, but so do interactions. Striking findings of this kind were reported by Wootton, Frick, Shelton, and Silverthorn (1997), who interviewed the parents of clinic-referred and non-referred six to 13-year olds, assessing parenting styles, the existence of callous-unemotional traits in the children, and conduct disorders. They found that "ineffective parenting" was unrelated to the incidence of conduct problems in children who were manipulative, emotionally constricted, and low on empathy and guilt. Children with such characteristics had high levels of conduct problems regardless of the degree of ineffective parenting they received. However, ineffective parenting was associated with increased conduct problems among children who did not possess these traits. Some kinds of children will apparently develop problems regardless of parental behavior, whereas others will develop problems only if they receive ineffective parenting. The child's personality determines whether and how parents matter, and whether a primary target for intervention should be the child or the parents.

The present chapter extends previous work by focusing on how child and adolescent personality characteristics moderate the impact of interparental conflict on psychopathology. The data and analytic techniques used for the present report were highly similar to those we used in a recent investigation of parenting styles (O'Connor & Dvorak, 2001). However, in the present chapter, general parenting styles are ignored in an attempt to focus solely on previously unreported data patterns for interparental conflict.

Personality-environment interactions may take a number of different forms. In contrast with the bad apple pattern reported by Wootton et al. (1997), children with some kinds of personality characteristics may be relatively immune to both interparental conflict and psychological disorders. Phrasing the possible interactions in the form of questions illustrates the possibilities more vividly. Does interparental conflict only sometimes matter? i.e., Does it matter only for some kinds of children and not others? Might some personality characteristics serve a protective function in some interparental conflict environments, and might the same characteristics increase vulnerability in other interparental conflict environments? What kinds of children are affected or unaffected by interparental conflict? If interparental conflict increases problems for some children, then does the absence of interparental conflict merely reduce the risk to normative levels, or does it reduce risk to lower-than-normative levels? Might the same level of interparental conflict be associated with increased risk in some children, and reduced risk in others? Might some exasperated parents be correct when they say that the problem seems to be with their child's personality and not with their interparental conflict? Counselors familiar with the bivariate relationships reported in the literature might mistakenly redirect blame back onto these parents, and their interventions may be distressing and futile (Turner & Dadds, 2001). The familiar-but-modest bivariate relationships may be hiding associations that are conditional and not universal. The identification of moderated relationships thus seems both theoretically and practically important (O'Connor & Dvorak, 2001).

O'Connor and Dvorak (2001, pp. 3-4) described five basic kinds or forms of linear interactions that can exist between two variables in the prediction of a third. These forms of interaction are depicted in Figure 1. The universe of possibilities may appear to include more than just these five kinds. For example, reversing the scoring for interparental conflict produces horizontal axis inversions of each of the five patterns in Figure 1. Similarly, reversing the scoring of the personality moderators causes the "high" and "low" lines to switch places. However, such reverse-scorings of variables do not increase the number of basic forms that the interactions can take, and it is conceptually and practically parsimonious to work with the reduced set of five basic forms of linear interaction. The verbal descriptions of the interactions that are provided in Figure 1 are "scoring-neutral" and should help illustrate these points.

For all five kinds of interactions, the relationship between interparental conflict and the development of problems depends on the personality characteristics of the children. However, the nature of this relationship is often dramatically different across kinds of interaction. Perhaps the biggest contrast is between Patterns A and B. In Pattern A, children will not develop problems unless they are exposed to interparental conflict, and, even then, the personality characteristics of some children make them immune to the otherwise negative effects of such conflict. In contrast, Pattern B depicts some children as prone to developing problems regardless of the kind of their exposure to interparental conflict, and other children as being likely to develop problems only if exposed to interparental conflict (as in the Wootton et al. study on ineffective parenting). In Pattern C, variation along the interparental conflict dimension increases or decreases problems beyond normative levels depending on the child's personality. In Pattern D, high levels of a interparental conflict result in normative levels of problems for all children, whereas low levels of interparental conflict can result in either high of low levels of problems depending on the child's personality. Pattern E represents the most dramatic kind of interaction between interparental conflict and child personality. Both high and low levels of interparental conflict can produce both high and low levels of problems, depending on the child's personality. It is thus seem important to learn about (1) the kinds of interparental conflict-child personality interactions that actually exist, (2) the kinds that are most common, (3) the interparental conflict variables on which the interactions occur, (4) the psychopathology variables for which the interactions occur, and (5) the personality variables that moderate interparental conflict effects.

Figure 1: Patterns of Linear Interaction

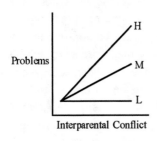

Pattern A: Personality can serve as a buffer against interparental conflict

Children with particular personality characteristics (L) will have low levels of problems regardless of exposure to interparental conflict; children who have the opposite kinds of traits (H) will only develop problems if exposed to interparental conflict.

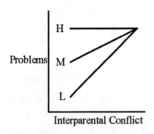

Pattern B: Personality can be a hopeless problem

Children with particular personality characteristics (H) will develop problems regardless of exposure to interparental conflict; children who have the opposite kinds of traits (L) will only develop problems if exposed to interparental conflict.

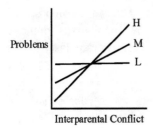

Pattern C: Responsive to interparental conflict or else moderately problematic

Children with particular personality characteristics (L) will develop average levels of problems regardless of exposure to interparental conflict; children who have the opposite kinds of traits (H) will develop either more than average or less than average problems depending on their exposure to interparental conflict.

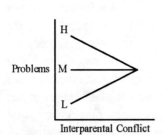

Pattern D: Moderately problematic or dramatically different

Children with average levels of particular personality characteristics (M) will have average levels of problems regardless of exposure to interparental conflict; children with high (H) or low (L) levels of these traits will also have average levels of problems when exposed to one level of interparental conflict, but they will develop either more than average (H) or less than average (L) problems when exposed to the opposite level of interparental conflict.

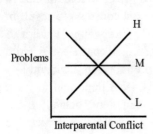

Pattern E: High levels of parental discrimination are required

Children with average levels of particular personality characteristics (M) will have average levels of problems regardless of exposure to interparental conflict; children with high (H) or low (L) levels of these traits will also have average levels of problems when they are exposed to average levels of interparental conflict; but when levels of interparental conflict are extreme, children with high and low levels of these particular traits will develop either high or low levels of problems depending on the level of interparental conflict.

The present study, closely following O'Connor and Dvorak (2001), was designed to provide a relatively thorough exploration of the range of potential interparental conflict-child personality interactions. Self-reports were collected from a large community sample of adolescents; three forms of interparental conflict were assessed (A: the occurrence of frequent, intense, and poorly resolved interparental conflict; B: the degree to which the adolescents felt threatened and unable to cope when interparental conflict occurred; and C: the frequency of child or adolescent-related conflict and the degree to which the adolescent respondents blamed themselves for the interparental conflict); we measured traits from the five-factor model (FFM) of personality; and we measured four kinds of adolescent problems (depression, anxiety, aggression, and delinquency). The FFM was used because of its comprehensiveness (Digman, 1990; McCrae & John, 1992). The five factors (neuroticism, extraversion, openness to experience, agreeableness, and conscientiousness) have repeatedly emerged from lexical and factor analytic investigations of personality traits, including studies of children and adolescents (Huey & Weisz, 1997; Robins, John & Caspi, 1994). Other personality characteristics, such as temperamental traits, are believed to be particular blends of the five dimensions and can be understood in terms of their locations in five-factor space (Digman, 1994). The debate over the comprehensiveness of the five-factor model is ongoing (O'Connor, 2002), but the model nevertheless provides a good starting point for a broad probe for moderated relationships.

The present tests for moderated relationships did not focus solely on scores on the five factors. The five factors are merely the dimensions of a multivariate space, and most of the personality variables that have been of interest to psychologists are blends of the five factors and exist in various regions of this space, i.e., in the spaces in between dimensional scores (O'Connor & Dvorak, 2001, p. 5). Focusing solely on dimensional scores provides a limited view of moderated relationships because (1) relatively few personality variables of interest fall squarely on dimensional scores, and (2) the strongest or most important moderators of interparental conflict may be for personality variables that are particular blends of dimensional scores. We therefore used the dimensional scores to construct a large number of vectors of scores reflecting blends of the five factors, providing a relatively comprehensive sweep of the five factor space. We were curious to see what interactions exist between personality vectors and adolescent problems.

In summary, our purpose was to identify the occurrence and nature of interparental conflict-child personality interactions that can be observed in data from a community sample. How common are such interactions and what forms do they take? Is it common for some kinds of child personality characteristics to be associated with problems regardless of interparental conflict (Pattern B)? Is it more common for child personality characteristics to serve as buffers against interparental conflict (Pattern A)? Are the interactions more complex and potentially challenging for parents and counselors (Patterns C, D, and E)?

METHOD

Participants and Procedure

The participants were 376 students from local schools and first year university classes (N = 25 in grade nine; 60 in grade ten; 102 in grade 11; 62 in grade 12; 36 in grade 13; and 91 in first year university). There were 130 males and 246 females. The ages ranged from 14 to 21, $M = 17.1$, $SD = 1.8$. All participants lived with at least one of their parents.

Individuals were asked to participate in a study on "parenting styles and behavior." They were informed that their participation was voluntary, that there were no risks or benefits associated with their participation, that their responses would remain anonymous and confidential, and that they were free to withdraw at any time. Individuals 16 years and under were given parental consent forms to be completed and returned before participation. Public and high school participants completed the questionnaires during class time, whereas the university students completed the questionnaires either during class or shortly afterwards at designated locations. The mean participation time was 45 minutes. All were debriefed upon completion. The advantages and disadvantages of self-report methodology in research on adolescent problems are reviewed in the Discussion section.

Measures

Interparental Conflict

Participants completed Grych, Seid, and Fincham's (1992) 51-item Children's Perception of Interparental Conflict Scale (CPIC). The measure contains three subscales: (1) Conflict Properties, which assesses the occurrence of frequent, intense, and poorly resolved interparental conflict; (2) Threat, which assesses the degree to which the adolescents felt threatened and unable to cope when interparental conflict occurred; and (3) Content, which assesses the frequency of child or adolescent-related conflict and the degree to which the adolescent respondents blamed themselves for the interparental conflict. The instructions that preceded the items in the present study were as follows: "In every family there are times when the parents don't get along. When their parents argue or disagree, people can feel a lot of different ways. We would like to know what kind of feelings you have when your parents have arguments or disagreements. If your parents don't live together in the same house with you, think about times that they are together when they don't agree or about times when both of your parents lived in the same house, when you answer these questions. If you have a step-parent or some other adult who has been living with you a long time, then you should answer the questions below while thinking about their disagreements."

The Cronbach alpha reliabilities for the present sample were .95 for Conflict Properties, .88 for Threat, and .92 for Content. The CPIC has good test-retest reliability and scores are significantly correlated with parental reports of interparental conflict (Grych et al., 1992). The measure is also appropriate for use with older children and adolescents (Bickham & Fiese, 1997; Harold, Fincham, Osborne, & Conger, 1997).

Five-Factor Model

Participants rated their personality characteristics on Saucier's (1994) markers of the big five personality dimensions, which were derived from a larger set carefully developed by Goldberg (1992). The measure consists of 40 unipolar trait adjectives, with eight internally consistent adjectives tapping each of the five dimensions. Saucier selected items that were relatively close to the prototypical cores of the five factors. The items are also more familiar and less difficult than items in other measures of the big five, and are thus better suited for use with younger populations. The items display low interscale correlations and higher within-scale correlations. Seven of Saucier's items are semantically redundant with other items in his list (e.g., organized, disorganized) and were therefore replaced with nonredundant items from the relevant factors in Goldberg's original list. The correlations between the items were subjected to a principal components analysis and the overall congruence between the loadings and a target matrix of ones and zeros representing the theoretical loadings of the adjectives on the five factors was .88. Factor scores on the five rotated dimensions were used in the analyses.

Depression

Participants completed the 27-item Child Depression Inventory (CDI; Kovacs, 1992), which assesses the cognitive, affective, behavioral, and vegetative symptoms of depression (sample item: "I am sad all the time"). Many of the CDI items were derived from the Beck Depression inventory, with wording adjustments for use with younger populations. The CDI items are internally consistent and moderately stable over time. CDI scores are correlated with clinicians' ratings of depression and with other measures of depression, and discriminate between nonreferred and clinical respondents (see Kovacs, 1992, for a review).

Anxiety

Participants completed the 28-item Revised Children's Manifest Anxiety Scale (Reynolds & Richmond, 1985), which assesses anxiety as manifested in somatic problems, worry and rumination, and problems with attention and concentration (sample item: "I often worry about something bad happening to me"). Many of the items were derived from the Taylor Manifest Anxiety Scale, with wording adjustments for use with younger populations. The items are internally consistent, and scores are highly stable over time. Scores are strongly correlated with other trait measures of anxiety, but not with state measures or IQ.

Aggressive and Delinquent Behavior

Achenbach's (1991) Youth Self-Report measure was used to measure aggressive behavior (19 items, sample item: "I am mean to others") and delinquent behavior (11 items, sample item: "I steal from places other than home"). These scales were developed from large, demographically diverse samples of clinically referred and nonreferred youths, and were designed to assess common presenting syndromes of problems. The scales were derived from principal components analyses of correlations among problem items. The items refer to problems occurring in the syndromes of both males and females, and in data from different informants. The aggression and delinquency scales of the Youth Self-Report are internally consistent, and scores are stable over time. Scores discriminate between demographically matched, clinically referred and nonreferred youths, and are correlated with parental and teacher judgments. It should be noted that only four of the items on the aggressiveness scale focus on physical aggression. The remaining 15 items focus on oppositional, defiant, and argumentative behaviors.

To reduce confusion, responses to all of the items were provided on eight-point Likert scales ranging from "extremely inaccurate" to "extremely accurate." The eight-point response format does not alter the meaning of scale scores for the present research purposes. The focus was on individual differences, and scale norms were not used in computing the participants' scores.

Statistical Analyses

Vectors of scores in five-factor space were computed by first selecting five possible weights, 1.0, .707, .00, -.707, and -1.0, that could each be given to each of the five dimensions. These weights are geometrically based and are perhaps most easily understood by reference to just two orthogonal dimensions, which would be at a 90 degree angle to one another and have a correlation of zero. A midpoint between the two dimensions, e.g., between zero and 90 degrees, would be 45 degrees, the cosine of which is .707. In correlation coefficient terms, .707 corresponds to 50% common variance. All possible combinations of these weights for five dimensions were derived. The all-zero weight set was eliminated, and sets of weights that were redundant with other weights due to opposite signs for all weights in a set were also eliminated, resulting in 1562 sets of weights for the analyses ($5^5 = 3125$, - 1 = 3124, /2 = 1562). However, many of the remaining weight sets are not geometrically meaningful and further pruning was possible. A careful consideration of geometrically valid and useful weight sets for two and three dimensional models revealed that the following two simple and logical rules can be used to prune less meaningful sets of weights:

(1) There can only be one value of "1" (or "-1") in a set of weights, and whenever there is a "1" (or "-1"), then all other weights must be "0". Values of "1" are reserved for vectors that point directly along one of the dimensions, which is necessarily orthogonal to the other dimensions. This simple two-part rule prunes very many vectors.

(2) For a five-dimensional model using our selected weight values, there cannot be more than three "0" values in a weight set that contains a value of .707 (or -.707). This is because whenever a vector bends even marginally away from one of the dimensional axes in a multidimensional space, then the vector necessarily protrudes into at least one other dimension of that space. Our desire to focus on 45 degree angle vectors, with values of .707 or -.707, means that there must always be at least two such values (and thus never more than three zeros) in a weight set.

(Readers are referred to Wiggins, Phillips, & Trapnell, 1989, for a two-dimensional depiction of some of these issues.) Applying these two rules reduced the number of vectors in our analyses from 1562 to 121. Composite scores were then computed by applying each set of weights to the five-factor model scores for each person. In summary, this procedure generated 121 vectors of scores, providing a relatively comprehensive sweep of the five-factor space. Each vector of scores can be thought of as a particular blend or recipe of five-factor scores. The use of more than five weights for each dimension yields an unmanageable number of composites, and five weights per dimension is probably sufficient to identify the major personality moderator variables

Moderated multiple regression (Aiken & West, 1991; Cohen & Cohen, 1983) was then used to test for interactions between interparental conflict variables and the five-factor composites in the prediction of the problem variables. For each tested interaction, the two predictors were first entered into a regression equation followed by their cross-product. A substantial increase in the variance accounted-for by the product term indicates an interaction. The independent variables were first "centered" (put in deviation score form so that their means were zero). We used an index of effect size to determine whether interactions were substantial or noteworthy (see Schmidt, 1996, for persuasive arguments favoring a focus on effect sizes rather than significance tests in psychological research). Specifically, we used the highest effect size reported by Wootton et al. (1997), Rsquared change = .031, as the minimum effect size for determining whether interactions occurred in our own data. Interactions of that magnitude were considered noteworthy in previous work; plots of Wootton et al.'s interactions revealed relationships between variables that appear distinctive upon visual inspection (see their pp. 306-307); and the present use of their maximum effect size as our own minimum effect size cut-off point is a conservative decision-rule. It is also worth noting that moderated regression is a notoriously conservative statistical technique for assessing interactions, especially for interactions in nonexperimental data (McClelland & Judd, 1993). "Significant" Rsquared change values of .01 have often been reported and discussed in psychological research, which again makes our chosen minimum cut-off point seem conservative.

Users of moderated regression have been urged to also test for the existence of curvilinear relationships in their data, which may provide an alternative explanation for the findings. The recommended practice is to have product terms (which carry the interaction) compete in a stepwise fashion with quadratic terms to determine which provides the greatest increment in the variance accounted for beyond the main effects. Interactions are said to exist when the R squared change values for product terms "win" the competition (Lubinski & Humphreys, 1990; MacCallum & Mar, 1995). In the present study a more conservative variant of this rule was used. The minimum effect size for a product term was .031, and the maximum effect size for either of the quadratic terms (for an interparental conflict variable or for a personality composite) was less than .015. All other occurrences were excluded from further analyses. Furthermore, once an interaction was deemed to exist, the full regression equation containing the main effects, the interaction term, and the two quadratic terms, was computed and any Rsquared change value for either of the quadratic terms that was greater-than or equal to .015 in this context caused all of the variables to be dropped from further moderated regression analyses.

The nature of an interaction that emerges from a moderated regression is typically elucidated by deriving regression equations for the dependent variable on the independent variable for different levels of the moderator (Aiken & West, 1991, p. 12; Cohen & Cohen, 1983, pp. 316-325). The overall regression equation is repeatedly solved using selected levels of the moderator variable (usually the mean, one SD below and one SD above the mean) and the independent variable (the highest and lowest scores). The computed values are then plotted. These simple slope analyses were conducted in the present study, but the interactions were too numerous for us to provide a plot for each one. Instead, in Figure 1 we provide a comprehensive depiction of the kinds of linear interactions that can occur, with a letter label (A, B, C, D, E) for each kind. We then used a set of decision rules to classify and letter-label each of the obtained interactions, and we provide counts of the kinds interactions that occurred for the various tested relationships.

The procedures for classifying each interaction into one of the five kinds of interaction depicted in Figure 1 were as follows. We computed: (1) the simple slopes for three levels of a moderator (the mean, one SD below, and one SD above); (2) the level of a moderator at which the slope of the DV on the IDV became zero; (3) the score of the IDV (parent variable) at which the high and low simple slopes intersect; and (4) the mean dependent variable levels of each of the simple slopes (see Aiken & West, 1991; Cohen & Cohen, 1983; Nye & Witt, 1995, for information on these computations). IF-statements were then applied to these four pieces of information to classify and label each interaction. For example, an interaction was labeled "A" if the slope of the DV on the IDV was flat at moderator values below one SD below the mean of the moderator; if the point of intersection of the high and low simple slopes was below one SD below the mean of the IDV; and if the mean DV score of the high-moderator simple slope was greater than the mean DV score of the low-moderator simple slope. Although five kinds of interaction are depicted in Figure 1, 18 kinds of linear interaction can actually emerge from the analyses. However, reverse-scorings of variables causes the larger set to collapse into the five basic forms. In the analyses we first categorized each interaction using the complete set of possibilities, and then collapsed the categories into the five kinds of interaction depicted in Figure 1 in order to simplify the presentation of the results. The set of decision rules for classifying interactions was comprehensive. All interactions that exceeded the minimum effect size fell into one (and only one) of the interaction categories.

The analyses were conducted using the MATLAB 5.3 software package. All of the computational procedures were carefully tested for accuracy by comparing the results with the results from SAS procedures.

RESULTS

Preliminary Analyses

The means, standard deviations, internal consistencies (Cronbach alphas) and intercorrelations between the variables are reported in Table 1. The intercorrelations between the interparental conflict variables and the problem variables were similar to those observed in previous work, and were generally the same for males and females. The positive correlations between depression, anxiety, aggression, and delinquency scores are consistent with previous findings regarding comorbidity of such disorders in children and adolescents (Brady & Kendall, 1992; McConaughy & Skiba, 1993; Russo & Beidel, 1994; Zoccolillo, 1992). Recent evidence indicates that comorbidities are due to overlapping risk factors (Fergusson, Lynskey, & Horwood, 1996).

Table 1. Means, Standard Deviations, Cronbach Alphas, and Pearson Correlations

	Mean	SD	Pearson Correlations											
			1	2	3	4	5	6	7	8	9	10	11	12
1. Depression	2.59	1.04	92	76	46	52	33	47	35	46	-20	-07	-25	-32
2. Anxiety	3.86	1.15	73	92	34	48	32	39	40	60	-22	-02	-11	-29
3. Aggression	3.03	1.16	52	30	90	66	19	49	12	37	17	03	-42	-28
4. Delinquency	3.06	1.21	50	32	69	82	29	50	25	51	32	06	-36	-28
5. Conflict Properties	3.42	1.48	18	22	37	31	95	43	80	16	-03	02	-03	-05
6. Conflict Threat	2.64	1.63	35	26	41	33	40	88	33	24	09	09	-17	-28
7. Conflict Content	2.58	1.78	21	26	32	32	76	29	92	22	-13	03	00	-08
8. Neuroticism	0.00	1.00	37	53	28	31	10	20	07	---	-06	-01	-22	-06
9. Extroversion	0.00	1.00	-25	-24	-05	18	-02	02	-07	10	---	00	02	-06
10. Openness	0.00	1.00	04	00	05	06	01	-01	05	02	03	---	-03	-02
11. Agreeableness	0.00	1.00	-20	-02	-42	-48	-20	-13	-15	09	-02	06	---	-04
12.Conscientiousness	0.00	1.00	-21	-08	-32	-16	-06	-19	03	-01	10	10	01	---

Note. Means for the first seven variables are on a 1-to-8 scale; variables 8-12 are factor scores; Cronbach alphas are on the diagonal; correlations for males are below the diagonal, correlations for females are above.

Moderated Regressions

The results of the moderated regressions are reported separately for males and females because of notable differences in the findings, and because the possible existence of gender differences in reaction to interparental conflict has been mentioned in previous work (Davies & Lindsay, 2001; Snyder, 1998). For males, 52 interactions exceeded the chosen minimum effect-size level (Rsquared change = .031), whereas only one interaction exceeded the same cut-off for females. We were concerned that a larger number of interactions may have existed in a bulge just below the cut-off point, and so the numbers of interactions were counted for a range of cut-off points. The results are plotted in Figure 2, and indicate that the number of effects increases dramatically with smaller effect sizes. This was particularly true for females, for whom there were few interactions for the .031 minimum effect size but dramatically more interactions for weaker minimum effect sizes.

To provide a further broad perspective on the results, the numbers of interactions were broken down by sex, interparental conflict behavior, and problem behavior, and are reported in Table 2. Findings are reported for analyses based on Rsquared change values of .031, and for analyses based on Rsquared change values of .015. Results for the weaker minimum effect size are reported because some readers may consider the .031 minimum effect size unusually stringent for interaction terms and may wonder whether some of the findings reported below are different for less stringent analyses. For males, and for both effect sizes, most of the interactions occurred for delinquency and aggression, with almost no effects for depression and anxiety. For females, there was only one interaction (for Conflict Threat and Aggression) for the .031 minimum effect size. However, there were 34 interactions for the .015 minimum effect size, almost all of which were for Aggression.

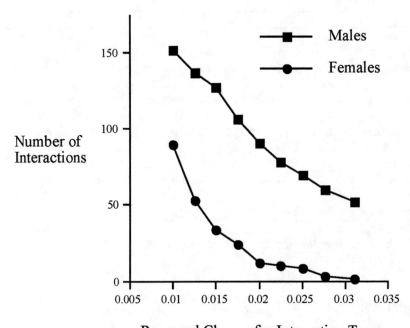

Figure 2. Number of Interactions Per Value of Rsquared Change

The numbers of interactions were then broken down by pattern, and these breakdowns are reported in Table 3. For males, the most striking finding was that Pattern C was by far the most common. This was true for both minimum effect sizes. Pattern B was two-to-three times more common than Pattern A. Patterns D and E were exceptionally rare, emerging only sparsely for the weaker minimum effect size. For females, interactions emerged primarily only for the weaker minimum effect size. Of these, 74% conformed to Pattern A, and 24% conformed to Pattern C.

The findings were then further broken down by problem behavior, interparental conflict behavior, and pattern. All of the interactions that reached the .031 level are listed in Table 4. The interaction patterns are those depicted in Figure 1. The legend in Figure 1 indicates which lines correspond to high, moderate, and low levels of the moderators and becomes important when interpreting the results. The "high" and "low" lines in Figure 1 represent high and low scores on the moderator composite variables listed in Table 4. For example, for males there was a significant Pattern A interaction for the prediction of Depression from Conflict Content. The moderator weights indicate that the effect occurred for low scores on Extraversion (the weight was -1.00) and moderate scores on the other five-factor variables (the weights were all zeros). Reference to Pattern A in Figure 1 reveals the nature of the effect: Introverted males scored increasingly higher on Depression as they felt more responsible for interparental conflict. In contrast, extraverted males scored low on depression regardless of whether or not they blamed themselves for interparental conflict.

Table 2. Total Numbers of Moderated Relationships for Males and Females

	Depression		Anxiety		Aggression		Delinquency	
	M	FM	M	FM	M	FM	M	FM
R squared Change = .031:								
Conflict Properties	0	0	0	0	0	0	12	0
Conflict Threat	0	0	0	0	4	1	8	0
Conflict Content	1	0	2	0	5	0	20	0
R squared Change = .015:								
Conflict Properties	10	0	0	3	0	0	29	0
Conflict Threat	0	0	0	0	10	17	21	0
Conflict Content	3	0	7	0	9	13	38	1

Note. "M" = males; "FM" = females.

Table 3. Numbers and Percentages of Moderated Relationships for Each Pattern

	Males		Females		Total	
	N	%	N	%	N	%
R squared Change = .031:						
Pattern A	5	10	0	0	5	9
Pattern B	13	25	0	0	13	25
Pattern C	34	65	1	100	35	66
Pattern D	0	0	0	0	0	0
Pattern E	0	0	0	0	0	0
Totals:	52		1		53	
R squared Change = .015:						
Pattern A	16	13	25	74	41	26
Pattern B	40	31	1	3	41	26
Pattern C	65	51	8	24	73	45
Pattern D	5	4	0	0	5	3
Pattern E	1	1	0	0	1	1
Totals:	127		34		161	

Note. The Patterns are those depicted in Figure 1.

It should be noted that reversing the coding of the FFM composites causes the "high" and "low" lines in Pattern A to switch places, whereas reversing the coding of the interparental conflict variable causes Pattern A to be inverted along the horizontal axis. This point is made because although such inversions can be challenging mental exercises, they are conceptually and empirically legitimate and possible. Numerous reverse-scorings of the personality moderators were actually performed in the present study in order to align the various findings that emerged with the relevant patterns that are depicted in Figure 1.

**Table 4: Moderated Relationships: Pattern, Effect Size, and Location
in Five-Factor Space**

	Pattern	Rsq.	Moderator Weights				
			N	E	O	A	C
Depression (males):							
Conflict Content	A	03	00	-100	00	00	00
Anxiety (males):							
Conflict Content	A	05	00	-100	00	00	00
Conflict Content	A	03	00	-71	00	00	71
Aggression (males):							
Conflict Threat	A	03	71	71	71	00	-71
Conflict Threat	A	04	00	71	71	00	-71
Conflict Threat	C	04	-71	71	00	00	-71
Conflict Threat	C	06	00	00	71	00	-71
Conflict Content	C	03	-71	00	-71	-71	-71
Conflict Content	C	06	-71	00	-71	-71	00
Conflict Content	C	04	-71	71	00	00	71
Conflict Content	C	04	00	-71	00	-71	00
Conflict Content	C	04	00	-71	00	-71	71
Delinquency (males):							
Conflict Properties	B	07	100	00	00	00	00
Conflict Properties	B	04	71	00	-71	00	-71
Conflict Properties	B	05	71	-71	00	00	00
Conflict Properties	B	05	71	-71	-71	00	00
Conflict Properties	C	03	-71	-71	00	00	-71
Conflict Properties	C	05	-71	-71	71	00	-71
Conflict Properties	C	04	-71	-71	71	00	00
Conflict Properties	C	06	-71	00	00	00	-71
Conflict Properties	C	06	-71	00	71	00	-71
Conflict Properties	C	07	-71	00	71	00	00
Conflict Properties	C	04	-71	71	00	00	-71
Conflict Properties	C	04	-71	71	71	00	-71

Note. Decimals omitted; the Patterns are those depicted in Figure 1; N = Neuroticism,
E = Extroversion, O = Openness to Experience, A = Agreeableness, C = Conscientiousness.

Table 4 continued: Moderated Relationships: Pattern, Effect Size, and Location in Five-Factor Space

	Pattern	Rsq.	Moderator Weights				
			N	E	O	A	C
Delinquency (males):							
Conflict Threat	B	05	100	00	00	00	00
Conflict Threat	B	04	71	00	-71	00	00
Conflict Threat	B	06	71	-71	00	00	00
Conflict Threat	B	05	71	-71	-71	00	00
Conflict Threat	B	04	71	-71	-71	00	-71
Conflict Threat	C	04	-71	00	00	00	-71
Conflict Threat	C	04	-71	71	00	00	-71
Conflict Threat	C	04	-71	71	71	71	-71
Conflict Content	B	04	71	00	71	00	00
Conflict Content	B	04	71	00	00	-71	71
Conflict Content	B	04	71	-71	00	00	00
Conflict Content	B	03	71	-71	-71	00	00
Conflict Content	C	09	-100	00	00	00	00
Conflict Content	C	03	-71	-71	-71	-71	-71
Conflict Content	C	04	-71	-71	-71	00	-71
Conflict Content	C	04	-71	-71	-71	00	00
Conflict Content	C	06	-71	-71	00	00	-71
Conflict Content	C	07	-71	-71	00	00	00
Conflict Content	C	03	-71	-71	00	71	-71
Conflict Content	C	04	-71	-71	71	-71	71
Conflict Content	C	06	-71	-71	71	00	-71
Conflict Content	C	06	-71	-71	71	00	00
Conflict Content	C	04	-71	-71	71	71	-71
Conflict Content	C	04	-71	00	-71	00	-71
Conflict Content	C	07	-71	00	00	00	-71
Conflict Content	C	07	-71	00	71	00	00
Conflict Content	C	04	-71	00	71	71	-71
Conflict Content	C	03	-71	71	00	00	-71
Aggression (females):							
Conflict Threat	C	03	-71	71	00	-71	00

Note. Decimals omitted; the Patterns are those depicted in Figure 1; N = Neuroticism, E = Extroversion, O = Openness to Experience, A = Agreeableness, C = Conscientiousness.

Another finding from Table 4 will be described to provide a further demonstration of how to interpret the coefficients. For delinquency and Conflict Properties in males, there was a Pattern B interaction with an *R*-squared change value of .04, and composite weights of .71 for N, .00 for E, -.71 for O, .00 for A, and -.71 for C. Males who were relatively neurotic, closed to experience, and disagreeable tended to score high on delinquency regardless of the level and intensity of interparental conflict they were exposed to. In contrast, males with the opposite personality characteristics scored low on delinquency when exposed to very little interparental conflict, and increasingly higher on delinquency as exposure to interparental conflict increased.

Perusal of the coefficients in Table 4 reveals considerable variability in the findings, especially for Pattern C. There was not a small number of personality composites that were responsible for most of the effects. Some broad patterns can nevertheless be discerned. All of the interactions for depression and anxiety conformed to Pattern A and involved extraversion. In these cases, extraversion served as a buffer against potentially harmful effects for interparental conflict. Lower scores on extraversion were associated with higher scores on depression and anxiety as interparental conflict increased.

However, there was also a cluster of Pattern A effects involving extraversion, openness, and agreeableness in the prediction of aggression. In these cases, low extraversion, low openness, and high agreeableness served as buffers against interparental conflict, whereas high extraversion, high openness, and low agreeableness were associated with increasing aggression as interparental conflict increased. There was also a tendency for the combination of neuroticism and low extraversion to be associated with high levels of delinquency regardless interparental conflict (Pattern B).

The moderator weights in Table 4 indicate that most of the moderator composites were based on strong weights for between two and four of the FFM dimensions. "Blends" of the FFM dimensions were thus common and important with regards to moderators of interparental conflict effects on problems. When the number of effects for a particular pattern (for a particular problem and interparental conflict variable) were small, the number of strongly weighted FFM dimensions in the composites could sometimes be relatively high (e.g., four). However, when there were a large number of effects for a particular pattern, there were usually only two strongly weighted FFM dimensions accompanied by notable variability for two or three of the remaining dimensions. In these cases, it seems like any personality composite that involved strong weights for the two or so key dimensions produced an effect, regardless of the weights for the other FFM dimensions. The region of important personality moderators in five-factor space was thus relatively large in these cases, and was anchored by a small number of strongly weighted dimensions.

Resiliency

Analyses were conducted to test predictions derived from recent findings regarding child personality characteristics and vulnerability to clinical problems. Huey and Weisz (1997) examined ego resiliency (adaptive, resourceful, and flexible responses to stress and novel situations, adaptive modulation of on one's impulses) in 116 clinic-referred children. They found that high scorers on ego resiliency displayed fewer internalizing and externalizing problems than low scorers. Although Huey and Weisz did not also assess parenting styles or interparental conflict, a straightforward prediction that could be derived from work is that resilient children should be less susceptible to clinical problems, even when exposed to interparental conflict. This prediction could be tested using the present data because Huey and Weisz reported correlations between ego resiliency and FFM scores for their participants (see their p. 409). We therefore used the signed squares of these correlations as weights that were applied to the FFM scores in the present study in order to produce "resiliency" scores. The weights, which reveal the nature of resiliency in FFM terms, were as follows: -.55 for neuroticism, .07 for extraversion, .22 for openness, .35 for agreeableness, and .41 for conscientiousness.

Two significant interactions for the resiliency prediction emerged. For females, there was a significant interaction between resiliency and Conflict Content in the prediction of aggression, R-squared change = .02, F (1, 242) = 9.35, p < .01, and between resiliency and Conflict Content in the prediction of delinquency, R-squared change = .015, F (1, 242) = 5.92, p < .05. Both interactions conformed to Pattern A, with flatter slopes for more resilient adolescents (the interaction for aggression is depicted in Figure 3). Resilient females were low in aggression when faced with interparental conflict for which they felt responsible. In contrast, less resilient females were increasingly aggressive as interparental conflict increased.

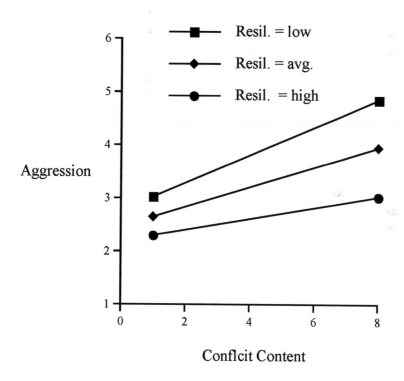

Figure 3. Interaction between Resiliency Scores and Conflict Content in the Prediction of Female Aggression

DISCUSSION

Personality-environment interactions have figured prominently in theories of development, in diathesis theories of psychopathology, and in person-environment fit models of psychological adjustment, but they have rarely been examined in empirical work. The vast majority of investigations into the role of interparental conflict in the subsequent development of problems has focused on simple bivariate relationships. Interparental conflict effects have proven to be quite consistent but often modest in size, thus further suggesting the possible importance of moderator variables. The present study was designed to provide a relatively thorough exploration of the role on one kind of person variable (personality characteristics) in altering the relationship between interparental conflict variables and problem behaviors. A comprehensive sweep of the multivariate space that is defined by the five-factor model of personality produced an array of interesting findings.

While the numbers of interactions that emerged were high, the interactions were limited in some important ways. The interactions occurred primarily for males and were relatively rare for females. They occurred for all three interparental conflict variables (Conflict Properties, Conflict Threat, and Conflict Content), but primarily for the prediction of delinquency. There were occasional effects for the prediction of aggression, and comparatively rare effects for the depression and anxiety. The nature of the interactions that did emerge, as well as the notable absence of interactions in other cases, confirms the importance of looking beyond bivariate effects for a more complete understanding of the development of problems. Personality-environment effects do matter, at least sometimes, and it is important to know when and how they matter. Personality and interparental conflict variables can both be viewed as "risk factors," with influences that are often conditional upon each other (Kazdin, Kraemer, Kessler, Kupfer, & Offord, 1997).

The present findings provide tentative answers to some of the questions about interparental conflict and problem behaviors that were raised at the outset of our paper. *Does interparental conflict only sometimes matter? i.e., Does it matter only for some kinds of children and not others?* The answer is "yes," because all of the moderated relationships involved flat slopes for some kinds of adolescents. However, there were combinations of interparental conflict variables and problem behaviors with sometimes very few personality moderators and for which there were notable bivariate effects (e.g., see the correlations in Table 1). Interparental conflict thus often does matter, even in the case of the moderated relationships, but it doesn't *always* matter.

Might some personality characteristics serve a protective function in some interparental conflict environments, and might the same characteristics increase vulnerability in other interparental conflict environments? The numerous interactions for Patterns A and C indicate that some personality characteristics operate in a protective fashion. However, the interactions for Patterns A and C also indicate that some personality characteristics increase vulnerability. *What kinds of children are affected or unaffected by interparental conflict?* This question has no simple answer. The effects are numerous, and they vary depending on the interparental conflict and problem variables. Readers may use the results presented in Table 4 as a preliminary road-map. *If interparental conflict increases problems for some children, then does the absence of interparental conflict merely reduce the risk to normative levels, or does it reduce risk to lower-than-normative levels?* The large number of effects for Pattern C indicate that the absence of interparental conflict often reduces risk to lower-than-normative levels, although the effects for Pattern A indicate that this effect is not universal.. *Might the same level of interparental conflict be associated with increased risk in some children, and reduced risk in others?* The answer is "no", due to the absence of effects for Patterns D and E. *Might some exasperated parents be correct when they say that the problem seems to be with their child's personality and not with their interparental conflict?* The answer is "yes", as indicated by the Pattern B effects, which occurred approximately 25% of the time. However, this hopeless "bad apple" view of some children and their problems should be viewed in context. The effects for Pattern A (which occurred 11-26% of the time) indicate that child personality characteristics also sometimes provided insulation or resiliency in the face of interparental conflict.

The numerous effects for Pattern C were not restricted to particular problems or interparental conflict variables. The effects for patterns A, B and C also complement the bivariate relationships that have been reported in previous work. In these patterns the effects of interparental conflict vary depending on child personality, but the mean of the lines for the personality variables (represented by the "average" lines) are nevertheless sloped, indicating general or overall effects for the interparental conflict variables.

Similarities and differences between the present findings and those reported by O'Connor and Dvorak (2001) for parenting variables (rather than interparental conflict) should be noted, especially given that the same analytic techniques were used in the two investigations. O'Connor and Dvorak (2001) reported 278 interactions for the .031 minimum effect size level, in contrast with the 53 interactions reported in the present study. However, O'Connor and Dvorak examined 10 parenting variables, in contrast to the three interparental conflict variables in the present study. The proportions of moderator effects for interparental conflict and parenting variables are thus roughly the same. In both investigations the effects occurred primarily for males, aggression, and delinquency, with relatively few effects for females, depression, and anxiety. Pattern C was the most common pattern in both studies, although a notably greater number of Pattern B effects emerged for interparental conflict than for parenting styles. There were also no Pattern D and E effects in the present study, whereas such effects occurred 14-17% of the time in the O'Connor and Dvorak (2001) research.

Limitations and Further Research

Our findings are based on self-reports from community samples and it is important that other methods and samples be used in further work. Our findings are based on the views of interparental conflict, personality and problems from the adolescent's perspective, and it would be interesting to see if and how the interactions vary when seen from the perspectives of parents. Adolescent reports of interparental conflict and problem behaviors undoubtedly have some validity. They are significantly associated with parent and expert reports, and potential problems with these reports have often been exaggerated (see Achenbach, McConaughy, & Howell, 1987; Brewin, Andrews, & Gotlib, 1993; Cantwell, Lewinsohn, Rohde, & Seeley, 1997; Fabrega, Ulrich, & Loeber, 1996; Metzler, Biglan, & Li, 1998; Schwarz & Mearns, 1989 for reviews). However, the overlap with parents' perceptions is not complete, and both perspectives must be known for a proper understanding and explanation of the interactions. The present findings provide a relatively comprehensive look at just one side of the picture.

The fact that data for all the variables were provided by the adolescents might raise concerns about method variance possibly inflating the findings. This may well be true for the bivariate associations reported in Table 1. However, the tests for interactions focused on whether bivariate relationships changed depending on the levels of moderator variables, and any method variance contamination would have served to reduce the likelihood of such interactions emerging. Similarly, the use of a community sample probably restricted the variation in the interparental conflict and problem variables, thus also attenuating the interaction effect sizes (Jouriles, Bourg, & Farris, 1991). We nevertheless used the most popular measures of clinical problems available, and it is unlikely that the patterns of findings would be dramatically different had clinical samples been used. In fact, the predictions regarding personality resiliency were confirmed in the present community sample even though the FFM composite weights used to create the "resiliency" scores were based on clinic-referred children (Huey & Weisz, 1997). The ideal investigation would include representative numbers of participants from both community and clinical samples in order to cover the full spectrum of personality, interparental conflict and problem behaviors.

Our measure of FFM traits was relatively brief, but the items were carefully drawn from larger pools (Goldberg, 1992; Saucier, 1994) and the factor structure for the measure in this study showed a high degree of correspondence with the theoretically based FFM structure. Our attempts to conduct a relatively comprehensive search for personality moderated relationships required using adequate but sometimes brief measures. Our broad scan of the universe of possibilities sets the stage for more specialized investigations of some of the promising effects.

The "effects of interparental conflict on problems" implies causal relationships that can obviously not be inferred from correlational data. The focus on moderated relationships, however, makes some alternative explanations less likely than would be the case in investigations focusing solely on bivariate relationships. For example, in bivariate terms there would be grounds for suspecting that children with particular personality characteristics evoke interparental conflict. However, this alternative interpretation becomes awkward and unlikely in the case of interactions with interparental conflict variables. This is because children with the same personality characteristics develop more or less problems depending on the interparental conflict they are exposed to. Proper tests for causal relationships are obviously required, but they are expensive and time consuming and it is important to first have some knowledge of the relationships that might exist before such efforts are undertaken (Rutter 1994).

It is also important for readers to recognize the exploratory, atheoretical nature of our work and the reliance on a statistical technique that has a controversial performance record. Moderated regression is the most widely and strongly recommended procedure for identifying interactions between variables (Aiken & West, 1991; Chaplin, 1997; Cohen & Cohen, 1983). It permits analyses of continuums of scores, and it is more powerful and appropriate than analyses based on relatively arbitrary categorizations of participants. However, the procedure is notoriously conservative and sensitive to the distributions of variables (Cohen & Cohen, 1983; McClelland & Judd, 1993). Our findings thus require replication in other data sets. Unfortunately, previous reports of interactions between variables have proven difficult to replicate (Chaplin, 1997; Dance & Neufeld, 1988; Goldberg, 1972). Successful replications have typically occurred for theoretically-based research focusing on carefully selected variables (Chaplin, 1997, p. 882). The results reported in the present exploratory study must thus be considered in relation to this historical record of research on interactions. Our findings are perhaps most properly viewed as a promising road map for more focused and theoretically based investigations.

It is also worth noting that, in contrast to much previous work on interactions, our primary focus was not on isolated, specific relationships that happened to be statistically significant (although previously reported effects for resiliency were replicated in this study). Instead, our primary focus was on the relative occurrences of conceptually important and dramatically different patterns of relations between personality and interparental conflict variables (re: Figure 1). Our results were based on not one or two interactions, but on 53 interactions. Many of the interactions also clumped together in large regions of the FFM factor space, which should increase the chances of replication in further work. Theoretically based research focusing on personality variables from these FFM regions is most likely to be successful.

The challenges for researchers are substantial, and involve not only specifying and refining knowledge of the interactions that do occur, but explaining them as well (Grych & Cardoza-Fernandes, 2001; Katz, 2001; Margolin, Oliver, & Medina, 2001). The variation in the nature of the interactions across problems, interparental conflict behaviors, and personality characteristics makes the task of explanation seem both daunting and enticing. Explanations are also required for the relatively small numbers of interactions for females (see Davies & Lindsay, 2001, and Snyder, 1998), especially at the higher minimum effect size level, and for depression and anxiety. Bivariate effects are undoubtedly important in these cases, but why are there so few interactions, especially in comparison to the numerous effects for males and delinquency? Finally, the present focus on two-way linear interactions constitutes only a small step beyond the traditional focus on bivariate associations. Numerous higher-order interactions probably also occur between interparental conflict, personality, and other variables in the prediction of problems.

REFERENCES

Achenbach, T. M. (1991). *Manual for the youth self-report.* Burlington, VT: University of Vermont Department of Psychiatry.

Achenbach, T. M., McConaughy, S. H., & Howell, C. T. (1987). Child/adolescent behavioral and emotional problems: Implications of cross-informant correlations for situational specificity. *Psychological Bulletin, 101,* 213-232.

Aiken, L. S., & West, S. G. (1991). *Multiple regression: Testing and interpreting interactions.* Newbury Park, CA: Sage.

Bickham, N. L., & Fiese, B. H. (1997). Extension of the Children's Perceptions of Interparental Conflict Scale for use with late adolescents. *Journal of Family Psychology, 11,* 246-250.

Brady, E. U., & Kendall, P. C. (1992). Comorbidity of anxiety and depression in children and adolescents. *Psychological Bulletin, 111,* 244-255.

Brewin, C. R., Andrews, B., & Gotlib, I. H. (1993). Psychopathology and early experience: A reappraisal of retrospective reports. *Psychological Bulletin, 113,* 82-98.

Buehler, C., Anthony, C., Krishnakumar, A., & Stone, G. (1997). Interparental conflict and youth problem behaviors: A meta-analysis. *Journal of Child & Family Studies, 6,* 223-247.

Cantwell, D. P., Lewinsohn, P. M., Rohde, P., & Seeley, J. R. (1997). Correspondence between adolescent report and parent report of psychiatric diagnostic data. *Journal of the American Academy of Child and Adolescent Psychiatry, 36,* 610-619.

Chaplin, W. F. (1997). Personality, interactive relations, and applied psychology. In R. Hogan, J. A. Johnson, & S. R. Briggs (Eds.), *Handbook of personality psychology* (pp. 873-890). New York: Academic Press.

Cohen, J., & Cohen, P. (1983). *Applied multiple regression/correlation. analysis for the behavioral sciences.* Hillsdale, N. J.: Erlbaum.

Cummings, E. M., & Davies, P. T. (2002). Effects of marital conflict on children: Recent advances and emerging themes in process-oriented research. *Journal of Child Psychology & Psychiatry & Allied Disciplines, 43,* 31-63.

Cummings, E. M., Goeke Morey, M. C., & Dukewich, T. L. (2001). The study of relations between marital conflict and child adjustment: Challenges and new directions for methodology. In J. H. Grych (Ed.), *Interparental conflict and child development: Theory, research, and applications* (pp. 39-63). New York, NY: Cambridge University Press.

Dance, K. A., & Neufeld, R. W. J. (1988). Aptitude-treatment interaction research in the clinical setting: A review of attempts to dispel the "patient uniformity" myth. *Psychological Bulletin, 104,* 192-213.

Davies, P. T., & Lindsay, L. L. (2001). Does gender moderate the effects of marital conflict on children? In J. H. Grych (Ed.), *Interparental conflict and child development: Theory, research, and applications* (pp. 64-97). New York, NY: Cambridge University Press.

Davies, P. T., & Windle, M. (2001). Interparental discord and adolescent adjustment trajectories: The potentiating and protective role of intrapersonal attributes. *Child Development, 72,* 1163-1178.

Digman, J. M. (1990). Personality structure: Emergence of the five-factor model. *Annual Review of Psychology, 41,* 417-440.

Digman, J. M. (1994). Child personality and temperament: Does the five-factor model embrace both domains? In C. F. Halverson, G. A. Kohnstamm, & R. P. Martin (Eds.), *The developing structure of temperament and personality from infancy to adulthood* (pp. 323-338). Hillsdale, NJ: Erlbaum.

Emery, R. E. (1982). Interparental conflict and the children of discord and divorce. *Psychological Bulletin, 92,* 310-330.

Fabrega, H., Ulrich, R., & Loeber, R. (1996). Adolescent psychopathology as a function of informant and risk status. *Journal of Nervous and Mental Disease, 184,* 27-34.

Fergusson, D. M., Lynskey, M. T., & Horwood, L. J. (1996). Origins of comorbidity between conduct and affective disorders. *Journal of the American Academy of Child and Adolescent Psychiatry, 35,* 451-460.

Goldberg, L. R. (1972). Student personality characteristics and optimal college learning conditions: An extensive search for trait-by-treatment interaction effects. *Instructional Science, 1,* 153-210.

Goldberg, L. R. (1992). The development of markers for the big-five factor structure. *Psychological Assessment, 4,* 26-42.

Grych, J. H., & Cardoza Fernandes, S. (2001). Understanding the impact of interparental conflict on children: The role of social cognitive processes. In J. H. Grych (Ed.), *Interparental conflict and child development: Theory, research, and applications* (pp. 157-187). New York, NY: Cambridge University Press.

Grych, J. H., Seid, M., & Fincham, F. D. (1992). Assessing marital conflict from the child's perspective: The Children's Perception of Interparental Conflict Scale. *Child Development, 63,* 558-572.

Harold, G. T., Fincham, F. D., Osborne, L. N., & Conger, R. D. (1997). Mom and dad are at it again: Adolescent perceptions of marital conflict and adolescent psychological distress. *Developmental Psychology, 33*, 333-350.

Hetherington, E. M., Bridges, M., & Insabella, G. M. (1998). What matters? What does not?: Five perspectives on the association between marital transitions and children's adjustment. *American Psychologist, 53*, 167-184.

Huey, S. J., & Weisz, J. R. (1997). Ego control, ego resiliency, and the five-factor model as predictors of behavioral and emotional problems in clinic-referred children and adolescents. *Journal of Abnormal Psychology, 106*, 404-415.

Jouriles, E. N., Bourg, W. J., & Farris, A. M. (1991). Marital adjustment and child conduct problems: A comparison of the correlation across subsamples. *Journal of Consulting and Clinical Psychology, 59*, 354-357.

Katz, L. F. (2001). Physiological processes and mediators of the impact of marital conflict on children. In J. H. Grych (Ed.), *Interparental conflict and child development: Theory, research, and applications* (pp. 188 212). New York, NY: Cambridge University Press.

Katz, L. F., & Gottman, J. M. (1997). Buffering children from marital conflict and dissolution. *Journal of Clinical Child Psychology, 26*, 157-171.

Kazdin, A. E., Kraemer, H. C., Kessler, R. C., Kupfer, D. J., & Offord, D. R. (1997). Contributions of risk-factor research to developmental psychopathology. *Clinical Psychology Review, 17*, 375-406.

Kelly, J. B. (2000). Children's adjustment in conflicted marriage and divorce: A decade review of research. *Journal of the American Academy of Child & Adolescent Psychiatry, 39*, 963-973.

Kerig, P. K. (1998). Moderators and mediators of the effects of interparental conflict on children's adjustment. *Journal of Abnormal Child Psychology, 26*, 199-212.

Kovacs, M. (1992). *Children's depression inventory.* North Tonawanda, NY: Multi-Health Systems.

Lubinski, D., & Humphreys, L. G. (1990). Assessing spurious "moderator effects:" Illustrated substantively with the hypothesized ("synergistic") relation between spatial and mathematical ability. *Psychological Bulletin, 107*, 385-393.

MacCallum, R. C., & Mar, C. M. (1995). Distinguishing between moderator and quadratic effects in multiple regression. *Psychological Bulletin, 118*, 405-421.

Margolin, G., Oliver, P. H., & Medina, A. M. (2001). Conceptual issues in understanding the relation between interparental conflict and child adjustment: Integrating developmental psychopathology and risk/resilience perspectives. In J. H. Grych (Ed.), *Interparental conflict and child development: Theory, research, and applications* (pp. 9-38). New York, NY: Cambridge University Press.

McClelland, G. H., & Judd, C. M. (1993). Statistical difficulties of detecting interactions and moderator effects. *Psychological Bulletin, 114*, 376-390.

McConaughy, S. H., & Skiba, R. J. (1993). Comorbidity of externalizing and internalizing problems. *School Psychology Review, 22*, 421-436.

McCrae, R. R., & John, O. P. (1992). An introduction to the five-factor model and its applications. *Journal of Personality, 60*, 175-215.

Metzler, C. W., Biglan, A., & Li, F. Z. (1998). The stability and validity of early adolescents' reports of parenting constructs. *Journal of Family Psychology, 12*, 600-619.

Nye, L. G., & Witt, L. A. (1995). Interpreting moderator effects: Substitute for the signed coefficient rule. *Educational and Psychological Measurement, 55*, 27-31.

O'Connor, B. P. (2002). A quantitative review of the comprehensiveness of the five-factor model in relation to popular personality inventories. *Assessment.*

O'Connor, B. P., & Dvorak, T. (2001). Conditional associations between parental behavior and adolescent problems: A search for personality-environment interactions. *Journal of Research in Personality, 35*, 1-26.

Reynolds, C. R., & Richmond, B. O. (1985). *Revised children's manifest anxiety scale.* Los Angeles, CA: Western Psychological Services.

Robins, R. W., John, O. P., & Caspi, A. (1994). Major dimensions of personality in early adolescence: The big-five and beyond. In C. F. Halverson, G. A. Kohnstamm, & R. P. Martin (Eds.), *The developing structure of temperament and personality from infancy to adulthood* (pp. 267-291). Hillsdale, NJ: Erlbaum.

Russo, M. F., & Beidel, D. C. (1994). Comorbidity of childhood anxiety and externalizing disorders: Prevalence, associated characteristics, and validation issues. *Clinical Psychology Review, 14*, 199-221.

Rutter, M. (1994). Beyond longitudinal data: Causes, consequences, changes, and continuity. *Journal of Consulting and Clinical Psychology, 62*, 928-940.

Saucier, G. (1994). Mini-markers: A brief version of Goldberg's unipolar big-five markers. *Journal of Personality Assessment, 63*, 506-516.

Schmidt, F. L. (1996). Significance testing and cumulative knowledge in psychology: Implications for training of researchers. *Psychological Methods, 1*, 115-129.

Schwarz, J. C., & Mearns, J. (1989). Assessing parental childrearing behaviors: A comparison of parent, child, and aggregate ratings from two instruments. *Journal of Research in Personality, 23*, 450-468.

Snyder, J. R. (1998). Marital conflict and child adjustment: What about gender? *Developmental Review, 18*, 390-420.

Turner, C. M., & Dadds, M. R. (2001). Clinical prevention and remediation of child adjustment problems. In J. H. Grych (Ed.), *Interparental conflict and child development: Theory, research, and applications* (pp. 387-416). New York, NY: Cambridge University Press.

Wiggins, J. S., Phillips, N., & Trapnell, P. (1989). Circular assumptions about interpersonal behavior: Evidence concerning some untested assumptions underlying diagnostic classification. *Journal of Personality and Social Psychology, 56*, 296-305.

Wootton, J. M., Frick, P. J., Shelton, K. K., & Silverthorn, P. (1997). Ineffective parenting and childhood conduct problems: The moderating role of callous-unemotional traits. *Journal of Consulting and Clinical Psychology, 65*, 301-308.

Zoccolillo, M. (1992). Co-occurrence of conduct disorder and its adult outcomes with depressive and anxiety disorders: A review. *Journal of the American Academy of Child and Adolescent Psychiatry, 31*, 547-556.

Chapter 4

THE RELATION OF SOCIAL INFLUENCES AND SOCIAL RELATIONSHIPS TO PROSOCIAL AND ANTISOCIAL BEHAVIOR IN HONG KONG CHINESE ADOLESCENTS

Hing Keung Ma
Hong Kong Baptist University
Daniel T. L. Shek and Ping Chung Cheung
The Chinese University of Hong Kong

ABSTRACT

The prosocial and antisocial behavior of Hong Kong Chinese adolescents were investigated in two studies. In Study 1, self-report questionnaires were used and the major findings were as follows: (1) negative peer influences were significantly stronger in boys than in girls, whereas positive peer influences were significantly stronger in girls than in boys. (2) antisocial adolescents tended to perceive their best friend as antisocial and exerting more negative influences on them, whereas prosocial adolescents tended to perceive their best friend as prosocial and exerting more positive influences on them. In Study 2, both intensive interviews and self-report questionnaires were used to investigate parental, peer, and teacher influences on the prosocial and antisocial behaviors of Hong Kong Chinese adolescents. Results indicated that perceived parental influence and parental relationships were positively associated with frequency of prosocial behavior and negatively associated with frequency of delinquent behavior. In addition, peer relationships were negatively associated with frequency of antisocial behaviors and teacher relationships were positively associated with frequency of prosocial behaviors. Adolescents in different identity statuses (achievement, moratorium, foreclosure, diffusion) showed different patterns of prosocial and antisocial behaviors. For example, adolescents in the identity achievement group exhibited high frequencies of prosocial behaviors and low frequencies of antisocial behaviors, but those in the identity moratorium group exhibited quite high frequencies of both prosocial and antisocial behaviors.

INTRODUCTION

Current research on adolescent behavior tends to emphasize on either the prosocial or antisocial behavior but seldom both in a single study (for prosocial behavior, see e.g., Radke-Yarrow, Zahn-Waxler, & Chapman, 1983; Staub, 1978, 1979; Staub, Bar-Tal, Karylowski, & Reykowski, 1984; for antisocial and delinquent behavior, see e.g., Cairns, Cairns, Neckerman, Ferguson, Gariepy, 1989; Gibbons & Krohn, 1986; Hindelang, Hirschi, & Weis, 1981; Kaplan, Martin, & Johnson, 1986; Parke & Slaby, 1983; Rutter & Giller, 1983; Widom, 1989). To fill this gap of research, the present study investigates both the prosocial and antisocial behavior of Chinese adolescents in one setting. It also explores the relation of these adolescent behaviors with social influences and social relationships.

PROSOCIAL AND ANTISOCIAL BEHAVIOR

Prosocial behavior in children and adolescents usually involves "sharing, cooperating, helping, feeling empathy and caring for others" (Radke-Yarrow, Zahn-Waxler, & Chapman, 1983, p. 528). In addition, altruistic behavior with some personal sacrifice and good-boy-nice-girl or normative behavior can also be regarded as prosocial behavior. In the present study, prosocial behavior refers to altruistic, socially acceptable or normative behavior. For examples, gave gifts to parents, helped handicapped people to cross the road, apologized to others after wrong-doing, and served as voluntary worker.

According to Hindelang, Hirschi and Weis (1981, pp. 54-55), the major antisocial and delinquent behavior in adolescents includes the followings: (1) general deviance such as theft, alcohol use, cheating on exams and came to school late; (2) drug usage; (3) parental defiance such as shouted at your father or mother or gone against your parents' wishes; and (4) aggressiveness such as group fist fighting. The antisocial and delinquent behavior measured in the present study are similar to above mentioned categories except the drug usage is not included. More emphasis is given to the investigation of the antisocial and aggressive acts in school and home settings in this study.

PARENTAL INFLUENCES

In an extensive review of the development of altruism, Moore and Eisenberg (1984) concluded that a variety of child-rearing practices such as inductive discipline, empathic preaching, modeling of positive behaviors, and assignment of responsibility contribute to prosocial development. Similar conclusions were reached in an early review by Staub (1979). On the other hand, poor family relationships have been found to be related to the antisocial or problem behavior of adolescents (Dilalla, Mitchell, Arthur, and Pagliocca, 1988; Jensen, 1972; LeCroy, 1988; Moos and Moos, 1986; Simons, Robertson, and Downs, 1989). Moos and Moos (1986) concluded in their review that families of delinquent adolescents are less cohesive and members are less independent; they also have more conflicts and stronger parental control (p. 26).

Yau and Smetana (1996) interviewed 120 lower-class Chinese adolescents in Hong Kong about their conflicts with parents and found that low maternal and paternal warmth were related to greater number of conflicts generated. In addition, greater parental control was associated with more serious conflicts. Shek and Ma (1997), in a study of perception of parental treatment styles on adolescent social behavior in Hong Kong, also found that adolescents who had a more positive perception of parental treatment style in terms of warmth and leniency showed less antisocial behavior. In addition, maternal treatment style was positively related to prosocial behavior.

Generally speaking, a good adolescent-parent relationship is positively related to frequency of prosocial behavior and negatively related to frequency of antisocial behavior.

PEER INFLUENCES

The influences of peers on adolescent behavior have been found to be quite significant (Berndt, 1979; Cheung and Ng, 1988; Hartup, 1983; Rutter and Giller, 1983). Many studies have found that peer groups serve as the training ground for antisocial and delinquent acts (see review by Patterson, DeBaryshe & Ramsey, 1989, p.331). In a study of adolescent behavior in Hong Kong, Cheung and Ng (1988) found that delinquent behavior was positively correlated with the association with delinquent friends. In other words, delinquent adolescents tended to cluster together. In a large scale study of adolescent behavior in Hong Kong, Ma, Shek, Cheung, and Lee (1996) concluded that "negative peer influence is significantly stronger for boys than for girls, whereas positive peer influence is significantly stronger for girls than for boys" (p.263). In addition, the best friends of antisocial adolescents tend to exert more negative influences on the antisocial adolescents, whereas the best friends of prosocial adolescents tend to exert more positive influences on the prosocial adolescents.

TEACHER INFLUENCES

The effects of schooling on the behavior of adolescents are also significant (Nicholls, 1989; Rest & Thoma, 1986). Generally speaking, teachers exert some influences on the prosocial and antisocial behavior of adolescents. The relationship between the teachers and adolescents is associated with the social behavior and conduct of the adolescents. Cheung, Ma, and Shek (1998), in their study of 673 adolescents in Hong Kong, found that the conceptions of success and achievement goals are related to prosocial behavior. They found that the beliefs that success involves gaining skills or understanding and that success involves working productively with some collaborators were positively associated with prosocial orientation and prosocial acts. They also argued that cultivation of prosocial orientation and behavior in family and classrooms is desirable at an early stage. In other words, it is important and essential for teachers to develop a prosocial orientation in their students starting when the students are quite young.

PERSONALITY

The relation of personality to delinquent or antisocial behavior is a popular topic in this area. Poor self-concepts or low self-esteem were found to be positively associated with frequency of delinquent behavior (Kaplan, 1978; Kaplan, Martin, & Johnson, 1986; Leung & Lau, 1989; Rosenberg & Rosenberg, 1978). On the other hand, Mussen, Harris, Rutherford, and Keasey (1970) found that altruism was positively related to self-esteem and positive ego strength. Gabrys (1983) found that prosocial children of ages from 9 to 16 years were rated low on both the Psychoticism and Neuroticism scales but high on the Lie scale of the Junior Eysenck Personality Inventory (Eysenck & Eysenck, 1975). He also found that antisocial children were rated high on both the Psychoticism and Neuroticism scales but low on the Lie scale. In other words, antisocial children tend to be more emotionally unstable and less socially desirable than the prosocial counterparts. In a Hong Kong study, Ma and Leung (1991) found that altruism was negatively related to psychoticism and positively related to social desirability. In addition, Radke-Yarrow, Zahn-Waxler, and Chapman (1983) in their review concluded that social competence including emotional stability and social adjustment was positively related to prosocial and altruistic behavior.

FOUR TYPES OF ADOLESCENT SOCIAL BEHAVIOR

Adolescent behavior can be classified into the following four types:

(1) Ambivalent - Active Type
    This group of adolescents is so active and energetic that they perform quite frequently both the prosocial and antisocial behavior. They are most probably in the stage of moratorium in the search for identity (Marcia, 1966).
(2) Undifferentiated - Passive Type
    This group of adolescents perform passively and quite infrequently both the prosocial and antisocial behavior. They tend to be diffused in their search for identity.
(3) Prosocial Type
    This group of adolescents tend to act prosocially and refrain from doing antisocial things. They are the good-boy-nice-girl in the family, school and society.
(4) Antisocial Type
    This group of adolescents usually act antisocially and only occasionally perform the prosocial acts. They are usually labeled as the antisocial or delinquent group that causes the family, school and society a lot of troubles.

SEX DIFFERENCES

In a meta-analytic review of sex differences in helping behavior, Eagly and Crowley (1986) concluded that men usually offered more help than women, while women got more help than men. They also argued males and females were not prosocial entirely on the same types of tasks; "male gender role fosters chivalrous acts and nonroutine acts of rescuing, both of which are often directed toward strangers, whereas the female gender role fosters acts of caring for others and tending to their needs, primarily in close relationships" (Eagly & Crowley, 1986, p. 300). Ma and Leung (1991) also found that there were significant sex differences in altruistic behavior in favor of females in Chinese primary school students. As for the aggressive and antisocial behavior, Eagly and Steffen (1986) concluded, in their review, that social norms tended to encourage some forms of aggression in males but not in females. Duke (1978) also concluded that girls committed fewer misbehaving acts in schools than boys. It is expected that female adolescents tend to be more prosocial and less antisocial than male counterparts.

ACADEMIC ACHIEVEMENT

Previous findings indicate that there is a positive relation between school failure and delinquent behavior (Grande, 1988; Lawrence, 1985). Antisocial children usually show poor academic achievement and "one explanation for this is that the child's noncompliant and undercontrolled behavior impedes learning" (Patterson, DeBaryshe & Ramsey, 1989, p.330). On the other hand, there is a close association between good academic achievement and prosocial or good behavior (Rutter, Maughan, Mortimore and Ouston, 1979). Ma, Shek, Cheung, and Lee (1996) concluded in their study of 2,862 Hong Kong Chinese adolescents, that academic achievement has a positive relation with prosocial behavior and a negative relation with antisocial behavior.

IDENTITY STATUS

According to Erikson's (1968) Stage 5 of Psychosocial Development, adolescents at this stage face some sort of identity crisis and strive hard to achieve a self-chosen identity. Marcia (1966, 1980), in his attempt to study Erikson's concept of identity, empirically classified the identity statuses of adolescents into the following four categories: (1) Identity achievement: Adolescents in the Identity Achievement status have gone through an identity crisis and have achieved a self-chosen identity. They have a clear career goal and a good sense of self-concept. (2) Identity Moratorium: Adolescents in the identity moratorium status have "generally experienced a delayed or drawn-out exploration of their identity. They have made few, if any, firm commitments to a career or personal values. Understandably, they have high levels of anxiety, suggesting the continued awareness of an unresolved life crisis" (Atwater, 1992, pp.236-237). (3) Identity Foreclosure: Adolescents at this status have not attempted to strive seriously the identity exploration. Instead, they accept the values and career decision endorsed by their parents or authorities such as their teachers. (4) Identity Diffusion or Confusion: Adolescents at this status neither attempt seriously to search an identity nor to accept one endorsed by their parents. They feel inadequate and often face some emotional problems such as anxiety, loneliness, and restlessness. The prosocial and antisocial behavioral patterns in each identity status were investigated in this study.

In this chapter, two studies on the social behavior of Hong Kong Chinese adolescents were reported here. These studies are based on Ma, Shek, Cheung, and Lee (1996) and Ma, Shek, Cheung, and Lam (2000). In Study 1, self-report questionnaires were used to investigate the relationship of prosocial and antisocial behavior to peer relationships, personality, and academic achievement. In Study 2, intensive interviews were used to investigate parental, peer, and teacher influences on the prosocial and antisocial behavior of Hong Kong Chinese adolescents.

STUDY 1

Method

Subjects

Subjects were recruited from 20 secondary schools in Hong Kong. There were 773 grade 7 students (385 males and 388 females, mean age 12.71 years), 707 grade 8 students (272 males and 435 females, mean age 13.84 years), 689 grade 9 students (293 males and 396 females, mean age 14.77 years), and 693 grade 10 students (281 males and 412 females, mean age 15.88 years). Totally there were 2862 subjects, 1231 of whom were males and 1631 of whom were females. There were 14 cases missing the age data in this sample. The average age of the total sample was 14.25 years, with a standard deviation of 1.41 years.

Instruments

Adolescent Behavior Questionnaire (ABQ)

Ma's (1988) ABQ measures the prosocial and antisocial/delinquent behavior of adolescents. Subjects were asked to report the frequency of 65 acts performed in the past one year on a 7-point scale: None, 1-2 times, 3-4 times, 5-6 times, 7-8 times, 9-10 times and more than 10 times. There are eight subscales in the ABQ: 1) Cognitive and academic performance (CA) - deviant or socially disapproved acts in classroom or school setting (e.g., playing truant); 2) Psychosocial activities (PS) - socially undesirable sexual activities (e.g., reading pornographic magazines); 3) Antisocial acts in school (AS1) - antisocial acts against one's teachers or school authority (e.g., told a lie to cheat the teacher); 4) Antisocial acts in one's family (AS2) - antisocial acts occurred in one's family (e.g., disobeyed parent's command); 5) Antisocial acts in other settings (AS3) - antisocial acts in general (e.g., gambling); 6) Aggression (AG) - aggressive or hostile acts (e.g., spoke foul language); 7) Normative acts (SN) - socially acceptable or normative acts (e.g., apologized to others); and 8) Altruistic acts (AL) - helping behavior (e.g., did voluntary work). In addition to the eight subscale scores, two general scores are usually generated from the responses to the ABQ: Antisocial/Delinquent Behavior (DB) score and Prosocial Behavior (PB) score. The DB score is the summation of six subscale scores (CA, PS, AS1, AS2, AS3, and SN) and it indicates the frequency of deviant or socially undesirable acts in the past one year. The PB score is the summation of the SN score and the AL score and it indicates the frequency of prosocial acts performed in the past one year. An overall score, Adolescent Behavior (AB) score can be generated by the following formula: AB = DB - PB. Only the DB and PB scores are presented in this study.

Peer Interaction Questionnaire

The Peer Interaction Questionnaire (PIQ) measures the subject's perception of the influences of his/her best friend on his/her prosocial and delinquent behavior, as well as the subject's perception of the amount of prosocial and delinquent acts performed by his/her best friend in the past year. Subjects were asked to rate on a 4-point scale (None, seldom, sometimes and frequently) how often his/her best friend would encourage him/her to perform prosocial and delinquent acts. The PI (Positive Influence) and NI (Negative Influence) indices measure the positive and negative influences of the subject's best friend on his/her behavior.

Subjects were also asked to estimate, according to what they know, on the same 4-point scale, the frequency of prosocial and delinquent acts performed by his/her best friend in the past year. The PDB (Peer's Delinquent Behavior) and PPB (Peer's Prosocial Behavior) indices assess the prosocial and delinquent behavior of the subject's best friend. A summary of these scores with some sample items is also given in Appendix 1.

Junior Eysenck Personality Questionnaire (JEPQ)

The Chinese version of the Junior Eysenck Personality Questionnaire has been standardized in Hong Kong by Eysenck and Chan (1982). There are four scales in the JEPQ: E (Extroversion), N (Neuroticism or Emotionality), P (Psychoticism or Toughmindedness) and L (Lying or Social Desirability). According to the EPQ manual (Eysenck & Eysenck, 1975), the typical extrovert is "sociable, likes parties, has many friends ..." and the typical introvert is "a quiet, retiring sort of person, introspective, fond of books rather than people ..." (p. 9). A high N scorer is described as "being an anxious, worrying individual, moody and frequently depressed" (p. 9). In addition, a high P scorer "may be described as being solitary, not carrying for people; he is often troublesome, not fitting in anywhere" (p. 11). A high P scorer may also be cruel, inhumane and hostile. The L scale attempts to measure dissimulation or a tendency to "fake good". Eysenck and Chan (1982) found that the internal consistency reliabilities of these four scales ranged from .63 to .85 (p. 157). The JEPQ subscores are computed by dividing the raw score by the number of relevant items. Thus, the range of these subscores is from 0.0 to 1.0.

Academic Achievement

There was no test of academic achievement used in this study. The allocation of high (secondary) school places to grade 6 students is administered by the Education Department of the Hong Kong Government. The elementary (primary) school students are classified into five bands by their performance in a Scholastic Aptitude Test and school examination results in the last three terms (second term in grade five and first and second terms in grade six) of their primary education. Band one students are supposed to have the best academic performance whereas the Band five students the poorest performance. With the help of the staff at the Education Department, 20 schools were randomly selected from all secondary schools (around 400 schools), 5 of them admitted Band 1 or 2 (i.e., above average academic achievement) students, 10 admitted mostly Band 3 (i.e., average academic achievement) students, and 5 admitted Band 4 or 5 (i.e., below average academic achievement) students.

Procedures

Subjects answered the questionnaires in their classroom during their normal class periods. The experimenter went through the test instruction with the subjects before they answered questions.

Results and Discussion

The internal consistency reliability (Cronbach alpha) of the DB (Delinquent Behavior) and PB (Prosocial Behavior) scores for a sample of 2522 subjects was .95 and .81; and that of the NI (Negative Influences), PI (Positive Influences), PDB (Peer's Delinquent Behavior) and PPB (Peer's Prosocial Behavior) scores for a sample of 940 subjects was .87, .81, .91 and .70 respectively. The result indicates that the reliability of the Adolescent Behavior Questionnaire (ABQ) and Peer Interaction Questionnaire (PIQ) was acceptable (Hindelang, Hirschi & Weis, 1982; Leung & Lau, 1989).

The means and standard deviations of the ABQ and PIQ scores are presented in Table 1.

The mean delinquent behavior (DB) score in the boy sample was significantly higher than that in the girl sample, which is consistent with the findings in literature (Duke, 1978; Eagly & Steffen, 1986). On the other hand, there was no significant sex difference in the prosocial behavior (PB) score. This finding is consistent with early reviews by Krebs (1970) and Maccoby and Jacklin (1974). Krebs (1970) found that there were no sex differences in most studies of altruism; and Maccoby and Jacklin (1974) in a review of studies on attachment, affiliation and positive interactions of all kinds also found little sex differences. However, Ma and Leung (1991) found that there were significant sex differences in altruistic behavior favoring females in Chinese Grade 2 to 6 students. Since the sample in the present study involving Grade 7 to 10 students, it seems that the sex differences pattern in young Chinese children is not the same as that in older children or adolescents. This is an interesting issue for future studies.

Table 1. Mean and Standard Deviations of Test Scores

Score	Total Sample		Boys		Girls		t
	M	SD	M	SD	M	SD	
Adolescent Behavior Questionnaire (N=2862; 1231 boys, 1631 girls)							
DB	1.88	.79	2.07	.90	1.74	.66	10.83**
PB	2.66	.79	2.65	.85	2.66	.74	-.60
	Peer Interaction Questionnaire (N=1102; 650 boys, 452 girls)						
NI	1.45	.38	1.51	.43	1.36	.29	7.18**
PI	2.39	.52	2.33	.53	2.48	.49	-4.77**
PDB	1.52	.48	1.59	.50	1.43	.43	5.68**
PPB	1.99	.59	2.01	.60	1.97	.56	1.20

$*p < .05.$ $**p < .001.$

Note. A *t-test* was performed on the means of the test scores in the male and female samples. DB = Delinquent Behavior; PB = Prosocial Behavior; PI = Positive Influences; NI = Negative Influences; PDB = Peer Delinquent Behavior; PPB = Peer Prosocial Behavior.

The negative peer influences (NI) were significantly stronger in boys than in girls; whereas, the positive peer influences (PI) were significantly stronger in girls than in boys. The peer delinquent behavior (PDB) was significantly higher in boys than in girls, but there was no significant sex difference in the peer prosocial behavior (PPB). The findings indicated that the best friend of the male subjects tended to exert stronger negative and weaker positive influences on their social behavior than their female counterparts. In addition, the male subjects perceived their best friend to be more delinquent and antisocial than the female subjects. In general, the result implied that the peer interaction among boys had a stronger tendency to reinforce delinquent and antisocial acts than the peer interaction among girls.

Peer Relationships and Personality

In order to simplify the discussion in this section, only the major scores DB and PB were used in the following analysis. The correlations of the DB (Delinquent Behavior) and PB (Prosocial Behavior) indices with PIQ (Peer Interaction Questionnaire) and JEPQ (Junior Eysenck Personality Questionnaire) scores for the total sample are presented in Table 2. Detailed correlational analyses for each grade sample, which were not reported here, also indicated that the correlations of DB and PB indices with PIQ and JEPQ scores are similar to those for the total sample. In addition, the partial correlations of DB and PB indices with PIQ and JEPQ scores controlling for grade effect differed from the corresponding simple correlations in Table 2 by a figure less than .03. The following discussion will therefore focus on the simple correlations in Table 2.

Table 2. Correlations of Adolescent Behavior Scores with Peer Interaction and Personality Scores

Score	Simple Correlation		Partial Correlation[a]	
	DB	PB	DB	PB
Peer Interaction Questionnaire (n=1102)				
PI	-.067	.366**	-.078	.364**
NI	.512**	.096**	.507**	.093*
PDB	.688**	.107**	.683**	.102**
PPB	-.016	.410**	-.024	.409**
Junior Eysenck Personality Questionnaire (n=425)				
P	.513**	.126*	.511**	.124
N	.268**	.081	.245**	.077
E	.215**	.242**	.231**	.244**
L	-.444**	.075	-.424**	.081

*p<.01. **p<.001.

[a]Partial correlations controlling for grade effect.

Note. DB = Delinquent Behavior; PB = Prosocial Behavior; PI = Positive Influences; NI = Negative Influences; PDB = Peer Delinquent Behavior; PPB = Peer Prosocial Behavior; P = Psychoticism; N = Neuroticism; E = Extroversion; L = Lying.

Generally speaking, the correlations of DB with NI (Negative Influences) and PDB (Peer Delinquent Behavior) were significant and positive, and the correlations of PB with PI (Positive Influences) and PPB (Peer Prosocial Behavior) were also significant and positive. In other words, subjects who were delinquent tended to perceive their best friend to be delinquent and to exert more negative influences on them. The positive correlation between DB and PDB is similar to Cheung and Ng's (1988) finding that delinquent behavior was positively correlated with the association with delinquent friends. The present finding also tends to support the general findings in other studies that the peer group serves as the training ground for antisocial and delinquent acts (see review by Patterson, DeBaryshe & Ramsey, 1989). On the other hand, subjects who were prosocial also tended to perceive their best friend to be prosocial and to exert more positive influences on them. Overall speaking, adolescents of similar characteristics tend to make good friends with each other (Cairns, Cairns, Neckerman, Gest & Gariepy, 1988).

Antisocial or delinquent behavior (DB) was significantly and positively related with psychoticism (P) and neuroticism (N), and significantly and negatively related with the Lie (L) score. While the correlation between PB and P was still significantly positive, the magnitude was much smaller, and there was no significant relation between PB and N or L. The results were similar to those found by Gabrys (1983). The present findings indicated that delinquent adolescents tended to be less emotionally stable in their personality.

Four Types of Adolescent Social Behavior

The means of the DB and PB scores for the total sample were 1.8781 and 2.6555 respectively. Those subjects scored higher than or equal to the both the means of DB and PB scores are classified as ambivalent; higher than or equal to DB and lower than PB classified as delinquent; lower than DB and higher than or equal to PB classified as Prosocial; and lower than both the means of DB and PB scores classified as passive. The PIQ and JEPQ scores in the above four groups of adolescents are presented in Table 3.

The negative peer influences (NI) and peer delinquent behavior (PDB) were significantly higher in the Ambivalent and Delinquent groups than in the Prosocial and Passive groups. In contrast, the positive peer influences (PI) and peer prosocial behavior (PPB) were significantly higher in the Prosocial and Ambivalent groups than in the Ambivalent and Delinquent groups. The Psychoticism (P) and Neuroticism (N) scores were significantly higher in the Ambivalent and Delinquent groups than in the Prosocial and Passive groups. On the other hand, the Lie score was significantly higher in the Prosocial and Passive groups than in the Ambivalent and Delinquent groups. In general, ambivalent and delinquent subjects tended to have stronger negative peer influences, higher peer delinquent behavior, more psychotic and neurotic, and less socially desirable than prosocial and passive subjects.

Table 3. Mean Score of Various Tests by Types of Adolescent Behavior

Score	Type				
	Ambivalent	Delinquent	Prosocial	Passive	F
	Peer Interaction Questionnaire(n=1102)				
N	228	183	275	416	--
NI	1.69	1.66	1.32	1.30	99.46**
PI	2.46	2.17	2.59	2.31	33.19**
PDB	1.87	1.91	1.33	1.29	189.46**
PPB	2.14	1.76	2.21	1.86	36.36**
Junior Eysenck Personality Questionnaire (n=425)					
N	86	43	115	181	--
P	.33	.37	.20	.16	36.48**
N	.66	.68	.53	.51	11.71**
E	.69	.61	.61	.57	7.11*
L	.37	.30	.52	.49	33.60**

*p<.001. **p<.0001.

The number and percentage of students of four different types of adolescent behavior are presented in Table 4.

**Table 4. Number and Percentage of Students of
Different Types of Adolescent Behavior**

Percentage	Grade				Sex		Number/ Row Total
	7	8	9	10	M	F	
			Ambivalent Type				
n	115	136	142	160	295	258	553
%	14.9	19.2	20.6	23.1	24.0	15.8	19.3
			Delinquent Type				
n	102	146	109	123	283	197	480
%	13.2	20.7	15.8	17.7	23.0	12.1	16.8
			Prosocial Type				
n	225	157	164	161	238	469	707
%	29.1	22.2	23.8	23.2	19.3	28.8	24.7
			Passive Type				
n	331	268	274	249	415	707	1122
%	42.8	37.9	39.8	35.9	33.7	43.3	39.2
Column Total	773	707	689	693	1231	1631	2862

There were more ambivalent subjects in the higher grades than in the lower grades. On the other hand, there were more prosocial and passive subjects in the lower grades than in the higher grades. The number of delinquent subjects was the largest in Grade 8 and the smallest in Grade 7. The number of male ambivalent or delinquent subjects was larger than the female counterparts. In contrast, the number of female prosocial or passive subjects was larger than the male counterparts. Generally speaking, older boys were ambivalent, and more younger girls were prosocial or passive.

Academic Achievement

The twenty schools participated in this study were classified into three categories according to their students' academic performance: above average, average, and below average. The relation of academic achievement and prosocial and antisocial behavior is presented in Table 5.

Table 5. Relation of Academic Achievement and Adolescent Behavior

Score	Academic Achievement						F
	Above Average (n=752)		Average (n=1438)		Below Average (n=672)		
	M	SD	M	SD	M	SD	
DB	1.77	.71	1.89	.79	1.98	.86	13.12*
PB	2.77	.83	2.63	.78	2.56	.77	15.93*

$*p < .0001$.

Note. DB = Delinquent Behavior; PB = Prosocial Behavior.

The mean of the DB score was the highest in subjects of below average academic achievement and the lowest in subjects of above average academic achievement, with the average academic achievement subjects in the middle. In contrast, the mean of the PB score was the lowest in subjects of below average academic achievement and the highest in subjects of above average academic achievement, with the average academic achievement subjects in the middle. In other words, academic achievement tended to have a positive relation with prosocial behavior and a negative relation with antisocial behavior. The above findings are consistent with current literature (Dishion, Patterson, Stoolmiller & Skinner, 1991; Grande, 1988; Lawrence, 1985; Patterson, DeBaryshe, & Ramsey, 1989). In a review of the socialization of Chinese children, Ho (1986) argued that Chinese parents placed much emphasis on obedience, proper conduct and moral behavior and discouraged their children to do adventurous or aggressive activities. They also set very high educational goals for their children and emphasized very much on their academic achievement in school (Mitchell, 1972). The parental pressure on Chinese adolescents to behave properly and to attain good academic results in school is usually high. It is argued that this kind of Chinese parenting may explain why prosocial adolescents tended to have better academic achievement.

STUDY 2

Method

Subjects
Participants included 19 grade 7 students (9 males and 10 females, mean age 12.74 years), 18 grade 8 students (9 males and 9 females, mean age 13.78 years), 21 grade 9 students (11 males and 10 females, mean age 15.05 years), and 13 grade 10 students (5 males and 8 females, mean age 15.46 years). Totally there were 71 subjects, 34 of whom were males and 37 of whom were females. The average age of the total sample was 14.18 years, with a standard deviation of 1.41 years. Participants came from 5 high schools, three of which admitted students of poor academic achievement and bad conduct; and two of which admitted students of good academic achievement.

Instruments

Adolescent Behavior Interview (ABI)
Interview Questions
This interview schedule was constructed by Ma, Shek and Cheung (1993). An intensive interview with each participant was conducted to explore his or her life experiences; value orientation; parental, peer, and teacher influences; and interpersonal relationships with parents, siblings, friends, teachers, and others. The major interview questions are as follows: (1) What sort of things have the greatest influences on your daily behavior (in school, at home, and outside school and home)? (2) Do your parents (siblings, friends, teachers, and mass media) exert influences on your behavior? (3) What sort of behavior you think is good, and what sort of behavior is bad? How do you define good and bad behavior? Have you done something that you just mentioned to be good (bad) behavior? How did you feel after performing the good (bad) behavior? What has influenced you to perform these behavior? (4) Please describe how you see your parents. Is your father (mother) good? Do you father and

mother have a good relation? How about your relationship with your parents? In what aspects do you have the greatest conflicts or disagreements with your parents? In what aspects do you have the same or similar views as your parents? (5) A similar set of questions as those in (4) were repeated for peers and teachers. (6) What are the happiest things in your experience? Please describe the details of the event and your feelings at that moment. What caused the event? Did the event change your feelings, self-esteem, or self-confidence? Did the event change the relationships between you and the people concerned? (7) A similar set of questions as those in (6) were repeated for the unhappiest experience. For each of the questions, the interviewer usually probed further after the participant gave the initial responses. Participants were free not to answer any of the questions.

ABI Scores

Three sets of scores were established from the interview data: (1) Influences Score: Parental, peer, and teacher influences on the social behavior of the adolescents are measured by the parental (PAI), peer (PEI), and teacher (TEI) influences scores, respectively. The average influence score, ALLI is equal to (PAI+PEI+TEI)/3, which indicates the mean influences on the social behavior of the adolescent by his or her parents, peers (best friends), and teachers. The range of the scores is from 1.0 to 5.0. A high score means greater influences. For example, a high PAI score indicates that the adolescent's social behavior (e.g., career choice, selection of arts or sciences streams in secondary school, studying hard, religious beliefs, and attitudes toward resolving interpersonal conflicts) is strongly influenced by his or her parents. (2) Relationships Score: The relationships between the adolescent and his or her parents, peer (best friends), and teacher were measured by the parental (PAR), peer (PER), and teacher (TER) relationships scores, respectively. The average relationships score, ALLR is equal to (PAR+PER+TER)/3, which indicates the mean relationships between the adolescent and his/her parents, peers (best friends) and teachers. The range of the scores is from 1.0 to 5.0. A high score means good relationships. For example, a high PAR score indicates that the relationship between the adolescent and his or her parents is harmonious; the parents understand their son or daughter and always talk to each other like good friends. A low PAR score indicates that the relationship is poor; the adolescent always quarrels with his or her parents and they do not understand each other; the parents sometimes physically punished the adolescent. (3) Identity Status: Participants were classified into one of the four identity statuses described by Marcia (1980), Identity Achievement, Identity Moratorium, Identity Foreclosure, and Identity Diffusion. The identity statuses are interpreted in terms of (a) moral identity: whether the adolescents are able to differentiate good behavior from bad behavior (e.g., whether they understand what are the normative or socially acceptable behavior, and whether they are committed to perform these behaviors), (b) vocational identity: to what extent they know their potential and personal interests (e.g., whether they are able to associate their personal interests with their possible future career); and (c) interpersonal relationships: the ability to resolve interpersonal conflicts with parents, peers, and teachers. The scope of the definition of the identity statuses is quite specific and fairly narrow. The classification of the identity status at this stage is quite exploratory.

Procedures

Participants answered the questionnaires in their classroom during their normal class periods. The experimenter went through the test instruction with the participants before they answered questions. Each participant also attended an individual interview (ABI) with a trained research assistant. The interview took about 30 to 45 minutes to complete. Participation in the study was on a voluntary basis.

Results and Discussion

A total of 17 ABI transcriptions were scored by two trained researchers. The inter-rater reliabilities of the PAI, PEI, TEI, PAR, PER, and TER scores were .86, .72, .82, .84, .72, and .85 respectively. In addition, the percentage of agreement in scoring the identity status classification between the two researchers was 76.50%. The inter-rater reliability of the ABI scores is regarded as satisfactory.

Participants were classified into two categories depending on their school type: (1) Those who came from schools which admitted high academic achievers, and (2) those who came from schools which admitted low academic achievers. A 2 (School type or ACAD: High Academic Achiever/Low Academic Achiever) X 2 (SEX: Male/Female) ANOVA of the ABQ and ABI scores was conducted and the results are given in Table 6. The findings indicated that there were significant school differences in the DB, $F(1, 69) = 7.46$, $p < .001$; and some ABI scores (PAI, $p < .001$; PEI, $p < .01$; ALLI, $p < .05$; PAR, $p < .001$; ALLR, $p < .001$). On the other hand, the sex differences and ACAD by SEX interaction effects were less salient.

The findings in Table 6 indicated that high academic achievers were significantly less delinquent than the low academic achievers. On the other hand, there was no significant difference in prosocial behavior between the high and low academic achievers, but results in Table 1 indicated that the reported frequency of prosocial behavior in high academic achievers was still higher than that in low academic achievers. This finding provides weak support for the previous findings that good academic achievement is positively related to prosocial (good) behavior (e.g., Rutter, Maughan, Mortimore & Ouston, 1979). It seems that academic achievement is more strongly related (in negative direction) to the delinquent behavior than prosocial behavior (in positive direction). Further studies in this area are required to find out the underlying causes or variables. In addition, the high academic achievers had larger influences from their parents and peers, and better relationships with their parents than the low academic achievers.

The sex differences and ACAD by SEX interaction effects were less salient in comparison to the ACAD effect. However, the following findings which involved significant interaction effects deserved some elaboration: (1) DB (Delinquent Behavior): Male low achievers scored significantly higher in the DB score than the male high achievers, but there were no significant differences in the DB score between the female high and low academic achievers. On the other hand, the finding indicated that, as far as Chinese girls are concerned, delinquent behavior does not seem to be linked closely with academic achievement. (2) PAI (Parental Influences): Parental Influences on the high male academic achievers were significantly greater than on the low male academic achievers. However, the differences were much smaller in the female groups. From Table 6, it is clear that parental influences on both male and female high academic achievers were very large, 4.00 and 4.06, respectively. The parental influences on female low academic achievers were still quite large, 3.79; but that on male low academic achievers were very low, 2.82 only. It seems that parental influences or parental control on female adolescents were quite large, whether they were high or low academic achievers. On the other hand, parental influences or parental control on low male academic achievers were the smallest among the four groups of academic achievers (i.e., high male, low male, high female, and low female academic achievers). This may be explained by the fact that Chinese parents exert much greater control and influence on their daughters than their sons. Chinese parents very often ask their daughters to spend their time at home and are less willing to let them go out to play with their peers. The control on girls by the parents is usually much stricter than the boys. (3) PEI (Peer Influences): The peer influences on the female high academic achievers were significantly larger than the low female academic achievers, but there were no significant differences in peer influences between the male high and male low academic achievers. The influences on female low academic achievers was greater from their parents than from their peers.

Table 6. Mean Scores in High and Low Academic Achievement

Score	High ACAD		Low ACAD		F-Ratio		
	Male (n=17)	Female (n=18)	Male (n=17)	Female (n=19)	ACAD	SEX	ACAD x SEX
Adolescent Behavior Questionnaire							
DB	1.36	1.50	2.25	1.50	13.65***	7.46**	15.40***
PB	2.84	3.13	2.51	2.81	3.74	2.97	.001
Adolescent Behavior Interview, influence							
PAI	4.00	4.06	2.82	3.79	11.15***	6.03*	4.68*
PEI	3.88	4.06	3.82	3.16	7.36**	1.89	5.26*
TEI	2.59	2.89	2.65	3.11	.32	2.34	.10
ALLI	3.49	3.67	3.10	3.35	5.34*	1.99	.06
Adolescent Behavior Interview, relationship							
PAR	4.12	4.11	2.94	3.21	24.55***	.41	.44
PER	3.94	4.44	3.71	3.95	3.43	3.41	.43
TER	3.06	3.61	3.06	3.16	1.91	3.56	1.76
ALLR	3.71	4.06	3.24	3.44	16.01***	4.06*	.29

*$p<.05$. **$p<.01$. ***$p<.001$.

Note. ACAD = Academic Achievement. DB = Delinquent Behavior. PB = Prosocial Behavior. PAI = Parental Influences. PEI = Peer Influences. TEI = Teacher Influences. ALLI = (PAI + PEI + TEI)/3. PAR = Parent-adolescent Relationships. PER = Peer Relationships. TER = Teacher-Student Relationships. ALLR = (PAR + PER + TER)/3.

Since the ACAD X SEX interaction effect is particularly strong in DB score, the following discussion focuses on this finding. The mean DB score in the male low academic achievers was significantly higher than that for the female counterparts, which is in line with the general results of previous research that male adolescents are more delinquent than the female adolescents (Duke, 1978; Eagly & Steffen, 1986; Ma, et al., 1996). On the other hand, the mean DB score in the female high academic achievers was higher than that for the male high academic achievers. This may be accounted for by the fact that Chinese parents tend to exert great pressure on the academic achievement of their children (Ho, 1986; Mitchell, 1972). In particular, the boys are usually under greater pressure than the girls. Therefore the male high academic achievers appeared to exhibit a fairly smaller frequency in delinquent or antisocial behavior in comparison with their female counterparts. Previous studies indicated that school failure is positively associated with delinquent behavior (Grande, 1988; Lawrence, 1985; Patterson, DeBaryshe, & Ramsey, 1989). Results in Table 6 support the previous findings for boys but not for girls. Generally speaking, high male academic achievers were less delinquent than the low male academic achievers in the present study. The competition for further education (e.g., admission to a good high school or a university) is keen in Hong Kong. In comparison with the low male academic achievers, high female academic achievers are more willing to spend a lot of time at their studies and tend to comply with school regulations. In addition, most high school students are taught the same curriculum. Low academic achievers usually find the curriculum too difficult and may not be able to catch up. Eventually, they lose interest in school and tend to misbehave during classes. On the other hand, there was no significant difference in delinquent behavior between the female high and low academic achievers. This may be accounted for by the fact that Chinese parents have high expectations in academic achievement in their sons but less so in their daughters. Male low academic achievers did not meet their parents' expectations and therefore were under greater pressure to study hard. The parents' high academic expectations might cause a lot of conflicts and unpleasant interactions between the male adolescents and their parents. Eventually, the male adolescents might choose to act out their frustration in academic failure in an antisocial way. The female low academic achievers were subject to less pressure from their parents and the society and therefore have less frustration and unhappiness than the male low academic achievers in facing the academic failure. They are more able to cope with the situation emotionally and do not tend to exhibit a high frequency of antisocial behavior.

The correlations of delinquent (DB) and prosocial behavior (PB) scores with influences and relationships scores are given in Table 7. Results indicated that the influence and relationship scores are, in general, negatively correlated with the delinquent behavior score and positively correlated with the prosocial behavior score.

The findings on the correlational analysis in Table 7 indicated that: (1) The correlations of parental influences (PAI) and parent-adolescent relationships (PAR) with delinquent behavior (DB) are significantly negative and those with prosocial behavior (PB) are significantly positive. Good parental influences and parent-adolescent relationships tend to reduce delinquent behavior and increase prosocial behavior. The present finding is in line with Shek and Ma's (1997) finding that negative perception of parental treatment was associated positively with reported frequency of antisocial behavior. In addition, Ho (1986), in his review on socialization of Chinese children, concluded that Chinese parents place great emphasis on "obedience, proper conduct, moral training, and the acceptance of social obligations, in contrast to the lack of emphasis placed on independence, assertiveness and creativity" (p.36). In other words, good and profound parental influences tend to reduce antisocial behavior and increase prosocial behavior in adolescents. (2) The correlation of peer relationships (PER) with delinquent behavior (DB) is significantly negative, and that of teacher-student relationships (TER) with prosocial behavior is significantly positive. Peer relationship is associated negatively with delinquent behavior and teacher-student relationship is associated positively with prosocial behavior. The finding indicated that delinquent adolescents tended to have poor relationships with their friends and peers. Previous findings showed that delinquent behavior is positively related with associating delinquent friends (Cheung & Ng, 1988; Patterson, DeBaryshe, &Ramsey, 1989). It appears that the friends of the delinquent adolescents are also delinquent youths and their relationship is usually poor. On the other hand, prosocial adolescents with a "good-boy-nice-girl orientation" usually had a good relationship with their teachers.

Table 7. Correlation of Social Behavior Scores with Influence and Relationship Scores

Score	DB	PB
Influences		
PAI	-.38***	.29**
PEI	.04	.05
TEI	-.16	.18
ALLI	-.26*	.26*
Relationships		
PAR	-.31**	.28*
PER	-.24*	.15
TER	-.15	.28**
ALLR	-.31**	.32**

*p<.05. **p<.01. ***p<.001.

Note. DB = Delinquent Behavior. PB = Prosocial Behavior. PAI = Parental Influences. PEI = Peer Influences. TEI = Teacher Influences. ALLI = (PAI + PEI + TEI)/3. PAR = Parent-adolescent Relationships. PER = Peer Relationships. TER = Teacher-Student Relationships. ALLR = (PAR + PER + TER)/3.

The mean ABQ and ABI scores by the four identity statuses (Identity Achievement, Identity Moratorium, Identity Foreclosure, and Identity Diffusion) are presented in Table 8. In order to simplify the discussion, we focus on the findings concerning the two ABQ scores (DB and PB), and the average influences (ALLI) and relationships (ALLR) scores by identity status.

From Table 8, the delinquent score (DB) was the lowest in the Achievement group and the highest in the Diffusion group, with the Moratorium and Foreclosure groups in the middle. However, the prosocial score (PB) was the highest in the Achievement group and the lowest in the Diffusion group, with the Moratorium and Foreclosure groups in the middle. The number of cases in the Achievement and Diffusion groups is two and nine respectively, which is very small. Further statistical analysis may not be appropriate. Overall speaking, adolescents in the Identity Achievement group tended to be the least delinquent and the most prosocial; and also had the largest influences from and the best relationships with their parents, peers, and teachers. On the other hand, adolescents in the diffusion group tended to be the most delinquent and the least prosocial; and also had the smallest influences from and the worst relationships with their parents, peers, and teachers. The patterns in the Moratorium and Foreclosure groups were in-between the Achievement and Diffusion groups.

The finding on the mean scores by identity status in Table 8 showed that adolescents in the Identity Diffusion group tended to have more social and psychological problems than the other groups, which is interesting and important and deserved further investigation. The overall finding is consistent with Marcia's (1980) classification of four identity statuses.

Table 8. Mean Scores by Identity Status

Measure	Identity		Status	
	Achievement (n=2)	Moratorium (n=25)	Foreclosure (n=35)	Diffusion (n=9)
	Adolescent Behavior Questionnaire			
DB	1.30	1.75	1.45	2.24
PB	3.89	3.02	2.69	2.56
	Adolescent Behavior Interview - influence			
PAI	5.00	3.96	3.69	2.56
PEI	5.00	3.84	3.51	3.89
TEI	4.00	2.92	2.74	2.56
ALLI	4.67	3.57	3.31	3.00
	Adolescent Behavior Interview - relationship			
PAR	5.00	3.76	3.69	2.44
PER	4.50	4.08	4.00	3.78
TER	4.00	3.24	3.20	3.11
ALLR	4.50	3.69	3.63	3.11

Note. DB = Delinquent Behavior. PB = Prosocial Behavior. PAI = Parental Influences. PEI = Peer Influences. TEI = Teacher Influences. ALLI = (PAI + PEI + TEI)/3. PAR = Parent-adolescent Relationships. PER = Peer Relationships. TER = Teacher-Student Relationships. ALLR = (PAR + PER + TER)/3.

GENERAL DISCUSSION

In summary, the major findings of the present study include the following. (1) boys were more antisocial than girls, (2) the negative peer influences were significantly stronger in boys than in girls; whereas the positive peer influences were significantly stronger in girls than in boys, (3) antisocial subjects tended to perceive their best friend to be antisocial and to exert more negative influences on them; whereas prosocial subjects tended to perceive their best friend to be prosocial and to exert more positive influences on them, (4) antisocial behavior was positively associated with psychoticism and neuroticism, (5) Male high academic achievers were less delinquent than the male low academic achievers, but there was no significant difference in delinquent behavior between the female high and low academic achievers. (6) Male high academic achievers are less delinquent than female high academic achievers but male low academic achievers are more delinquent than female low academic achievers. (7) There is no significant difference in prosocial behavior between the high and low academic achievers in both sexes; but the reported frequency of prosocial behavior in high academic achievers is still higher than that in low academic achievers, and females are more prosocial than males. (8) The high academic achievers have larger influences from their parents and peers, and better relationships with their parents than the low academic achievers. (9) The characteristics of the four identity statuses in terms of prosocial and delinquent behavior; and relationships between the adolescent and his or her parents, peers, and teachers are interesting. They are as follows: (a) Identity Achievement: Adolescents are able to differentiate what are good behaviors and what are bad behaviors; and they tend to exhibit high frequency of prosocial behavior and low frequency of antisocial behavior. They know their own potential and interests and are able to decide which career path they should follow. They usually have good relationships with their parents, peers, and teachers. (b) Identity Moratorium: They are in the stage of struggling hard for an identity and tend to be a bit ambivalent. They usually exhibit quite high frequency in both prosocial and antisocial behavior. Their relationships with parents, peers, and teachers are fairly good. (c) Identity Foreclosure: They are usually obedient and tend to follow the opinion of their parents and teachers. They usually exhibit low frequency of antisocial behavior and fairly high frequency of prosocial behavior. Their relationships with parents, peers, and teachers are quite good. (d) Identity Diffusion: This is a stage at which the adolescents neither have an identity nor have the motivation to search for an identity. It is a stage of diffusion and "getting lost". They are not able to differentiate good behavior from bad behavior, and tend to exhibit high frequency of antisocial behavior and low frequency of prosocial behavior. Their relationships with parents, peers, and teachers are usually poor.

The general findings on the antisocial behavior of Hong Kong Chinese adolescents in this study appear to be similar to those in the western societies. For examples, boys were more antisocial than girls (Eagly & Steffen, 1986); and antisocial behavior was positively associated with psychoticism and neuroticism (Gabrys, 1983), but negatively associated with academic achievement (Grande, 1988; Lawrence, 1985; Patterson, DeBaryshe & Ramsey, 1989). However there are few altruism or prosocial behavior scales for studying children and adolescents' behavior (Ma & Leung, 1991; Radke-Yarrow, Zahn-Waxler & Chapman, 1983); and as mentioned before, current research on adolescent behavior seldom emphasizes on both the prosocial and antisocial behavior in a single study; thus the present study makes a contribution to fill this gap of research. The use of self-report method in the study of prosocial and antisocial behavior has some limitations. For example, subjects may not give the true responses. However, this method is found to be useful and acceptable, especially in finding out the correlations among a large number of variables (Cheung & Ng, 1988; Hindelang, Hirschi & Weis, 1982; Ma & Leung, 1991). Some of the following findings may be interesting and meaningful to be replicated in future studies: (1) the negative peer influences were significantly stronger in boys than in girls; whereas the positive peer influences were significantly stronger in girls than in boys, (2) antisocial subjects tended to perceive their best friend to be antisocial and to exert more negative influences on them; whereas prosocial subjects tended to perceive their best friend to be prosocial and to exert more positive influences on them, and (3) academic achievement tended to have a positive relation with prosocial behavior and a negative relation with antisocial behavior. Finally, the classification of adolescent behavior into four types by using the means of the prosocial and antisocial behavior scores appears to generate some interesting and consistent findings. It is a useful and comprehensive perspective for studying the prosocial and antisocial behavior of adolescents.

In particular, the findings in Study 2 provide good empirical evidence for understanding the parental, peer, and teacher influences on the prosocial and delinquent behavior between the high and low academic achievers in Hong Kong. The finding of the social behavior pattern of the Chinese adolescents in the four identity statuses is new and interesting. However, there are two major limitations in the present study. First, the number of cases in the Identity Achievement group is very small ($n = 2$). Since it is natural that young adolescents (Grade 7 to 10 students in this study) are usually not in the status of identity achievement, further study should include a sample of older adolescents (e.g., Grade 11 to 12 or university students). The present findings on identity status should be regarded as exploratory at this stage. Second, the present study is a cross-sectional one, further study should include a longitudinal study to explore the causes and effects among the variables. Finally, the scoring system of the Adolescent Behavior Interview instrument should be further refined and standardized. It is also interesting to conduct a cross-cultural study to investigate the differences in the development of prosocial and delinquent behavior in adolescents from different cultures.

AUTHOR'S NOTES

This research was funded by two earmarked research grants from the Research Grant Council of the Universities Grant Committee, Hong Kong (Grant # CUHK 4/92H and RGC/95-96/07) to Hing Keung Ma, Daniel Shek and Ping Chung Cheung. The authors thank the staff at the Educational Research Unit of Education Department for their help in sampling, Royce Y. P. Lee and Christina O. B. Lam for their help in data collection, and Zhang Lu-Fei and Tam Ka Keung for their help in scoring the interview data. Correspondence should be addressed to Hing Keung Ma, Department of Education Studies, Hong Kong Baptist University, Kowloon Tong, Hong Kong (E-mail addresss: hkma@hkbu.edu.hk).

Thanks are due to Heldref Publications for granting permission to reproduce materials in two papers published in the *Journal of Genetic Psychology* (Ma, Shek, Cheung & Lee, 1996; Ma, Shek, Cheung & Lam, 2000).

REFERENCES

Atwater, E. (1992). *Adolescence* (3rd Ed.). Englewood Cliffs, NJ: Prentice Hall.

Berndt, T. J. (1979). Developmental changes in conformity to peers and parents. *Developmental Psychology, 15*, 608-616.

Cairns, R.B., Cairns, B.D., Neckerman, H.J., Ferguson, L.L., & Gariepy, J.L. (1989). Growth and Aggression: 1. Childhood to early adolescence. *Developmental Psychology, 25*, 320-330.

Cheung, P. C., Ma, H. K., & Shek, D. T. L. (1998). Conceptions of success: Their correlates with prosocial orientation and behaviour in Chinese adolescents. *Journal of Adolescence, 21*, 31-42.

Cheung, Y. W., & Ng, A. M. C. (1988). Social factors in adolescent deviant behavior in Hong Kong: An integrated theoretical approach. *International Journal of Comparative and Applied Criminal Justice, 12*, 29-45.

DiLalla, L.F., Mitchell, C.M., Arthur, M.W., & Pagliocca, P.M. (1988). Aggression and delinquency: Family and environmental factors. *Journal of Youth and Adolescence, 17*, 233-246.

Dishion, T. J., Patterson, G. R., Stoolmiller, M., Skinner, M. L.(1991). Family, school, and behavioral antecedents to early adolescent involvement with antisocial peers. *Developmental Psychology, 27*,172-180.

Duke, D. L. (1978). Why don't girls misbehave more than boys in school? *Journal of Youth and Adolescence, 7*, 141-157.

Eagly, A.H., & Crowley, M. (1986). Gender and helping behavior: A meta-analytic review of the social psychological literature. *Psychological Bulletin, 100*, 283-308.

Eagly, A. H., & Steffen, V. J. (1986). Gender and aggressive behavior: A meta-analytic review of the social psychological literature. *Psychological Bulletin, 100*, 309-330.

Erikson, E. H. (1968). *Identity: Youth and Crisis*. New York: W. Norton.

Eysenck, H. J., & Eysenck, S. B. G. (1975). *Manual of the Eysenck Personality Questionnaire (Junior & Adult)*. Kent, UK: Hodder & Stoughton.

Eysenck, S. G. B., & Chan, J. (1982). A comparative study of personality in adults and children: Hong Kong vs. England. *Personality and Individual Differences, 3*, 153-160.

Gabrys, J. B. (1983). Contrasts in social behavior and personality of children. *Psychological Reports, 52*, 171-178.

Gibbons, D. C., & Krohn, M. D. (1986). *Delinquent behavior* (4th Ed.). Englewood Cliffs, NJ: Prentice-Hall.

Grande, C. G. (1988). Delinquency: The learning disabled student's reaction to academic school failure? *Adolescence, 89*, 209-219.

Hartup, W. W. (1983). Peer relations. In P. H. Mussen (Series ed.) and E. M. Hetherington (Volume ed.), *Handbook of Child Psychology, Vol. IV. Socialization, personality, and social development* (pp. 103-196). New York: John Wiley.

Hindelang, M.J., Hirschi, T., & Weis, J.G. (1981). *Measuring delinquency*. Beverly Hills, CA: Sage.

Ho, D. Y. F. (1986). Chinese patterns of socialization: A critical review. In M. H. Bond (Ed.), *The Psychology of the Chinese People* (pp. 1-37). Hong Kong: Oxford University Press.

Kaplan, H. B. (1978). Deviant behavior and self-enhancement in adolescence. *Journal of Youth and Adolescence, 7*, 253-277.

Kaplan, H.B., Martin, S.S., & Johnson, R.J. (1986). Self-rejection and the explanation of deviance: specification of the structure among laten constructs. *American Journal of Sociology, 92*, 384-411.

Krebs, D. L. (1970). Altruism - an examination of the concept and a review of the literature. *Psychological Bulletin, 73*, 258-302.

Jensen, G.F. (1972). Parents, peers, and delinquent action: A   test of the differential association perspective. *American Journal of Sociology*, 78, 562-575.

Lawrence, R. (1985). School performance, containment theory, and delinquent behavior. *Youth & Society, 17*, 69-95.

LeCroy, C.W. (1988). Parent-adolescent intimacy: Impact on adolescent functioning. *Adolescence*, 23, 137-147.

Leung, K, & Lau, S. (1989). Effects of self-concept and perceived disapproval of delinquent behavior in school children. *Journal of Youth and Adolescence,18*, 345-359.

Ma, H. K. (1988). *Adolescent Behavior Questionnaire: An introduction.* Unpublished manuscript, The Chinese University of Hong Kong.

Ma, H. K., & Leung, M. C. (1991). Altruistic orientation in children: Construction and validation of the Child Altruism Inventory. *International Journal of Psychology, 26*, 745-759.

Ma, H. K., Shek, D. T. L., & Cheung, P. C. (1993). *Adolescent Behavior Interview.* Unpublished manuscript, Hong Kong Baptist University.

Ma, H. K., Shek, D. T. L., Cheung, P. C., & Lee, R. Y. P. (1996). The relation of prosocial and antisocial behavior to personality and peer relationships of Hong Kong Chinese adolescents. *Journal of Genetic Psychology, 157*, 255-266.

Ma, H. K., Shek, D. T. L., Cheung, P. C., & Lam, C. O. B. (2000). Parenatal, peer, and teacher influences on the social behavior of Hong Kong Chinese adolescents. *Journal of Genetic Psychology, 161*,65-78.

Maccoby, E. E., & Jacklin, C. N. (1974). *The psychology of sex differences Vol. I. Text. Vol. II. Annotated bibliography.* Stanford, CA: Stanford University Press.

Marcia, J.E. (1966). Development and Validation of ego identity status. *Journal of Personality and Social Psychology, 3*, 551-558.

Marcia, J. E. (1980). Identity in adolescence. In J. Adelson (Ed.), *Handbook of adolescent psychology* (pp.159-177). New York: Wiley.

Mitchell, R. E. (1972). *Pupil, parent, and school: A Hong Kong study.* Taipei, Taiwan: Orient Cultural Service.

Moore, B.S., & Eisenberg, N. (1984). The development of altruism. In G.J. Whitehurst (ed.), *Annals of Child Development: A Research Annual Volume 1.* (pp.107-174). Greenwich, Connecticut: JAI Press.

Moos, R.H., & Moos, B.S. (1986). *Family environment scale manual.* 2nd ed. Palo Alto, CA: Consulting Psychologists Press.

Mussen, P., Harris, S., Rutherford, E., & Keasey, C. B. (1970). Honesty and altruism among preadolescents. *Developmental Psychology, 3(2)*, 169-194.

Nicholls, J. G. (1989). *The competitive ethos and democratic education.* Cambridge, MA: Harvard University Press.

Parke, R.D., & Slaby, R.G (1983). The development of aggression. In E.M. Hetherington (Ed.) & P.H. Mussen (Series Ed.), *Handbook of child psychology: Vol IV. Socialization, personality and social development.* (4th ed.) (pp. 547-641). NY: John Wiley.

Patterson, G. R., DeBaryshe, B. D., & Ramsey, E. (1989). A developmental perspective on antisocial behavior. *American Psychologist, 44*, 329-335.

Radke-Yarrow, M., Zahn-Waxler, C., & Chapman, M., (1983). Children's prosocial dispositions and behavior. In E.M. Hetherington (Ed.) & P.H. Mussen (Series Ed.),

Handbook of child pshchology: Vol IV. Socialization, personality and social development. (4th ed.) (pp.469-545). NY: John Wiley.

Rest, J. R., & Thoma, S. J. (1986). Educational programs and interventions. In J. R. Rest (Ed.), *Moral development: Advances in research and theory.* (pp.59-88). New York: Praeger.

Rosenberg, F. R., & Rosenberg, M. (1978). Self-esteem and delinquency. *Journal of Youth and Adolescence, 7,* 279-294.

Rutter, M., & Giller, H. (1983). *Juvenile delinquency: Trends and perspectives.* Harmondsworth, Middlesex: Penguin.

Rutter, M., Maughan, B., Mortimore, P., & Ouston, J. (1979). *Fifteen thousand hours: Secondary schools and their effects on children.* Cambridge, MA: Harvard University Press.

Shek, D. T. L., & Ma, H. K. (1997). Perceptions of parental treatment styles and adolescent antisocial and prosocial behavior in a Chinese context. *Psychologia, 40,* 233-240.

Simons, R.L., Robertson, J.F., & Downs, W.R. (1989). The nature of the association between parental rejection and delinquent behavior. *Journal of Youth and Adolescence, 18,* 297-310.

Staub, E. (1978). *Positive social behavior and morality: Vol.1. Social and personal influences.* New York: Academic Press.

Staub, E. (1979). *Positive social behavior and morality, Vol. 2. Socialization and development.* NY: Academic Press.

Staub, E. (1980). Social and prosocial behavior: Personal and situational influences and their interactions. In E. Staub (Ed.), *Personality: Basic aspects and current research.* Englewood

Staub, E., Bar-Tal, D., Karylowski, J., & Reykowski, J. (eds.) (1984). *Development and maintenance of prosocial behavior.* NY: Plenum Press.

Widom, C.S. (1989). Does violence beget violence? A critical examination of the literature. *Psychological Bulletin, 106,* 3-28.

Yau, J., & Smetana, J. G. (1996). Adolescent-Parent conflict among Chinese adolescents in Hong Kong. *Child Development, 67,* 1262-1275.

Chapter 5

SELF-CONCEPT, WEIGHT ISSUES AND BODY IMAGE IN CHILDREN AND ADOLESCENTS

Jennifer A. O'Dea
Senior Lecturer in Education
University of Sydney, Australia

INTRODUCTION

A child's self-concept is constructed throughout childhood and adolescence from several different domains. Self-concept theorists have identified the multi-dimensional nature of self-concept in children and adolescents including different individual domains such as academic self-concept, athletic competence, social acceptance and romantic appeal.

General self-esteem is used to describe and measure the overall sense of self and sense of self-worth among young people. Influences on self-concept include gender, age and stage or pubertal development. Self-concept and body image are interrelated and are associated with gender, body weight and pubertal development, particularly among female adolescents. Various programs aimed at improving self-esteem have been implemented among children and adolescents and a recent program, titled "Everybody's Different" was successful at improving body image in young male and female adolescents.

SELF-CONCEPT AND SELF-ESTEEM IN CHILDREN AND ADOLESCENTS

Children work to construct their self-concept from the pre-school period through adolescence. Constructing the self-concept is like piecing together a "personal theory" of what the self is like as an experiencing and functioning individual (Berk, 1991, pp.434-435). The self-concept is subject to continual change as it is exposed to new information and experiences and as the child learns more about himself or herself and the surrounding world. An additional component of self-concept is self-esteem which refers to the judgment we make about the worth of ourselves (Coopersmith, 1967; Rosenberg, 1979; Harter, 1983; Harter,

1988) Children and adolescents with high self-esteem are fundamentally satisfied with themselves as a person, whilst still able to identify weaker characteristics that may require work to overcome. High self-esteem envelops a realistic appraisal of the selfs' characteristics and competencies coupled with an attitude of self-acceptance, self-respect and self worth (Berk, 1991, p.437).

The self-concept of adolescents is influenced by several variables. The adolescent self-concept decreases slightly on entry into secondary school and then gradually increases with age (Wylie, 1979; Berk, 1991) and becomes increasingly differentiated into separate categories related to roles with age (Harter and Monsour, 1992; Marsh, 1992). Theorists categorize the adolescent self-concept as encompassing several different domains such as academic and scholastic competence, physical and athletic competence, physical appearance, close friendship, romantic appeal, perception of personal behavior and global self worth (Shavelson, Hubner and Stanton, 1976; Harter, 1982). Shavelson classifies academic self-concept further by having separate categories for mathematics, english, science and history (Shavelson et al., 1976). Reviews of the adolescent self-concept agree that self-concept is multidimensional and measurement must address the many separate dimensions of the total self-concept, (Marsh, 1990; Kimm et al., 1991; Harter and Monsour, 1992; Marsh, 1992) rather than try to allocate one self-esteem score.

Harter's Perceived Competence Scale for Children (Harter, 1982) includes a scale for measurement of importance ratings. This instrument assumes that the importance a child gives to certain areas of self-concept determines the overall effect upon their self-concept. For example, a child may score low on the physical ability/athletic competence subscale of the Harter Perceived Competence Scale, but may also assign a low level of importance to that area of self-concept. The discrepancy between perception and importance of the various dimensions of self-concept in comparison to the actual score affects the overall self-concept. Measurement of the importance assigned to each dimension of self-concept is therefore essential in order to assess general self-concept.

The self-concept of adolescents is also influenced by gender. A study of 14-16 year old adolescents showed that girls scored lower on the Rosenberg Self-esteem Scale than boys (Harper and Marshall, 1991). The authors suggest that the lower level of self-esteem among girls was the cause of their higher level of reported problems. Similar differences between the self-concept of girls and boys have reported that differences in specific components of self-concept may exist, and that these effects are lost when forming a total score (Wylie, 1979). Marsh (1990) presented a review of self-concept research and theory and states that global measures of self-concept tend to favor boys. This suggestion is supported by the literature. Girls tend to score higher on self-concept measures of reading and general schoolwork, but score lower on physical ability, maths and physical appearance. Physical appearance self-concept (physical self-esteem) scores decline significantly after preadolescence. Girls also score higher than boys for self-concept related to verbal competence, honesty and trustworthiness and same sex relationships. Boys score higher than girls on perceived emotional stability scales and perceived problem solving ability. Marsh states that these trends are consistent with traditional gender stereotypes.

Self-concept studies of Australian adolescents (O'Dea & Abraham, 1999a; O'Dea & Abraham, 1999b) produced similar findings to the studies of Marsh. The self-concept scales ranked as most important by male and female students were in order, Close Friendship, Scholastic Competence and job competence. Females rated their ability to form close friendships significantly higher and of greater importance than did males. Males had a more positive self-concept related to physical appearance, scholastic competence, and athletic competence than did females, although both boys and girls rated athletic competence as the least important of all the aspects of self-concept. Boys also scored higher than females for the discrepancy between self-concept and importance, showing that the boys felt more capable of achieving in the areas of self-concept that were important to them.

A number of studies have identified factors associated with low self-concept in adolescents. Renouf and Harter (1990) and Harter, Marold and Whitesell (1992) measured self-concept, depression and social support among 346 young adolescents. Findings showed that depressed adolescents and those who had expressed suicidal thoughts had low self-concept scores and in particular, low scores for physical appearance, peer likability, athletic competence, scholastic competence and behavioral conduct. Other researchers have identified the negative impact that depression, anxiety and mood have upon the adolescent self-concept (Teri, 1982; Taylor and Cooper, 1992)

Growth retardation, particularly height stunting has been linked to low self-concept in adolescents. Studies of growth retarded adolescents (Shurka, Galatzer and Baizerman, 1983) adolescents with achondroplasia (short stature) (Csapo, 1991) and children with spina bifida (Andrade, Kramer, Garber and Longmuir, 1991) have shown that adolescents with conditions for which there is no available treatment have lower self-concept and higher levels of emotional problems. Other adolescent groups in which low self-concept has been detected include young adolescents in after school sibling care (Berman, Winkelby, Chesterman and Boyce, 1992) and children attending schools for the gifted (Marsh and Parker, 1984). The latter study demonstrated a clear separation between different facets of self-concept and found that adolescents from low socioeconomic status/low ability schools had higher self-concepts than adolescents from high socioeconomic status/high ability schools. The authors have termed this phenomenon the "large fish/small pond effect" and suggest that it may be more beneficial for the development of self-concept if children study in less competitive environments. The effect on self-concept was demonstrated to be larger after controlling for academic ability and an individual's socioeconomic status, suggesting that the general self-concepts of children in competitive or selective school environments are adversely affected by continual peer competition.

Research shows that low ability children benefit from being placed in a classroom with other low ability students, but high ability children do not (Brookover, 1989).

A study of Australian teenaged girls showed no differences in global self-esteem scores between girls from middle and lower socioeconomic backgrounds (O'Dea, 1994).

THE RELATIONSHIP BETWEEN SELF-CONCEPT AND BODY IMAGE

Research linking physical attractiveness reported by others, perceived physical attractiveness, body weight and height to self-concept has shown that adolescent self-concept is strongly influenced by body weight and perceived body weight.

Lerner, Lerner, Hess and Schwab, (1991) showed that 12 year olds with high physical attractiveness scores rated by others and self perceived, also had better scores on peer/parent relationships, classroom behavior and general self-concept. Similar results were found by Kenealy, Gleeson, Frude and Shaw, 1991, who studied 1,018 adolescents. They found that respondents with low self-attractiveness scores had low self-esteem. Thornton and Ryckman (1991) examined the relationship between physical attractiveness, physical effectiveness and self-esteem. This study showed that adolescents with higher self-attractiveness and self-effectiveness scores had higher self-esteem.

Numerous researchers have investigated the effect of height and weight on adolescents' self-concept. Height has not been shown to be a particularly potent influence on the self-concept of adolescents. Hensley (1983) found no distinct pattern for height and self-esteem of male and female late adolescents, although Rienzi, Scrams and Uhles (1992) found that self-acceptance was positively related to the average academic score (grade point average (GPA)) and negatively related to height for female adolescents. The most potent influence on self-concept is body weight, and this has a particularly negative influence on the self-concept of females. The association between self-concept and body weight in children and adolescents will be discussed in detail later in this chapter.

LINKS BETWEEN SELF-CONCEPT, AGE AND GENDER

Self-concept and self-esteem has been studied extensively among adolescents. A large study of 12,266 Australian adolescents (Marsh, 1989) found gender and age differences in self-concept. Marsh found that the self-concept scores of pre-adolescents were lower than those of children who had entered adolescence and that there was a significant decrease in self-concept scores in pre and very early adolescence. He suggested that some time in early to middle adolescence, the self-concept begins to rise and this continues during late adolescence and early adulthood. This trend has been confirmed by other authors (O'Malley and Bachman, 1983; Savin-Williams and Demo, 1984; Wallace, Cunningham and Del Monte, 1984) and this decline of self-concept in preadolescence is partly attributed to the transition from primary school to high school (Marsh, 1989; Rosenberg, 1979, Simmons, Blyth, Van Cleave and Bush, 1979). Changing to a new school environment and adjusting to new expectations from teachers and peers may cause adolescents to question their ability to cope with their behavior and performance and this may affect their self-concept (Berk, 1991, p.440). It has been suggested that younger children and preadolescent children have an unrealistically high self-concept which becomes more realistic with age and that this "reality testing" may also account for the decline in self-concept at entry into adolescence (Marsh, Barnes, Cairns and Tidman, 1984). Self-concept (self-esteem) tends to rise after early adolescence contradicting the long held belief that adolescence is a time of serious emotional trauma and turmoil.

Gender differences are apparent between the self-concepts of male and female adolescents. Males tend to score higher on most self-concept categories and on measures of general self-esteem than females. The large Marsh study (1989) found boys to score higher on physical ability, physical appearance, mathematics, emotional stability, problem solving and general self-esteem. Girls scored higher on verbal and reading competency, school related self-concept, honest/trustworthiness and religious/spiritual values. Marsh commented that these gender differences were consistent with traditional sex stereotypes. Scores of male and female adolescents on the Harter Self Perception Profile for Adolescents (Harter, 1988) confirm Marsh's findings. Males in Harter's study scored higher than females on all categories of self-concept except for behavioral conduct. The physical appearance scores of male and female adolescents in the Australian study was the only category of self-concept on which gender differences varied substantially with age (Marsh, 1989). The younger females in Marsh's study had greater physical appearance scores than older females. These studies suggest that adolescents' self-concept is already affected by cultural sex stereotypes in preadolescence and that the effects are relatively stable throughout the adolescent years. The studies of Marsh (1989), Harter (1988), Kimm et al. (1991) and O'Dea & Abraham (1999a) highlight the importance of measuring different aspects of the adolescent self-concept rather than using one overall measure of general self-esteem. Using a multidimensional instrument enables examination of gender, pubertal and body weight interactions with different categories of self-concept. A one-dimensional instrument would not be able to detect such variations. Measuring change in the self-concept must therefore take into account the fact that separate dimensions must be measured and that the overall self-concept is expected to improve from early to late adolescence.

SELF-CONCEPT AND PUBERTY

Several studies have shown that pubertal development affects physical self-concept with early developing females having a less positive physical self-concept than their "on time" or late-maturing peers (Alsaker, 1992; Folk et al., 1993; O'Dea & Abraham, 1999a; Abraham & O'Dea, In Press; Attie & Brooks-Gunn, 1989; Cauffman & Steinberg, 1996; Graber et al, 1994; Swarr 7 Richards, 1996). In studies of young adolescents aged 11–14 years old, we consistently found post-menarcheal females to have poorer self-esteem than their pre-menarcheal counterparts (O'Dea & Abraham, 1995; O'Dea & Abraham, 1999b; O'Dea & Abraham, In Press). The female adolescents who were post-menarcheal had poorer general self-esteem as well as poorer self-esteem related to athletic competence, physical appearance and behavioral conduct. The opposite trend for self-esteem was observed among the young males in the studies with post-pubertal males having the greatest global self-esteem of all adolescents in the studies and post-pubertal females having the poorest. Similar effects of pubertal development upon self-concept have been aspects of the adolescent reported in other studies (Blyth et al., 1981; Brooks-Gunn, 1984; Alasaker, 1992; Folk et al., 1993) and support the suggestion that stage of pubertal development may be more influential than age in influencing the self-concept of adolescents, particularly females.

SELF-CONCEPT AND BODY WEIGHT

Body weight and in particular overweight has been consistently found to be a potent predictor of lower self-esteem in both female and male children and adolescents.

Studies of the relationship between self-esteem and body weight in young pre-adolescent children aged below 12 years have generally found an inverse relationship between self-esteem and measures of body weight, body mass index, overweight or obesity (Coopersmith, 1967; Felker, 1968; Felker & Kay, 1971; Sallade, 1973; Strauss, 1985; Kaplan & Wadden, 1986).

Similar results have been found in studies of adolescents with general self-esteem being lower in overweight or obese adolescents (Sheslow, Hassink, Wallace et al., 1993; Pierce & Wardle, 1993; French, Story & Perry, 1995; French, Perry, Leon et al., 1996; Kimm, Barton, Berhane et al., 1997; Pritchard, King, Czai, Ka-Narins, 1997; O'Dea & Abraham, 1999a;

Strauss, 2000). Studies that have failed to find a relationship between self-esteem and body weight may have been limited by the use of a one-dimensional instrument for measuring self-esteem rather than using a multi-dimensional instrument. For example, studies of weight and self-concept among adolescents using single dimensional tools such as the Rosenberg self-esteem scale (Rosenberg, 1965) have not been able to detect any impact of weight upon self-esteem (Lawson, 1980; White, 1982; Mendelsen & White, 1985; Wadden et al., 1989, Mendelsen & El-Mofty, 1991; Gortmaker et al., 1993) and this may simply be due to the insensitivity of the instrument being used. Studies which have included a sub-scale measure of general self-esteem such as body esteem or physical self-esteem have reported strong inverse relationships between actual body weight and these sub-scale measures of physical self-esteem, showing that children and adolescents of greater body weight have poorer body esteem (Hill et al., 1992; Mendelsen & White, 1982; Mendelsen & white, 1985), poorer body image (O'Dea, Abraham & Heard, 1996; Gardner, Friedman, Stark et al., 1999) and poorer physical self-esteem (Newell et al., 1990; French et al., 1995; O'Dea & Abraham, 1999a)

IMPACT OF SPORT AND EXERCISE ON SELF-CONCEPT

Several studies worldwide have reported greater general self-esteem and physical self-esteem in young people who participate in sports or physical activity (Zanatopoulos & Hodge, 1991; Guyot et al., 1981; Salokun, 2000). Participation by children and adolescents in physical activity and exercise has been found to be associated with greater self-esteem and physical self-esteem in several studies and in both sexes (Schumaker et al., 1986; Sherrill et al., 1989; Salokun, 1990). Various types of sports and physical activity have been shown to be related to higher global self-esteem and greater physical self-esteem in children and adolescents including participation in swimming (Miller, 1989; Frankl, 1996), creative dance (Radel et al., 1993), baseball (Hawkins & Gruber, 1982) and Karate and martial arts (Richman & Rehberg, 1986).

Interventions to improve self-esteem have successfully employed physical activities in children and adolescents aged 9-16 years old (Parishplass & Lufi, 1997; Boyd & Hrycaiko, 1997; Goni & Zulaika, 2000). The recent successful intervention study of Goni & Zulaika differed from the usual physical education classes in that they focused on identifying individual goals, promoted participative and non-competitive games and praised students at every chance possible during the classes. This type of non-competitive, cooperative approach to physical activity and sport has been previously found to improve self-concept in high school girls (Marsh & Peart, 1988) and young children (Emmanouel et al., 1992; Grant & Roberts, 1982).

BODY IMAGE AND BODY SATISFACTION
AMONG CHILDREN AND ADOLESCENTS

The concept of body image refers to the mental picture we have of our bodies and how we feel about our bodies. Body image is a general term described as a concept or scheme incorporating a collection of feelings and perceptions such as overall awareness of the body, perception of body boundaries, attention to parts of the body as well as the whole, perception of size and parts and the whole, position in space and gender-related perceptions (Fisher, 1986, p.633; Thompson, 1990). Body image includes an individual's perception and judgment of their size, shape, weight and any other aspect of the body that relates to body appearance. The physical appearance construct can be divided into body perception such as the accuracy of reporting one's weight, subjective judgment such as satisfaction with the body and may be related to behavioral components such as dietary restraint (Thompson, 1990).

Body image incorporates terms such as body perception, body satisfaction and body esteem. Physical self-esteem is measured as a subscale of general self-esteem.

Research into body image among adolescents since the 1960's has shown a progression toward a more inaccurate and negative perception of the body, despite most adolescents possessing a normal body weight. Early studies documented a high frequency of middle to late adolescents who were dissatisfied with their bodies and perceived themselves as overweight despite the majority being of normal weight. That dissatisfaction with weight and shape is more prevalent among girls was demonstrated in an early study from Berkeley, California, which found that 43-56% of early adolescent girls perceived themselves as fat and 63-70% wanted to lose weight, despite only 25% being classified as overweight (Huenemann, Shapiro, Hampton and Mitchell, 1966). In later studies Dwyer and co-workers (Dwyer, Feldman, Selzer and Mayer, 1969/a, 1969/b) found 60% of 17 year old girls had already dieted and that most had commenced dieting at an average age of 14.5 years. These studies demonstrated that girls were actively dieting, despite the majority having normal body weights.

There have been numerous studies in several different countries since the early studies from the USA which have replicated the findings that adolescents, particularly girls, incorrectly perceive themselves as overweight and that this trend has increased among adolescents since the 1960's. (Killen, Taylor, Telch, Saylor, Maron and Robinson, 1986; Rosen and Gross 1987; Gralen, Levine, Smolak and Murnen, 1990; Patton, Johnson-Sabine, Woods, Mann and Wakeling, 1990; Koff, Rierdan and Stubbs, 1990; Paxton, Wertheim, Gibbons, Szmukler, Hillier and Petrovich, 1991; Lautenbacher, Thomas, Roscher, Strian, Pirke and Krieg, 1992; Moore, 1993; Fisher, Pastore, Schneider, Pegler and Napolitano, 1994; Levine, Smolak, Moodey, Shuman and Hessen, 1994; Wichstrom, 1995; Mueller et al., 1995; Page and Allen, 1995; O'Dea et al., 1996; Shisslak et al., 1998; sands et al., 1997).

GENDER DIFFERENCES IN BODY SATISFACTION AND BODY PERCEPTION

Several studies have shown that adolescents have a poor body image and that the body image of girls is more inaccurate and negative than that of boys. Biddulph, Elliot, Faldt, Fowler and Dugdale, (1984) surveyed 277 girls aged 15-16 years and found that 63% were dissatisfied with their weight and wanted to lose weight despite only 15% being overweight. This study showed that a significant proportion of girls whose weight fell below the normal reference level wanted to lose weight. Of the girls with weights below the reference levels, 37% wanted to lose weight. This study also stated that the majority of adolescent girls perceived themselves to be overweight, were actively attempting to lose weight, and that normal weight girls desired ideal weights significantly below recommended references. This inaccurate body perception is characteristic of adolescent girls to a greater extent than among boys. Wadden, Foster, Stunkard and Linowitz (1989) point out that while obese girls are less satisfied with their weight and shape, in comparison to non obese girls, this dissatisfaction is not associated with symptomatology of depression or anxiety. There was no overall difference between the mean scores of obese and non-obese girls for anxiety and depression. They found that whilst there was no relationship between the girls' Body Mass Index (BMI) and their mean scores for anxiety or depression, the girls' perceived overweight correlated significantly with anxiety and depression.

This study showed that obese girls are not necessarily more unhappy than non-obese girls, but those with an inaccurate perception of their body image may be.

A study of 130 obese children in the USA (Kimm, Sweeney, Janosky, 1991) showed that whilst their mean overall score on the Piers-Harris Children's Self-concept Scale was within the norms, certain sub-groups scored low, with non-white children displaying the lowest self-esteem. The lowest self-esteem scores were among younger girls and adolescent males.

A sample of adolescents from Brisbane, Australia in 1985 showed that while only 14% of girls aged 11-19 years were actually overweight or obese, 36% of normal weight girls perceived themselves to be overweight. Dissatisfaction with and misperception of weight increased with age (Carroll, Gleeson, Ribsby and Dugdale, 1986). In comparison, of the adolescent boys in Carroll's study, 22% were overweight or obese, and 17% of normal weight boys perceived themselves to be overweight. A concerning finding in this study was that 1% of underweight girls perceived themselves as overweight. None of the underweight boys perceived themselves as overweight. The body image of adolescents, particularly girls, leads them to attempt weight loss, often by dangerous and ineffective means.

The difference in body image between males and females has become clearer over the past two decades. Studies have shown that girls have poorer body image and are more dissatisfied with their weight than boys (Dwyer, Feldman, Seltzer and Mayer, 1969b; O'Dea et al., 1996). Adolescent boys are more likely than girls to perceive themselves as too thin and generally want to be larger although boys' perceptions are not as inaccurate as that of adolescent girls (Blyth, Simmons, Bulcroft, Felt, van Cleave and Bush, 1981; Stager and Burke, 1982; Rosen, Gross and Vara, 1987; Koff et al., 1990; Tiggemann and Pennington, 1990; Page 1992; Moore, 1993; Page and Allen, 1995; Nowak et al., 1996; O'Dea et al., 1996). A study of Australian school children illustrates these gender differences with 22% of girls and 31% of boys wanting to have their current body size, 71% and 34% wanting to be smaller and 7% and 35% wanting to be larger (Wertheim et al., 1992). A study of 895 adolescent boys found that the majority of boys dissatisfied with their weight perceived themselves as underweight and wanted to increase arm and chest size and decrease abdomen size (Moore, 1990).

BODY IMAGE ISSUES IN BOYS

Body image research among adolescent males shows that these young males perceive themselves to be thinner than they actually are (O'Dea et al., 1996; Tucker, 1983; Tucker, 1984; McCreary & Sasse, 2000) and several studies have found that male adolescents are actively trying to gain weight. The study of McCeary & Sasse (2000) found that adolescent males' drive for muscularity resulted in them trying to gain weight and muscle mass and that the drive was related to poor self-esteem. The recent study of O'Dea & Rawstone (2001) studied the weight gain practices of 397 male adolescents aged 13-19 years. Males in the study had tried to gain weight in the previous 12 months (26%); were currently trying to build up their bodies (59%); felt that they should develop their muscles (75%) and received advice from others that they should gain weight (23%). The majority of adolescent males who were trying to gain weight were using relatively sensible methods of weight gain such as eating healthy food and exercise (54%) but a significant percentage (34%) were using ineffective and/or potentially dangerous methods of weight gain including dietary supplements (for example, creatine monohydrate), "pills" (which were not specifically identified by the participants), steroids, fluid pills and insulin (O'Dea & Rawstorne, 2001).

Clearly, the body image concerns of young males encompasses a drive for slimness (Blyth et al., 1981; Koff, Rierden & Stubbs, 1990; O'Dea, 1999a; O'Dea et al., 1996) as well as a drive for muscularity (McCreary & Sasse 2000; Moore, 1990) which may adversely affect their physical and/or psychological health if taken to extremes.

AGE AND PUBERTAL DIFFERENCES IN BODY IMAGE AMONG ADOLESCENTS

The desire to become slimmer and the presence of weight losing behaviors have been observed in preadolescent children as young as seven years old (Maloney, McGuire, Daniels and Specker, 1989; Hill, Oliver and Rogers, 1992). The majority of studies have shown that body image and eating disturbances among girls increase in older age groups and in particular, dissatisfaction with upper thighs, buttocks and stomach measurements (Davies and Furnham, 1986; Salmons, Lewis, Rogers and Gatherer, 1988; Robinson, Bacon and O'Reilly, 1993). Boys generally want to be bigger (Rosen and Gross, 1987; Tiggemann and Pennington, 1990) and taller (Morrow, 1984; Harmatz, Gronendyke and Thomas, 1985; Koff et al., 1990; Booth, 1990) and are more likely to exercise for weight control than to use other dangerous methods (Drewnowski and Yee, 1987; Wardle and Beales, 1988; O'Dea & Rawsforne, 2001). Among a large sample of 36,320 adolescents, the percentage of subjects reporting dieting and disordered eating was significantly less among younger adolescents than their older peers (Story, Rosenwinkel, Himes, Resnick, Harris and Blum, 1991).

Similar results have been found in other studies of adolescents (Crowther, Post and Zaynor, 1985; Eisele, Hersgaaird and Light, 1986; Davies and Furnham, 1986; Whitaker, Davies, Shaffer, Johnson, Abrams and Walsh, 1989; Richards, Casper and Larson, 1990; Killen et al., 1992), with this trend being particularly marked among females.

The relationship between the stage of pubertal development and body image, body satisfaction and disordered eating has been examined in several studies. The majority of findings show that post-menarcheal girls have poorer body image and higher levels of dieting and eating disturbances related to weight control than pre-menarcheal girls and that this relationship is independent of age (Fabian and Thompson, 1989; Killen et al., 1992; O'Dea and Abraham, 1995; O'Dea & Abraham, 1999b; O'Dea & Abraham, In Press). A study by Killen et al., (1992) of 971 Californian girls found pubertal development (as measured by self-reported Tanner stage) to be associated with eating disorder symptoms (Killen et al., 1992). Girls who were more developmentally advanced were more likely to manifest eating disorder symptoms than their less developed counterparts and this relationship was independent of age. The normal pubertal changes that occur among girls in this age group, such as increased body weight and percentage of body fat may account for the higher rates of body dissatisfaction observed in pubertal girls (Alsaker, 1992).

In contrast, studies of adolescent boys show that male body satisfaction increases after pubertal development begins (Alsaker, 1992; Folk, Pedersen and Cullari, 1993).

ETHNIC DIFFERENCES IN BODY SATISFACTION AND BODY PERCEPTION

Adolescents from different ethnic backgrounds living in their home countries hold similar perceptions and attitudes towards body satisfaction and body weight as those held by adolescents from developed countries and Caucasian backgrounds (Erkolahti, Jansson, Offer and Steinhausen, 1992; O'Dea 1998; O'Dea, 1999a). Studies of Japanese (Lerner, Iwanaki, Chihara and Sorell, 1980; Pang, Mizokawa, Morishima and Olstad, 1985; Saitoh, O'Dea & O'Brien, 1997; Lerner, Iwawaki, Chihara and Sorell, 1981) African (Alawiye, Alawiye and Thomas, 1990) Chinese (Lau, 1990) Spanish (Toro, Castro, Gracia and Perez, 1989) Indian (Suman, 1990) German (Gutezeit and Marake, 1984) South African (Theron, Nel and Lubbe, 1991) French (Boudaroud and Herren, 1991) Italian (Molinari, 1986) and American Indian (Story, Hauck, Broussard, White, Resnick and Blum, 1994) adolescents showed similar results to those of the Australian, British and American studies discussed earlier. The Japanese children in the studies of Pang and Lerner scored lower than their American counterparts on body image scales with regard to height and the shape of their noses. Studies comparing the body image of African American and white American adolescents have shown that African American girls and boys are less likely to perceive themselves as overweight (Desmond, Price, Hallinan and Smith, 1989) and are more satisfied with their bodies (Wade, 1991; Harris, 1994). In the study of Wade (1991) African American boys scored higher than African American girls on measures of body image and attractiveness.

An analysis of the influence of ethnic and cultural differences on the body perception of adolescents by Worsley (1981) showed that ethnicity can affect self-perception and the perception of body image. In this study the daughters of migrants reported more independent and stronger self-aspirations than their peers and the sons of European migrants rated the "fat young woman" figure more positively than other participants. Ethnic influences on self-perception and body image have not been thoroughly investigated among Australian adolescents, but it does seem that the slim ideal for females and the larger ideal for males exist throughout cultural and ethnic groups.

SOCIAL CLASS INFLUENCES ON BODY WEIGHT AND BODY IMAGE

Body weight and the prevalence of overweight and obesity have been shown to be related to socioeconomic factors. Studies have shown that people of lower socioeconomic status have a higher prevalence of overweight and obesity (Garn and Clarke, 1975; Mustajoki, 1987; Dawson, 1988; Sobal and Stunkard, 1989). Studies of (Gliksman, Dwyer and Wlodarczyk, 1990; O'Dea, 1994; Garn and Clarke, 1975).

Few studies have examined the relationship between socio-economic status and body image. The literature presents conflicting results on this issue. The majority of studies have found that socioeconomic status is not related to eating disorders, low body satisfaction, poor body image, dieting to lose weight or disordered eating among females (Lowe, Miles and Richards, 1985;

Crowther et al., 1985; Williams, Schaefer, Shisslak, Gronwaldt and Comerci, 1986; O'Dea, 1994). Story et al. obtained body image information from adolescents in the USA and found no difference among any measure between urban, suburban or rural youth (Story et al., 1991). Other studies have found that females of higher socio-economic status were more likely to display the desire to lose weight and dieting behaviors (Duncan, Ritter, Dornbusch, Gross and Carlsmith, 1985; Wardle and Marsland, 1990; Moore, 1993). A study of Australian teenaged girls found no difference between girls from upper or lower socioeconomic groups for measures of body image or eating behaviors (O'Dea, 1994). An average of 37% of girls from both groups perceived themselves as 'too fat' and 42% of girls from both groups reported currently dieting to lose weight. Health professionals working with eating disorder patients believe that the prevalence of distorted body image and eating disorders is similar between all social classes (Abraham and Llewellyn-Jones, 1991).

BODY IMAGE AMONG YOUNG ADULTS

Body image research among adults has focused largely on gender differences and its relationship to eating disturbances. Among young adults' poor self-concept relating to physical appearance (low physical self-esteem) and misperception of body weight has been reported by numerous authors (Thompson and Thompson, 1986; Galgan and Mable, 1986; Powers and Erickson, 1986; Harmatz, 1987; O'Dea, 1999a). Concern about and dissatisfaction with body size and shape has increased in both sexes since the 1960's (Cash, Winstead, and Janda, 1986). Gender differences have been observed in all studies of young adults. Women tended to overestimate their body size and specific body parts, particularly thighs, abdomen and hips (Thompson, 1986; Robinson et al., 1993), whereas men tended to perceive themselves as being underweight. Men wanted to be bigger, taller and more muscular (Tucker, 1984; Harmatz, Gronendyke and Thomas, 1985; Thompson and Thompson, 1986; Mishkind, Rodin, Silberstein and Striegel-Moore, 1986; Booth, 1990; O'Dea, 1999a). Loosemore, Douglas, Mable, Galgan, and Balance, (1989) found that body image distortion and dissatisfaction was greatest among male college body builders compared to other groups of college males. Mishkind et al., study suggested that the pressures for men to conform to the ideal of muscular mesomorphy may contribute to physical and psychological damage to health. These studies indicate that concerns about body shape and size affect men as well as women (O'Dea, 1999a).

The study by Thompson and Thompson (1986) demonstrated that seemingly normal adults with no history of eating disorders tended to overestimate their body size and it also found that females were more likely than males to do so. The researchers obtained significant positive correlations between self-esteem scores and inaccurate perception of males' waist measurements and significant negative correlations between self-esteem and inaccurate perception of females' thigh measurements. Women and men who possessed the most inaccurate perception of their bodies had the lowest self-esteem. This trend has also been demonstrated in studies of eating disordered women and normal women (Bell, Kirkpatrick and Rinn, 1986; Birtchnell, Dolan and Lacey, 1987) and one study linked negative attitudes towards the body to greater proneness to depression (Mintz and Betz, 1986). Powers and Erickson (1986) suggest that inaccurate body perception has become a normal feature of the female population and this is supported by other authors (Bell et al., 1986; Harmatz, 1987; Silberstein, Striegal-Moore, Timko and Rodin, 1988; O'Dea, 1998; O'Dea 1999a). A study of overweight young adults (Stake and Lauer, 1987) showed that being overweight had a negative effect on the quality and quantity of women's relationships with men, but had little effect on men's relationships with women. The misperception of the self as overweight in normal and underweight women was related to lower self-esteem among the group possessing the greatest misperception (Harmatz, 1987). The author describes these subjects as "being in a permanent state of frustration."

Sexual orientation and its relationship to body image has been studied very little. Herzog, Newman and Warshaw (1991) studied groups of young homosexual and heterosexual men's perceptions of their ideal weight. Heterosexual men desired a heavier weight than the ideal standard and homosexual men desired a weight below the ideal. Homosexual men perceived the underweight ideal as most desirable.

A study of young homosexual, bisexual and heterosexual women showed few differences between groups for personality and self-esteem but found that bisexual women were more satisfied with their bodies (La Torre and Wendenburg, 1983).

The existence of eating disorders, particularly bulimia nervosa among young college women was noted by several studies in the late 1980's (Pertschuk, Collins, Kreisberg and Fager, 1986; Brauers, 1988; Holleran, Pascale and Fraley, 1988; Mintz and Betz, 1988; Silverstein and Perdue, 1988). The authors suggest that the combination of low physical esteem, vulnerable general self-esteem caused by the transition from high school to college and role concerns may culminate in bulimia in the early college years.

Clearly, young women are at risk of developing poor physical self-esteem, poor general self-esteem and dissatisfaction with their bodies that may lead to eating disorders if no intervention is undertaken. Recent research shows that men are also at risk of damaging their general and physical self-esteem through the development of body dissatisfaction and pursuit of gender stereotypes. Interventions aimed at improving body image, physical and general self-esteem, and the incidence of eating disorders must address these gender issues and focus on the causes of inaccurate body perception and body dissatisfaction.

INTERVENTIONS AIMED AT IMPROVING SELF-IMAGE

Interventions to raise self-esteem have been implemented among adults, children and adolescents. Programs developed for adults have mostly focused on physical activity programs or endurance training. Skrinar, Bullen, Cheek and McArthur, (1986) measured the effects of endurance training on body consciousness in women. They found that a six to eight week training program decreased the body weight and body fat composition of young women and that aerobic fitness increased. Self-perception of body competence and internal body consciousness increased significantly but the perception of public body consciousness remained unchanged. This study demonstrated that physical training can help to improve women's perception of how others see them. Similar results were found among women by Ben Shlomo and Short (1986) and Wiltey and Kunce (1986). Tucker demonstrated that a 16 week weight training program could improve the self-concept of college males compared to controls and Ford, Puckett, Reeve and Lafavi, (1991) obtained similar results among college males using body building and jogging, but not strength development exercises (e.g. push-ups). Conversely, Melnick and Mookerjee (1991) achieved a rise in self-esteem and improved body image among college students (males and females) after delivering a 16-week course in weight training.

A physical rehabilitation program for young males measured the effects of physical training upon behavior and self-attitudes. Twenty-five young males attended a four-week training program in which they were coached to break personal records every day. Despite the lack of a control group, the author reported significant improvements in physical fitness, body image, self-concept and behavioral conduct. (Collingwood, 1972).

The use of various counseling therapies for the improvement of body image among women has been shown to be effective. Butters and Cash (1987) demonstrated that a cognitive-behavioral program was effective in improving self-esteem and body image in a group of college women compared to controls. Dworkin and Kerr (1987) compared three different interventions for women experiencing body image problems - cognitive therapy, cognitive-behavioral therapy and reflective therapy. They found that while all participants improved, cognitive therapy participants showed the most improvement in body image as measured by Body Cathexis and Self-Cathexis Scales (Secord and Jourard, 1953) compared to controls. Participants in cognitive-behavioral therapy showed the most improvement in total self-concept.

Programs designed to improve personal appearance (Fiore and DeLong, 1990) and provide therapy and yoga (Engelman, Clance and Imes, 1982) have reported improvement in general self-esteem among women although neither included control groups. The results of these studies should be analyzed with caution because of this failure to include a comparison group.

The effect of an "undieting" program for use among 18 overweight women who were apparently depressed, disliked themselves and had disordered eating patterns and negative feelings about their bodies was tested by Polivy and Herman (1992). Participants underwent 10 two-hour sessions conducted by a social worker, with the main aim of preventing dieting and establishing normal eating behavior. Results showed that there were significant reductions in scores from the Eating Disorders Inventory (Garner, Olmstead and Polivy, 1983) with the exception of Body Dissatisfaction. Scores from the Body Dissatisfaction subscale were not significantly reduced. All other scores that had been elevated at pretest were reduced to within normal ranges. Depression and restraint scores as measured by the Beck Depression Inventory (Beck, 1967) and the Restraint Scale (Herman and Polivy, 1980) were normalized and there were significant increases for scores on the Janis-Field Self-esteem Scale (Pliner, Chaiken and Flett, 1990) and State Self-esteem Scale (Heatherton and Polivy, 1991).

Whilst there was no change in body weight over the 10 week intervention time, the authors concluded that the "undieting" program was successful in improving body image and self-esteem among overweight women with poor body image and lower than average self-esteem.

Other studies of adults have shown no significant effect of programs aimed at improving self-concept (Ventura and Dundon, 1974; Ewert, 1977; Ford, Puckett, Blessing and Tucker, 1989; Caruso and Grill, 1992). A review of self-concept programs suggest that the lack of success of programs is due to the use of weak interventions, small sample sizes, non-multidimensional self-concept instruments and a poor fit between intended goals and self-concept dimensions used to evaluate the intervention (Marsh, 1990).

Self-concept programs for children and adolescents have shown that most programs have utilized physical activity and outdoor adventure activities.

Anshell, Muller and Owens (1986) measured the effect of sports camp experience on the multidimensional self-concepts of boys aged 6-9 years. Participants were helped to experience persistent success at sports and develop positive peer relations. Results showed that athletic and physical competence improved as opposed to other dimensions of self-concept. Programs including activities such as precision jump rope (Hatfield, Vaccaro and Benedict, 1985), an

Outward Bound Academic Bridging Course (Marsh and Richards, 1986), swimming programs (Miller, 1989), non aerobic weight training (McGowan, Jarom and Pedersen, 1974), Outward Bound Adventure Programs (Svobodny, 1979; Marsh, Richards and Barnes, 1986/a), strength training for girls (Holloway, Beuter and Duda, 1988) and physical fitness training for girls (Marsh and Peart, 1988) can all significantly improve the self-concept of adolescents. The Outward Bound Program of Marsh, Richards and Barnes (1986/a) was shown to maintain significant long-term effects on self-concept at 18 month follow-up (Marsh, Richards and Barnes, 1986/b).

A physical fitness training program conducted with 137 Sydney high school girls (Marsh and Peart, 1988) demonstrated that both competitive and cooperative programs enhanced physical fitness, but only the cooperative program enhanced physical self-concept. Girls participating in the competitive program showed a statistically significant decline in self-concept scores in comparison with the cooperative and control groups. The results of this study have important implications for programs aimed at raising the self-esteem among adolescents and strongly suggest that intervention activities should not be competitive.

Providing positive feedback to students has been shown to raise academic self-concept (Craven, Marsh and Debus, 1991) and this study strongly suggested that programs aimed at raising self-concept should include methods that provide positive feedback to children.

PROGRAMS AIMED AT IMPROVING
BODY IMAGE AMONG ADOLESCENTS

Several large, randomized and controlled programs specifically aimed at improving disturbed eating and body satisfaction among adolescent females have been tested in Australia, the USA, Israel and Switzerland (Paxton, 1993; Killen et al., 1993; Neumark-Sztainer, Butler and Palti, 1995; Buddeberg-Fischer et al., 1998; Neumark-Sztainer, Sherwood, Collier et al., 2000). Paxton (1993) developed a prevention program for disturbed eating and body dissatisfaction in adolescent girls which aimed to reduce moderate and extreme weight loss behaviors, disordered eating and low body image. The five session program was conducted among 107 females and 29 control females in Australia. There were no significant changes for measures of eating and dieting behavior, body dissatisfaction or self-esteem. The author concluded that no interaction effects were found on body image variables, indicating no effect of the intervention program. Suggested explanations by the author for the failure of this program to impact these girls was the short term nature of the intervention, the use of small numbers and the fact that beliefs and attitudes are already entrenched among girls by this age suggesting that early interventions, perhaps led by peer leaders may be more successful. In addition, the author suggests that a combination of early intervention and yearly reinforcement throughout secondary school may be more effective.

A long term, controlled study evaluating the effectiveness of a prevention program designed to modify eating attitudes and unhealthful weight regulation practices of young adolescent girls was tested in California (Killen et al., 1993). A total of 931 girls participated as experimental and control groups with an age range of 11-13 years. The aims of the program were to provide information about the harmful effects of unhealthful weight regulation, promote healthy nutrition and exercise and develop coping skills for resisting the sociocultural influences that appear linked to the desire for thinness and dieting. The 18 lesson intervention consisted of a slide show about seven girls who demonstrated both healthy and unhealthy approaches to weight regulation with lesson activities and discussion following the slide shows. Results showed that participants displayed increases in knowledge but there were no significant differences between treatment and control groups for measures of bulimia, appearance, dietary restraint, weight concerns, purging behaviors or Body Mass Index (BMI). Secondary analysis which divided participants into high and low risk groups according to their degree of weight concerns showed beneficial effects for high-risk participants on the knowledge score only. The authors concluded that this specific curriculum aimed at reducing unhealthful eating, dieting, restraint and poor body image should not be targeted at the whole female adolescent population of a school, as was the case in this study, but may benefit selected high risk adolescent females.

Similar results were obtained in a study of 341 Jewish-Israeli girls aged 14-16 years old (Neumark-Sztainer et al., 1995). The girls who participated in the Israeli study improved their nutritional knowledge and reported more regular meal patterns and exercise. The authors also reported a short-term reduction in self reported unhealthy dieting and bingeing but there were no significant changes in the girls' body dissatisfaction, recent dieting or attitudes to weight loss. Other similar controlled educational interventions aimed at preventing eating problems have produced increases in the adolescent participants' knowledge of eating disorders (Moriarty, Shore and Maxim, 1990; Shisslak, Crago and Neal, 1990; Moreno and Thelan, 1993) but no significant changes to their eating disorder behaviors and attitudes or self perceptions.

The recent study of Neumark-Stainer et al. (2000) evaluated a community-based intervention aimed at the primary prevention of disordered eating among preadolescent girls aged 10-11 years attending Girl Scout groups. The program focused on media literacy and advocacy skills. The media literacy training focused on helping girls develop skills for recognizing media advertising strategies in order to understand the potential effect of images portrayed in the media on body image, and to take action toward modifying negative media messages and promoting positive media messages. The intervention program did not have a statistically significant effect on dieting behaviors, weight loss attempts, unhealthful dieting, binge eating or body satisfaction. The program produced modest improvements in knowledge about puberty and acceptance of a range of body sizes. An important feature of the study was the statistically significant improvement in self-efficacy related to the girls' ability to impact weight-related social norms, showing that the intervention helped them to feel more able to resist media influences about social norms.

A study conducted among male and female adolescents aged 14-19 years in Switzerland (Buddeberg-Fisher et al., 1998) aimed to develop an awareness of issues concerning eating behavior, body image and physical and mental well-being. School lessons included a video about eating disorders, written information about eating disorders, pubertal development, social body image norms and disturbed eating behavior. Whilst the intervention produced no statistically significant effects in students' measures of eating disorder attitudes and behaviors the direction of scores suggested improvement.

An intervention among elementary school children in Ohio (Smolak, Levine & Schermer, 1998) did not significantly improve students' body esteem or weight loss behaviors, but it did produce modest improvements in knowledge of nutrition, cause of body fat and effects of dieting.

Previous interventions to prevent eating disturbances and improve body image have had generally poor or very modest results other than improvements in adolescents' knowledge. It has been argued that improving children's knowledge of eating disorders and unhealthful methods of weight control is ineffective in changing their behaviors and that focusing on problem behaviors may serve to be iatrogenic by introducing young people to undesirable weight loss practices and may simply heighten food concerns or body concerns and inadvertently glamorize eating problems (Garner, 1985; Carter, Stewart, Dunn et al., 1997; Mann et al., 1997; Dixey, 1998; O'Dea, 1999b; O'Dea & Maloney, 2000; O'Dea, 2000).

INTERVENING TO IMPROVE BODY IMAGE AND SELF-ESTEEM

Many adolescents exhibit poor body image and low self-esteem. This negative self-perception may lead both boys and girls towards health damaging behaviors such as dieting, vomiting, laxative abuse and the use of diet drugs and anabolic steroids. Low self-esteem may be found among adolescents who are dissatisfied with their body weight and shape. These children suffer much unhappiness and trauma with regard to their body weight and shape and some adolescents, particularly girls, may develop disordered eating or eating disorders such as anorexia nervosa and bulimia nervosa.

Programs aimed at raising general self-esteem among adolescents have focused on outdoor adventures, sporting programs and physical education activities. Unfortunately, not all students can participate in such activities, because of lack of interest in physical activities, time and financial restraints. The Outward Bound Program, for example, has proven to be efficacious in raising self-esteem among adolescents, but requires a significant time commitment from staff and participants and is only available to those who can afford to pay the registration fees. Whilst there are benefits in raising self-esteem, the logistics of implementing successful programs make it difficult to involve adolescents, particularly those who need it most.

INTERACTIVE EDUCATIONAL APPROACHES TO BODY IMAGE PROGRAMS

The cooperative learning approach states that children and adolescents respond more favorably in a cooperative, interactive, student-centered learning environment (Hill & Hill, 1990). The benefits of a cooperative, group learning environment for children and adolescents have been shown to result in higher achievement, development of leadership skills, promoting positive attitudes toward learning, promotion of self-esteem, tolerance, a sense of belonging and the development of skills for the workplace (Hill & Hill, 1990). Doise and Mugny (1994) have conducted research which supports their contentions that social interaction in classroom settings can lead to more advanced cognitive development. Johnson and Johnson (1981, 1987) found clear evidence of significantly higher academic achievement in 21 of their 26 studies. A meta-analysis of the 122 studies that had been conducted in this area between 1924 and 1981 was undertaken by Johnson, Maruyama, Johnson, Nelson and Skon (1981). Cooperative learning experiences promoted higher achievements than did individualized, instructional or competitive learning experiences. Cooperative and interactive learning experiences have been shown to encourage students to develop more positive attitudes towards themselves, other students and the learning experience (Cooper, Johnson, Johnson and Wilderson, 1980; Slavin, 1990, 1991) to promote self-esteem (Norem-Hebeison and Johnson, 1981; Wilkinson, 1988-1989) and to enhance the management of classroom discipline problems (McInerney and McInerney, 1994).

For a classroom situation to be classified as cooperative it must include certain criteria. Johnson and Johnson (1989) describe positive interdependence, face to face interaction, individual accountability, collaborative skills and group processing as essential classroom features if the students are to derive the benefits of cooperative learning. Slaven (1991) incorporates the use of teamwork, quizzes and games. Kagan (1992) encourages the incorporation of "content-free" curriculum, which encourages the development of skill development (thinking and communication skills), information sharing and team building. Sharan and Sharan (1992) suggest a group investigation model of cooperative learning, which incorporates group investigation, interaction, interpretation and intrinsic motivation.

In all of these cooperative learning approaches, students learn by working together as a productive, cohesive and supportive group.

The development of a general self-esteem and body image education program should incorporate these methodologies in order to enhance student learning and self-esteem. The content of the lessons in the educational program should focus upon building self-esteem and the cooperative classroom environment should be designed in order to enhance this major objective.

This new approach to the enhancement of adolescent self-esteem and body image is in stark contrast to previous interventions which have employed more traditional pedagogical approaches which instructed students about the dangers of fad diets and eating disorders (Paxton, 1993; Killen et al., 1994; Neumark-Sztainer et al., 1995; Smolak et al., 1998; Buddeberg-Fischer et al., 1998).

Adopting a more cooperative, interactive, student-centered educational approach may be more effective at building students' self-esteem, improving their body image and preventing eating problems than the more traditional approaches, all of which have previously had little or limited success.

It is argued that in order to change the health damaging behaviors of adolescents such as weight loss behaviors and eating problems, one must firstly change the beliefs, values and attitudes which precede such behaviors (Bandura, 1986). Bandura's social cognitive theory states that in particular, the self-perceptions of people must initially change in order to precipitate behavioral change. In order to reduce adolescents' eating problems, one must therefore initially aim to improve their body image.

THE NEW SELF-ESTEEM APPROACH TO PREVENTION

A new approach to the prevention of eating problems and body image concerns was introduced in response to the poor results of previous studies. As low self-esteem has been repeatedly shown to be associated with eating disorders and body image concerns (Button et al., 1997; O'Dea & Abraham, 1999b; Shisslak et al., 1998) an intervention (O'Dea & Abraham, 2000) based on promoting self-esteem was developed. The design of the self-esteem program was characterized by the following features:

Study Design

- **Large, randomized, controlled intervention**
- Inclusion of male and female adolescents

- Long-term 12 month follow-up
- Inclusion of an analysis of high-risk adolescents (those with low self-esteem and high Trait anxiety)
- Single blind trial
- Very high retention rate of participants
- Use of standardized testing instruments
- Positive involvement of teachers, parents and significant others

Design of Educational Intervention

- Based on educational theories of cooperative, interactive and student-centered learning
- Avoidance of didactic, authoritarian teaching styles
- No content related to eating disorders, food habits, and weight control behaviors, healthy eating or any reference to students' bodies or their body image. This was done in order to reduce any sensitivity students may have felt about their bodies
- No attempt to effect students' knowledge about eating disorders, food habits, weight control behavior, healthy eating or body image.

Table 1. An Outline of the Everybody's Different Program

Lesson 1: Dealing with stress
  Rela Rexation tape. Ways of dealing with stress. Feeling good in your body.
Lesson 2: Building a positive sense of self
  Building your self-esteem. Identifying your unique features and self-image and how it might be destroyed. "I am OK" self-esteem-building activity.
Lesson 3, 4, 5: Stereotypes in our society
  Collage posters of stereotypes. Male and female stereotypes.
  Being an individual – being yourself. Learning to accept and value differences
Lesson 6: Positive self-evaluation
  Exploring individuality. What is unique about you?
  Self-advertisement activity. Learning to value uniqueness.
Lesson 7: Involving significant others
  Ways of improving your self-image. Receiving positive feedback from others. Hand outline activity.
  Learning to seek positive feedback from significant others.
Lesson 8: Relationship skills
  How other people affect our self-image. Dealing with relationships. Video of self-esteem. Role-plays.
Lesson 9: Communication skills
  Games and activities to build self-esteem
  Pictionary game. Program evaluation by students and teachers.

*Lessons lasted 50-80 minutes and were conducted by the students' regular health education teacher.

The focus of this new preventative approach is self-esteem development among adolescents in order to foster a positive sense of self which encompasses a positive body esteem. The self-esteem program titled "Everybody's Different" (O'Dea, 1995) (Table 1) was delivered in high schools by regular teachers using a controlled, randomized and single blind study design. The teachers and students were unaware that the self-esteem program in which they were participating was linked to the aim of improving body satisfaction. This was instigated in order to reduce students making deliberately favorable responses on the eating disorder, depression, anxiety and body satisfaction test instruments. In addition, this new approach completely ignored any attempt to directly instruct students about eating disorders, food habits or eating behaviors, body image or body weight issues so that the intervention could purely test whether a self-esteem approach alone could affect adolescents' body image and body esteem.

The results of the self-esteem program were consistently positive in both the short term and long term as 12 months after the intervention and were positive among male and female adolescents. The Everybody's Different intervention significantly improved students' beliefs, attitudes and unhealthy behaviors. Statistically significant improvements were achieved in the intervention group for the body dissatisfaction scale of the Eating disorders Inventory (Garner, Olmstead & Polivy, 1983), physical appearance ratings, and self-concept scores. Female students who participated in the intervention participated less in weight loss behaviors and did not lose weight compared to girls in the control group who lost significant amounts of body weight. Similar positive results were achieved among those students considered to be at high risk of developing eating problems and who had low self-esteem and high Trait anxiety (Spielberger, Gorsuch & Lushene, 1970). The majority of intervention effects were still present at the 12 month follow-up, showing that the self-esteem intervention produces a long-term benefit to young people. Importantly, the new self-esteem approach to the prevention of eating problems was proven to be both efficacious and safe, as there were no adverse effects on students' measures of depression, State or Trait Anxiety or eating disorder attitudes and behaviors. It is important to make certain that such interventions do no harm to vulnerable young participants.

SUMMARY

The self-concept of children and adolescents is effected by many variables, age, gender, puberty, body weight and involvement in sports and physical activity. Programs to improve self-esteem among children and adolescents have been successful, particularly if they focus on positive self-appraisal and are delivered in a non-competitive, non-threatening environment. Improvement of body image and eating disturbances in children and adolescents has previously resulted in mainly modest increases in knowledge with very little convincing attitudinal or behavioral change. The new self-esteem approach for the prevention of body image concerns, eating disturbances and eating disorders has produced significant and long-lasting improvements in body satisfaction, dieting, weight loss and eating disorder attitudes in adolescents. The success of educational initiatives to prevent body image concerns and eating problems in adolescents appears to rest on the introduction of programs with a strong self-esteem component, delivered in a cooperative supportive and non-threatening educational environment with positive input from teachers, parents and the community environment. Educational and preventive interventions must be duly cautious and must take care that they do not inadvertently do more harm than good when intervening among vulnerable children and adolescents.

REFERENCES

Abraham, S. & O'Dea, J. (In Press). Body mass index, menarche and perceptions of dieting among pre and post pubertal adolescent females. *International Journal of Eating Disorders*.

Abraham, S. & Llewellyn-Jones, D. (1991). *Eating Disorders - The Facts*. London: Oxford University Press.

Alawiye, O., Alawiye, C. & Thomas, J. (1990). Comparative self concept variances of school children in two English-speaking West African nations. *Journal of Psychology, 124(2)*, 169-176.

Alsaker, F. (1992) Pubertal timing, overweight and psychological adjustment. *Journal of Early Adolescence. 12*, 396-419.

Andrade, C., Kramer, J., Garber, M. & Longmuir, P. (1991). Changes in self concept, cardiovascular endurance and muscular strength of children with spina bifida aged 8-13 years in response to a 10 week physical activity program: A pilot study. *Childcare, Health and Development, 17(3)*, 183-196.

Anshel, M., Muller, D. & Owens, V. (1986). Effect of a sports camp experience on the multidimensional self concepts of boys. *Perceptual Motor Skills, 63(2:1)*, 363-366.

Attie, I. & Brooks-Gunn, J. (1989). Development of eating problems in adolescent girls: a longitudinal study. *Development Psychology, 25*, 70-79.

Bandura, A. (1986). *Social foundations of thought and action: a social cognitive theory*. Englewood Cliffs, N.J.: Prentice-Hall.

Beck, A., Ward, C., Mendelson, M., Mock, J. & Erbaugh, J. (1961). An Inventory for Measuring Depression. *Archives of General Psychiatry, 4*, 61-71.

Bell, C., Kirkpatrick, S. & Rinn, R. (1986). Body image of anorexic, obese and normal females. *Journal of Clinical Psychology, 42(3)*, 431-439.

Ben Shlomo, L. & Short, M. (1986). The effects of physical conditioning on selected dimensions of self concept in sedentary females. *Occupational Therapy in Mental Health, 5(4)*, 27-46.

Berk, L. (1991). *Child Development*. (2nd ed.). Needham Heights, Massachussetts: Allyn and Bacon, 432-447.

Berman, B.D., Winkelby, M., Chesterman, E. & Boyce, W.T. (1992). After school chid care and self esteem in school age children. *Paediatrics, 89(4:1)*, 654-659.

Biddulph, J., Elliott, K.V., Faldt, J.E., Fowler, P. & Dugdale, A.E. (1984). The body image and health-related behaviour of teenage girls. *Journal of Food and Nutrition, 41*, 33-36.

Birtchnell, S., Dolan, B. & Lacey, H. (1987). Body image distortion in non eating disordered women. *International Journal of Eating Disorders, 6(3)*, 385-391.

Blyth, D., Simmons, R., Bulcroft, R., Felt, D., van Cleave, E. & Bush, D. (1981). The effects of physical development on self image and satisfaction with body image for early adolescent males. *Research in Community & Mental Health, 2*, 43-73.

Booth, N. (1990). The relationship between height and self esteem and the mediating effect of self consciousness. *Journal of Social Psychology, 130(5)*, 609-617.

Boudoroud, A. & Herren, H. (1991). Relation between physical appearance and the choice of values attached to the self, in the present and in the future, during adolescence. *Enfance, 45(3)*, 241-253.

Boyd, K. R., and Hrycaiko, D. W. (1997). The Effect Of A Physical Activity Intervention Package On The Self-Esteem Of Pre-Adolescent And Adolescent Females. *Adolescence, 32*(127), 693-708.

Brookover, W.B. (1989). Self concept of ability scale - a review and further analysis. *Paper presented at the Annual meeting of the American Educational Research Association.*

Brooks-Gunn, J. (1984). The psychological significance of different pubertal events to young girls. *Journal of Early Adolescence, 4(4)*, 315-327.

Brouwers, M. (1988). Depressive thought content among female college students with bulimia. *Journal of Counselling and Development, 66*, 425-428.

Buddeberg-fischer, B., Klaghofer R., Gnam G., Buddeberg C. (1998) Prevention of disturbed eating behaviour: a prospective intervention study in 14-19 year ols Swiss students. *Acta Psychiatrica Scandinavica, 98*, 146-155.

Butters, J.W. & Cash, T.F. (1987). Cognitive-Behavioural Treatment of Women's body image dissatisfaction. *Journal of Consulting and Clinical Psychology, 55(6)*, 889-97.

Button, E. (1990). Self-Esteem In Girls Aged 11-12: Baseline Findings From A Planned Prospective Study Of Vulnerability To Eating Disorders. *Journal Of Adolescence, 13*(4), 407-13.

Button, E. J., Loan, P., Davies, J., and Sonuga-Barke, E. J. (1997). Self-Esteem, Eating Problems, And Psychological Well-Being In A Cohort Of Schoolgirls Aged 15-16: A Questionnaire And Interview Study. *International Journal Of Eating Disorders, 21*(1), 39-47.

Carroll, D., Gleeson, C., Ribsby, B. & Dugdale, A.E. (1986). Body build and the desire for slenderness in young people. *Australian Paediatric Journal, 22*, 121-125.

Carter, J.C., Stewart, D.A., Dunn, V.J., Fariburn, C.G. Primary prevention of eating disorders: might it do more harm than good? *International journal of Eating Disorders, 22*, 167-172.

Caruso, C.M. & Gill, D.L. (1992). Strengthening physical self-perceptions through exercise. *Journal of Sports Medicine and Physical Fitness, 32(4)*, 416-27.

Cash, T., Winstead, B. & Janda, L., (1986). The great American Shape Up. *Psychology Today, 20(4)*, 30-37.

Cauffman, E. & Steinberg, L. (1996). Interactive effects of menarchial status and dating on dieting and disordered eating among adolescent girls. *Developmental Psychology, 32(4)*, 631-635.

Collingwood, T. (1972). The effects of physical training upon behaviour and self attitudes. *Journal of Clinical Psychology, 28(4)*, 583-585.

Cooper, L., Johnson, D., Johnson, R. & Wilderson (1980). The effects of cooperation, competition and individualization on cross-ethnic, cross-sex and cross-ability friendships. *Journal of Social Psychology, 111*, 243-52.

Coopersmith, S. (1967). *The antecedents of self-esteem.* San Franciso: W. H. Freeman.

Craven, R., Marsh, H. & Debus, R. (1991). Effects of internally focussed feedback and attributional feedback on enhancement of academic self concept. *Journal of Educational Psychology, 83(1)*, 17-27.

Crowther, J.H., Post, G. & Zaynor, L. (1985). The prevalence of bulimia and binge eating in adolescent girls. *International Journal of Eating Disorders, 4*, 29-42.

Csapo, M. (1991). Psychosexual adjustment of children with short stature (Achondroplasia): Social competence, behavioural problems, self esteem, family functioning, body image and reaction to frustrations. *Behavioural Disorders, 16(3)*, 219-224.

Davies, E. & Furnham, A. (1986). Body satisfaction in adolescent girls. *British Journal of Medical Psychology, 59(3)*, 279-287.

Dawson, D.A. (1988). Ethnic differences in female overweight: data from the 1985 National Health Interview Survey. *American Journal of Public Health, 78*, 1326-1329.

Dixey, R. (1998). Healthy Eating In Schools, Overweight And Eating Disorders - Are They Connected. *Educational Review, 50(1)*, 29-35.

Drewnowski, A. & Yee, D.K. (1987). Men and body image: are males satisfied with their body weight? *Psychosomatic Medicine, 49*, 626-634.

Duncan, P., Ritter, P., Dornbusch, S., Gross, R. & Carlsmith, J. (1985). The effects of pubertal timing on body image, school behaviour and deviance. *Journal of Youth and Adolescence, 14(3)*, 227-235.

Dworkin, S.H. & Kerr, B.A. (1987). Comparison of interventions for women experiencing body image problems. *Journal of Counselling Psychology, 34(2)*, 136-140.

Dwyer, J., Feldman, C., Seltzer, C. & Mayer, J. (1969/a). Adolescent attitudes toward weight and appearance. *Journal of Nutrition Education, 1*, 14-19.

Dwyer, J.T., Feldman, J.J., Seltzer, C.C. & Mayer, J. (1969/b). Body image in adolescents: attitudes towards weight and perception of appearance. *American Journal of Clinical Nutrition, 20*, 1045-1056.

Eisele, J., Hersgaaird, D. & Light, H. (1986). Factors related to eating disorders in young adolescent girls. *Adolescence, 21*, 283-290.

Emmanouel, C., Zerevas, Y. & Vagenas, G. (1992). Effects of four physical education teaching methods on development of motor skill, self concept and social attitudes of fifth grade children. *Perceptual Motor Skills, 74(3:2) Special Issue*, 1151-1167.

Engelman, S., Clance, P. & Imes, S. (1982). Self and body cathexis change in therapy and yoga groups. *Journal of the American Society of Psychosomatic Dentistry and Medicine, 29(3)*, 77-88.

Erkolahti, R., Jansson, J., Offer, D. & Steinhausen, H.C. (1992). Comparison of the self image of teenagers in Finland, the United States and Germany. *Journal of Adolescent Health, 13(5)*, 392-395.

Ewert, A. (1977). The Effects of Outdoor Adventure Activities Upon Self Concept. *Master's Thesis*, Eastern Washington University.

Fabian, L. & Thompson, J. (1989). Body image and eating disturbance in young females. *International Journal of Eating Disorders, 8(1)*, 63-74.

Felker D.W. (1968) relationship between self-concept, body build and father's interest in sport in boys. *Research Quarterly, 39*, 513-517.

Felker D.W. & Kay R.S. (1971) Self-concept, sports interests, sports participation and body type of seventh and eighth grade boys. Journal of Psychology, 78, 223-228.

Fiore, A. & DeLong, M. (1990). A personal appearance program for displaced homemakers. *Journal of Career Development, 16(3)*, 219-226.

Fischer, M., Pastore, D., Schneider, M., Pegler, C. & Napolitano, B. (1994). Eating attitudes in urban and suburban adolescents. *International Journal of Eating Disorders, 16(1)*, 67-74.

Fisher, S. (1986). *Development and Structure of the Body Image*. (Vol. 2.). Hillsdale: Lawrence Erlbaum Publishing Co. Pty Ltd.

Folk, L., Pedersen, J. & Cullari, S. (1993). Body satisfaction and self concept of third and sixth grade students. *Perceptual Motor Skills. 76*, 547-553.

Ford, H., Puckett, J., Reeve, T. & Lafavi, R. (1991). Effects of selected physical activities on global self concept and body cathexis scores. *Psychological Reports, 68(3:2)*, 1339-1343.

Ford, T., Puckett, J., Blessing, D. & Tucker, L. (1989). Effects of selected physical activities on health related fitness and psychological well being. *Psychological Reports, 64(1)*, 203-208.

Frankl, D. (1996) Swimming and diving project for youth: Aquatic skills and the development of self-esteem. *Kinesiology, 28* (1), 14-19.

French, S. A., Perry, C. L., Leon, G. R., and Fulkerson, J. A. (1996). Self-Esteem And Change In Body Mass Index Over 3 Years In A Cohort Of Adolescents. *Obesity Research, 4*(1), 27-33.

French, S. A., Story, M., and Perry, C. L. (1995). Self-Esteem And Obesity In Children And Adolescents - A Literature Review [Review]. *Obesity Research. 3*(5):479-490.

Galgan, R. & Mable, H. (1986). Body satisfaction in college women: a survey of facial and body size components. *College Student Journal, 20(3)*, 326-328.

Gardner, R. M., Friedman, B. N., and Jackson, N. A. (1999). Body Size Estimations, Body Dissatisfaction, And Ideal Size Preferences In Children Six Through Thirteen. *Journal Of Youth and Adolescence. 28*(5):603-618.

Garn S.M., Clarke, D.C. (1975). Nutrition, growth, development and maturation: findings from the Ten-State Nutrition Survey of 1968-1970. *Paediatrics, 56*, 306-319.

Garner, D.M. (1985). Iatrogenesis in anorexia nervosa and bulimia nervosa. *International Journal of Eating Disorders, 4*, 701-726.

Garner, D.M., Olmstead, M.P. & Polivy, J. (1983). Development and validation of a multidimensional eating disorder inventory for anorexia nervosa and bulimia. *International Journal of Eating Disorders, 2*, 15-34.

Gliksman, M.D., Dwyer, T. & Wlodarczyk, J. (1990). Differences in modifiable cardiovascular disease risk factors in Australian school children: the results of a nationwide survey. *Preventative Medicine, 19*, 291-304.

Gortmaker, S.L., Dietz, W.H. & Sobol, A.M. (1987). Increasing paediatric obesity in the United States. *American Journal of Diseases in Childhood, 141*, 535-540.

Gortmaker, S. L., Must, A., Perrin, J. M., Sobol, A. M., and Dietz, W. H. (1993). Social And Economic Consequences Of Overweight In Adolescence And Young Adulthood [See Comments]. *New England Journal Of Medicine, 329*(14), 1008-12.

Graber, J.A., Brooks-Gunn, J., Paikoff, R.L. & Warren, M. (1994). Prediction of eating problems: An eight year study of adolescent girls. *Developmental Psychology, 30(6)*, 823-834.

Gralen, S.J., Levine, M.P., Smolak, L. & Murnen, S.K. (1990). Dieting and disordered eating during early and middle adolescence: Do the influences remain the same? *International Journal of Eating Disorders, 9*, 501-512.

Grant, C. & Fodor, I. (1986). Adolescent attitudes toward body image and anorexic behaviour. *Adolescence, 21(82)*, 269-281.

Gutezeit, G. & Marake, J. (1984). Studies of the effects of various factors upon the self perception of children and juveniles. *Praxis der Kinderpsychologie und Kindersychiatrie, 33(4)*, 133-141.

Guyst, G., Fairchild, L. & Hill, M. (1981). Physical fitness, sport, participation, body build and self concept of elementary school children. *International Journal of Sport Psychology, 12(2)*, 105-116.

Guyot, G.W., Fairchild, L., Hill, M. (1981) Physical fitness, sport participation, body build, and self-concept of elementary school children. *International Journal of Sport Psychology, 12*, 105-116.

Harmatz, M., Gronendyke, J. & Thomas, T. (1985). The underweight male: the unrecognised problem of body image research. *Journal of Obesity and Weight Regulation, 4(4)*, 258-267.

Harmatz, M.G. (1987). The misperception of overweight in normal and underweight women. *Journal of Obesity and Weight Regulation, 6(1)*, 38-54.

Harper, J.F. & Marshall, E. (1991). Adolescent's problems and their relationship to self esteem. *Adolescence, 26(104)*, 799-808.

Harter, S. (1982). The perceived competence scale for children. *Child Development, 53(1)*, 87-97.

Harter, S. (1983). Developmental perspectives on the self system. In Heatherington, E.M. (Ed.) *Handbook of Child Psychology: Vol 4. Socialization, personality and social development* (4th Ed. pp.275-385). New York: Wiley.

Harter, S. (1988). *Manual for the Self Perception Profile for Adolescents*. Colorado: University of Denver.

Harter, S. & Monsour, A. (1992). Development analysis of conflict caused by opposing attributes in the adolescent self-portrait. *Der Psych, 28(2)*, 251-260.

Harter, S., Marold, D. & Whitesell, N. (1992). Model of psychosocial risk factors leading to suicidal inclination in young adolescents. *Developmental and Psycho Pathology, 4(1)*, 167-188.

Hatfield, B., Vaccaro, P. & Benedict, G. (1985). Self concept responses of children to participation in an eight week precision jump rope program. *Perceptual Motor Skills, 61(3:2)*, 1275-1279.

Heatherton, T.F. & Polivy, J. (1991). Development & validation of a scale for measuring state self-esteem. *Journal of Personality & Social Psychology, 60*, 895-910.

Hensley, W. (1983). Gender, self esteem and height. *Perceptual and Motor Skills, 56(1)*, 235-238.

Herman, C.P. & Polivy, J. (1980). Restrained eating. In A. Stunkard (Ed). *Obesity*, Philadelphia: Sauders. 208-225.

Herzog, D., Newman, K. & Warshaw, M. (1991). Body image dissatisfaction in homosexual and heterosexual males. *Journal of Nervous and Mental Disease, 179(6)*, 356-359.

Hill, A.J., Oliver, S. & Rogers, P.J. (1992). Eating in the adult world: the rise of dieting in childhood and adolescence. *British Journal of Clinical Psychology, 31(1)*, 95-105.

Hill, S. & Hill, T. (1990). *The collaborative classroom - A guide to cooperative learning*. South Yarra: Eleanor Curtain Publishing.

Holleran, P.R., Pascale, J. & Fraley, J. (1988). Prevalence and correlates of eating disordered behaviours among undergraduate women. *Journal of Counselling Psychology, 35*, 463-471.

Holloway, J., Beuter, A. & Duda, J. (1988). Self efficacy and training for strength in adolescent girls. *Journal of Applied Social Psychology, 18(8:2)*, 699-719.

Huenemann, R., Shapiro, L.R., Hampton, M.C. & Mitchell, B.W. (1966). A longitudinal study of gross body composition and body conformation and their association with food and activity in a teenage population. *American Journal of Clinical Nutrition, 18*, 325-338.

Johnson, D. & Johnson, R. (1981). Effects of cooperation and individual learning experiences on inter-ethnic interaction. *Journal of Educational Psychology, 73.* 454-9.

Johnson, D. & Johnson, R. (1987). *Cooperation and Competition.* Hillsdale: Lawrence Erlbaum.

Johnson, D., Maruyama, G., Johnson, R., Nelson, D, & Skon. (1981). Effects of cooperative, competitive and individualistic goal structures on achievement: a meta-analysis. *Psychological Bulletin, 89,* 47-62.

Kagan, D. (1992). Professional growth among preservice and beginning teachers. *Review of Educational Research, 62,* 129-69.

Kaplan, K. M., and Wadden, T. A. (1986). Childhood Obesity And Self-Esteem. *Journal Of Pediatrics, 109*(2), 367-70.

Kenealy, P., Gleeson, K., Frude, N. & Shaw, W. (1991). The importance of the individual in the "causal" relationship between attractiveness and self esteem. *Journal of Community and Applied Social Psychology, 11(1),* 45-56.

Killen J.D., Hayward, C., Litt, I., Hammer, L., Wilson, D.M., Miner, B., Barr-Taylor, C., Varady, A. & Shisslak, C. (1992). Is puberty a risk factor for eating disorders? *American Journal of Diseases in Childhood, 146,* 323-325.

Killen, J.D., Hayward, C., Wilson, D.M., Taylor, C.B., Hammer, L.D., Litt, I., Simmonds, B. & Haydel, F. (1994). Factors associated with eating disorder symptoms in a community sample of 6th and 7th grade girls. *International Journal of Eating Disorders, 15(4),* 357-367.

Killen, J.D., Taylor, C.B., Hammer, L.D., Litt, I., Wilson, D.M., Rich, T., Hayward, C., Simmonds, B., Kraemer, H. & Varady, A. (1993). An attempt to modify unhealthful eating attitudes and weight regulation practices of young adolescent girls. *International Journal of Eating Disorders, 13(4),* 369-384.

Killen, J.D., Taylor, C.B., Telch, M.T., Saylor, K.E., Maron, D.J. & Robinson, T.N. (1986). Self induced vomiting and laxative and diuretic use among teenagers: Precursors of the binge-purge syndrome? *Journal of the American Medical Association, 255,* 1447-1449.

Kimm, S., Sweeney, C. & Janosky, J. (1991). Self concept measures and childhood obesity: a descriptive analysis. *Journal of Developmental and Behavioural Paediatrics, 12(1),* 19-24.

Kimm, S. Y. S., Barton, B. A., Berhane, K., Ross, J. W., Payne, G. H., and Schreiber, G. B. (1997). Self-Esteem And Adiposity In Black And White Girls - The Nhlbi Growth And Health Study. *Annals Of Epidemiology, 7*(8), 550-560.

Koff, E., Rierdan, J. & Stubbs, M. (1990). Gender, body image and self concept in early adolescence. *Journal of Early Adolescence, 10(1),* 56-68.

La Torre, R. & Wendenburg, K., (1983). Psychological characteristics of bisexual, heterosexual and homosexual women. *Journal of Homosexuality, 9(1),* 87-97.

Lau, S. (1990). Crisis and vulnerability in adolescent development. *Journal of Youth and Adolescence, 19(2),* 111-131.

Lautenbacher, S., Thomas, A., Roscher, S., Strian, F., Pirke, K.M. & Krieg, J.C. (1992). Body size perception and body satisfaction in restrained and unrestrained eaters. *Behavioral Research and Theory, 30(3),* 243-250.

Lerner, R.M., Iwanaki, S., Chihara, T., Sorell, G. (1980). Self concept, self esteem and body attitudes among Japanese male and female Adolescents. *Child Development, 51(3),* 847-55.

Lerner, R., Iwawaki, S., Chihara, T. & Sorell, G. (1981). Self concept, self esteem, and body attitudes among Japanese male and female adolescents. *Annual Progress in Child Psychiatry and Child Development,* 494-507.

Lerner, R., Lerner, J., Hess, L. & Schwab, J. (1991). Physical attractiveness and psychosocial functioning among early adolescents. *Journal of Early Adolescence, 11(3)*, 300-320.

Levine, M.P., Smolak, L., Moodey, A.F., Shuman, M.D. & Hessen, L.D. (1994). Normative developmental challenges and dieting and eating disturbances in middle school children. *International Journal of Eating Disorders, 15(1)*, 11-20.

Loosemore-Douglas, J., Mable, H.M., Galgan, R.J. & Balance, W.D. (1989). Body image disturbance in selected groups of men. *Psychology: A Journal of Human Behaviour, 26(2-3)*, 56-59.

Lowe, H.C., Miles, S.W., & Richards, C.G. (1985). Eating attitudes in an adolescent schoolgirl population. *New Zealand Medical Journal, 98*, 330-331.

Maloney, M.J., McGuire, T., Daniels, S.R. & Specker, B. (1989). Dieting behaviour and eating attitudes in children. *Pediatrics, 84(3)*, 482-487.

Mann, T., Nolen-Hoeksema, S., Huang, K., Burgard, D., Wright, A., & Hanson, K. (1997) Are two interventions worse than none? Joint primary and secondary prevention of eating disorders in college females. *Health Psychology, 16*, 214-225.

Marsh, H. (1989). Age and Sex Effects in Multiple Dimensions of Self Concept: Preadolescence to Early Adulthood. *Journal of Educational Psychology, 81(3)*, 417-430.

Marsh, H.W., Barnes, J., Cairns, L. & Tidman, M. (1984). The Self Description Questionnaire (SDQ): Age affects in the structure and level of self concept for preadolescent children. *Journal of Educational Psychology, 76*, 940-956.

Marsh, H. & Parker, J. (1984). Determinants of student self-concept: Is it better to be a relatively large fish in a small pond even if you don't learn to swim as well? *Journal of Personality and Social Psychology, 47(1)*, 213-231.

Marsh, H. & Peart, N. (1988). Competitive and cooperative physical fitness training programs for girls: Effects on physical fitness and multidimensional self concepts. *Journal of Sport and Exercise Psychology, 10(4)*, 390-407.

Marsh, H. & Richards, G. (1986). The Outward Bound bridging course for low achieving High School Males: Effect on academic achievement and multidimensional self concepts. *Australian Journal of Psychology, 40(3)*, 281-298.

Marsh, H., Richards, G. & Barnes, J. (1986). Multidimensional self concepts: A long term follow-up of the effect of participation in an Outward Bound program. *Personality and Social Psychology Bulletin, 12(4)*, 475-492.

Marsh, H.W. (1984). Age and Sex Effects in Multiple Dimensions of Preadolescent Self Concept. EDRS Price - MF01/PC01.

Marsh, H.W. (1990). A multidimensional, hierarchical model of self concept: theoretical and empirical justification. *Educational Psychology Review, 2(2)*, 77-173.

Marsh, H.W. (1992). Content specificity of relations between academic achievement

McCreary, D. R., and Sasse, D. K. (2000). An Exploration Of The Drive For Muscularity In Adolescent Boys And Girls. *Journal Of American College Health. 48(6):297-304.*

McGowan, R., Jarom, B. & Pedersen, D. (1974). Effects of a competitive endurance training program on self concept and peer approval. *Journal of Psychology, 86(1)*, 57-60.

McInerney, D. & McInerney, I. (1994). *Educational psychology. Constructing learning.* Sydney: Prentice Hall.

Melnick, M. & Mookerjee, S. (1991). Effects of advanced weight training on body cathexis and self esteem. *Perceptual and Motor Skills, 72(3:2)*, 1335-1345.

Mendelson, B.K. & White, D.R. (1982). Relation between body esteem and self esteem of obese and normal children. *Perceptual and Motor Skills, 54(3:1)*, 899-905.

Mendelson, B.K. & White, D.R. (1985). Development of self-body esteem in overweight youngsters. *Developmental Psychology, 21(1)*, 90-96.

Mendelson, B.K., White, D.R. & Mendelson, M.J. (1995). Children's global self esteem predicted by body esteem but not by weight. *Perceptual Motor Skills, 80(1)*, 97-98.

Miller, R. (1989). Effects of sports instruction on children's self concept. *Perceptual and Motor Skills, 68(1)*, 239-242.

Mintz, L.B. & Betz, N.E. (1986). Six differences in the nature, realism and correlates of body image. *Sex Roles, 15(3-4)*, 185-195.

Mintz, L.B. & Betz, N.E. (1988). Prevalence and correlates of eating disordered behaviours among undergraduate women. *Journal of Counselling Psychology, 35*, 463-471.

Mishkind, M., Rodin, J., Siberstein, L. & Striegel-Moore, R. (1986). The embodiment of masculinity: Cultural, psychological and behavioural dimensions. *American Behavioural Scientist, 29(5)*, 545-562.

Molinari, E. (1986). Body image and self image in a group of obese adolescents. *Acta Medica Auxologica, 18(1)*, 45-53.

Moore, D.C. (1990). Body image and eating behaviour in adolescent boys. *American Journal of Diseases in Childhood, 144*, 475-478.

Moore, D.C. (1993). Body image and eating behaviour in adolescents. *Journal of the American College of Nutrition, 12(5)*, 505-10.

Moreno, A.B. & Thelan, M.H. (1993). A preliminary prevention program for eating disorders in a Junior High School population. *Journal of Youth and Adolescence, 22(22)*, 109-124.

Moriarty, D., Shore, R. & Maxim, N. (1990). Evaluation of an eating disorder curriculum. *Evaluation and Program Planning, 13*, 407-413.

Morrow, J. (1984). Deviational salience: Application to short stature and relation to perception of adolescent boys. *Perceptual and Motor Skills, 59(2)*, 623-633.

Mueller, C., Field, T., Yando, R., Harding, J., Gonzalez, K.P., Lasko, D. & Bendell, D. (1995). Under-eating and over-eating concerns among adolescents. *Journal of Child Psychology and Psychiatry, 36(6)*, 1019-25.

Mustajoki, P. (1987). Psychosocial factors in obesity. *Annual of Clinical Research, 19*, 143-146.

Neumark-Sztainer, D., Butler, R. & Palti, H. (1995). Eating disturbances among adolescent girls: Evaluation of a school-based primary prevention program. *Journal of Nutrition Education, 27*, 24-31.

Neumark-Sztainer, D., and Hannan, P. J. (2000). Weight-Related Behaviors Among Adolescent Girls And Boys - Results From A National Survey. *Archives Of Pediatrics and Adolescent Medicine. 154*(6):569-577.

Neumark-Sztainer, D., Sherwood, N.E., & Coller, T. (2000) Primary prevention of disordered eating among preadolescent girls: feasibility and short-term effect of a community-based intervention. *Journal of the American Dietetic Association, 100* (2), 1466-1473.

Newell, K., Hamming, C., Jurich, A. & Johnson, D. (1990). Self concept as a factor in the quality of diets of adolescent girls. *Adolescence, 25(97)*, 117-130.

Norem-Hebeison, A. & Johnson, D. (1981). Relationships between cooperative, competitive and individualistic attitudes and differential aspects of self esteem. *Journal of Personality, 49*, 415-25.

Nowak, M., Speare, R. & Crawford, D. (1996). Gender differences in adolescent weight and shape-related beliefs and behaviours. *Journal of Paediatrics and Child Health, 32*, 148-152.

O'Dea, J. (1994). Food habits, body image and self esteem of adolescent girls from disadvantaged and non-disadvantaged backgrounds. *Australian Journal of Nutrition and Dietetics, 51*, 74-78.

O'Dea, J. (1995). *Everybody's Different - A self esteem program for young adolescents*, NSW: University of Sydney.

O'Dea, J., Abraham, S. (1995). Should Body Mass Index be used in young adolescents? *The Lancet* (Letter), *345: 657.*

O'Dea, J., Abraham, S. & Heard, R. (1996). Food habits, body image and weight control practices of young male and female adolescents. *Australian Journal of Nutrition and Dietetics, 53*, 32-38.

O'Dea, J. A., and Abraham, S. (1999a). Association Between Self-Concept And Body Weight, Gender, And Pubertal Development Among Male And Female Adolescents. *Adolescence. 34*(133):69-79.

O'Dea, J. A., and Abraham, S. (1999b). Onset Of Disordered Eating Attitudes And Behaviors In Early Adolescence: Interplay Of Pubertal Status, Gender, Weight, And Age. *Adolescence. 34*(136):671-679.

O'Dea, J. A., and Abraham, S. (2000). Improving The Body Image, Eating Attitudes, And Behaviors Of Young Male And Female Adolescents: A New Educational Approach That Focuses On Self-Esteem. *International Journal Of Eating Disorders. 28*(1):43-57.

O'Dea, J., and Maloney, D. (2000). Preventing Eating And Body Image Problems In Children And Adolescents Using The Health Promoting Schools Framework. *Journal Of School Health. 70*(1):18-21.

O'Dea J. & Rawstorne, P. (2001) Male adolescents identify their weight gain practices, reasons for desired weight gain, and sources of weight gain information. *Journal of the American Dietetic Association. 101(1),* 12-23.

O'Dea, J. (2000) School-based interventions to prevent eating problems: first do no harm. *Eating Disorders: The Journal of Treatment and Prevention, 8* (1), 123-130.

O'Dea, J. (1999b). Children and adolescents identify food concerns, forbidden foods, and food-related beliefs. *Journal of the American Dietetic Association, 99*, 1-11.

O'Dea, J.A. (1998) The body size preferences of underweight young women from different cultural backgrounds. *Australian Journal of Nutrition and Dietetics, 55*, 75-80.

O'Dea, J. (1999a). Cross-cultural, body weight and gender differences in the body size perceptions and body ideals of university students. *Australian Journal of Nutrition and Dietetics, 56(3),* 144-150.

O'Malley, P.M. & Bachman, J.G. (1983). Self esteem: Change and stability between ages 13 and 23. *Developmental Psychology, 19*, 257-268.

Page, R. (1992). Feelings of physical unattractiveness and hopelessness among high school students. *High School Journal, 75(3),* 150-155.

Page, R.M. & Allen, O. (1995). Adolescent perceptions of body weight and weight satisfaction. *Perceptual Motor Skills, 81(1),* 81-82.

Pang, V., Mizokawa, D., Morishima, J. & Olstad, R. (1985). Self concepts of Japanese-American children. *Journal of Cross Cultural Psychology, 16(1),* 99-109.

Parishplass, J., and Lufi, D. (1997). Combining Physical Activity With A Behavioral Approach In The Treatment Of Young Boys With Behavior Disorders. *Small Group Research, 28*(3), 357-369.

Patton, G.C., Johnson-Sabine, E., Woods, K., Mann, A.H. & Wakeling, A. (1990). Abnormal eating attitudes in London schoolgirls: Outcome at twelve month follow-up. *Psychological Medicine, 20*, 383-394.

Paxton, S.J. (1993). A prevention program for disturbed eating and body dissatisfaction in adolescent girls: a one year follow-up. *Health Education Research, 8(1)*, 43-51.

Paxton, S.J., Wertheim, E.H., Gibbons, K., Szmukler, G., Hillier, L. & Petrovich, J.L. (1991). Body image satisfaction, dieting beliefs and weight loss behaviours in adolescent girls and boys. *Journal of Youth and Adolescence, 20(3)*, 361-379.

Pertschuk, M., Collins, M., Kreisberg, J. & Fager, S.S. (1986). Psychiatric symptoms associated with eating disorders in a college population. *International Journal of*

Pierce, J. W., and Wardle, J. (1993). Self-Esteem, Parental Appraisal And Body Size In Children. *Journal Of Child Psychology and Psychiatry and Allied Disciplines. 34*(7):1125-1136.

Pliner, P., Chaiken, S. & Flett, G.L. (1990). Gender differences in concern with body weight and physical appearance over the life span. *Personality and Social Psychology Bulletin, 16*, 263-273.

Polivy, J. & Herman, C.P. (1992). Undieting: a program to help people stop dieting. *International Journal of Eating Disorders, 11(3)*, 26-268.

Powers, P., & Erickson, M. (1986). Body image in women and its relationship to self image and boyd satisfaction. *Journal of Obesity and Weight Reduction, 5(1)*, 37-50.

Pritchard, M. E., King, S. L., and Czajkanarins, D. M. (1997). Adolescent Body Mass Indices And Self-Perception. *Adolescence, 32*(128), 863-880.

Radell, S. A., Adame, D. D., Johnson, T. C., and Cole, S. P. (1993). Dance Experiences Associated With Body-Image And Personality Among College Students - A Comparison Of Dancers And Nondancers. *Perceptual and Motor Skills. 77*(2):507-513.

Renouf, A. & Harter, S. (1990). Low self worth and anger as components of the depressive experience in young adolescents. *Development and Psychopathology, 2(3)*, 293-310.

Richards, M.H., Casper, R.C. & Larson, R. (1990). Weight and eating concerns among preadolescents and young adolescent boys and girls. *Journal of Adolescent Health Care, 11*, 203-209.

Richman C.l., Rehberg, H. (1986) The development of self-esteem through martial arts. International Journal of Sports Psychology, 17, 234-239.

Rienzi, B., Scrams, D. & Uhles, P. (1992). GPA and height are related to self acceptance scores of female college students. *Perceptual and motor skills, 74(2)*, 354.

Robinson, B.E., Bacon, J.G. & O'Reilly, J. (1993). Fat phobia: measuring, understanding and changing anti-fat attitudes. *International Journal of Eating Disorders, 14(4)*, 467-80.

Rosen, J.C. & Gross, J. (1987). Prevalence of weight reducing and weight gaining in adolescent girls and boys. *Health Psychology, 6*, 131-147.

Rosen, J.C., Gross, J. & Vara, L. (1987). Psychological adjustment of adolescents attempting to lose or gain weight. *Journal of Consulting Psychology, 55(5)*, 742-47.

Rosenberg, M. (1965). Measurement of self-esteem. In Rosenberg, M. (ed). *Society and the Adolescent Self Image*. New York: Princeton University. 297-307.

Rosenberg, M. (1979). *Conceiving the self*. New York: Basic Books.

Saitoh, S., O'Dea, J. & O'Brien, C. (1997). Body shape preference in university freshmen: A comparative study between the University of Tsukuba and the University of Sydney. *Bulletin of Physical Education Tsukuba, 53*, 32-38 (Japanese).

Salokun, S.O. (1990) Comparison of Nigerian high school male athletes and non-athletes on self-concept. *Perceptual & Motor Skills, 70*, 865-866.

Sallade, J. (1973) A comparison of the psychological adjustment of obese vs. non-obese children. *Journal of Psychosomatic Research,17*, 89-96.

Salmons, P., Lewis, V., Rogers, P. & Gatherer, A. et al. (1988). Body shape dissatisfaction in school children. *British Journal of Psychiatry, 153(Suppl 2)*, 27-31.

Sands, R., Tricker, J., Sherman, C., Armatas, C., and Maschette, W. (1997). Disordered Eating Patterns, Body Image, Self-Esteem, And Physical Activity In Preadolescent School Children. *International Journal Of Eating Disorders, 21*(2), 159-166.

Savin-Williams, R.C. & Demo, D.H. (1984). Developmental change and stability in adolescent self concept. *Developmental Psychology, 20*, 1100-1110.

Schumaker, J.F., Small, L & Wood, J. (1986) Self-concept, academic achievement and athletic participation. *Perceptual and Motor Skills, 62*, 387-390.

Secord, P.F. & Jourard, S.M. (1953). The appraisal of body cathexis and the self. *Journal of Consulting Psychology, 17*, 343-347.

Sharan, Y. & Sharan, S. (1992). *Expanding cooperative learning through group investigation.* New York: Teachers College Press.

Shavelson, R.J., Hubner, J.J. & Stanton, G.C. (1976). Validation of construct interpretations. *Review of Educational Research, 46*, 407-441.

Sherrill, C., Holguin, O., Caywood, A.J. (1989) Fitness, attitude toward physical education and self-concept of elementary school children. *Perceptual and Motor Skills, 69*, 411-414.

Sheslow, D., Hassink, S., Wallace, W. & De Lancey, E. (1993). The relationship between self esteem and depression in obese children. *Annals New York Academy of Sciences, 699*, 289-291.

Shisslak, C.M., Crago, M. & Neal, M.E. (1990). Prevention of eating disorders among adolescents. *American Journal of Health Promotion, 5(2)*, 100-106.

Shisslak, C. M., Renger, R., Sharpe, T., Crago, M., Mcknight, K. M., Gray, N., Bryson, S., Estes, L. S., Parnaby, O. G., Killen, J., and Taylor, C. B. (1999). Development And Evaluation Of The Mcknight Risk Factor Survey For Assessing Potential Risk And Protective Factors For Disordered Eating In Preadolescent And Adolescent Girls. *International Journal Of Eating Disorders. 25*(2):195-214.

Shurka, E., Galatzer, A. & Baizerman, M. (1983). The self concept of growth retarded children, adolescents and youth: An exploratory study. *International Journal of Eclectic Psychotherapy, 2(3)*, 21-35.

Silberstein, L., Striegel-Moore, R. Timko, C. & Rodin, J. (1988). Behavioural and psychological implications of body dissatisfaction: Do men and women differ? *Sex Roles, 19(3-4)*, 219-232.

Silverstein, B. & Perdue, L. (1988). The relationship between role concerns, preferences for slimness and symptoms of eating problems among college women. *Sex Roles, 18*, 101-106.

Simmons, R.G., Blyth, D.A., Van Cleave, E.F. & Bush, D.M. (1979). Entry into early adolescence: the impact of school structure, puberty and early dating on self esteem. *American Sociological Review, 44*, 948-967.

Skrinar, G., Bullen, B., Cheek, J., McArthur, J. (1986). Effects of endurance training on body consciousness in women. *Perceptual Motor Skills, 62(2)*, 483-490.

Slavin, R. (1990). *Cooperative learning. Theory, research and practice.* Massachussets: Allyn and Bacon.

Slavin, R. (1991). Group rewards make groupwork work. *Educational Leadership, 48*, 71-82.

Smolak L., Levine, M., & Schermer, F. (1998) A controlled evaluation of an elementary school primary prevention program for eating problems. *Journal of Psychosomatic Research, 44* (3-4), 339-353.

Sobal, J., & Stunkard, A. J. (1989). Socioeconomic status and obesity: a review of the literature. *Psychological Bulletin, 105*, 260-75.

Speilberger, C., Gorsuch, R. & Lushene, R. (1970). *Manual for the State-Trait Anxiety Inventory.* Palo Alto: Consulting Psychologists Press.

Stake, J. & Lauer, M. (1987). The consequences of being overweight: A controlled study of gender differences. *Sex Roles, 17 (1-2)*, 31-47.

Story, M., Hauck, F.R., Broussard, B.A., White, L.L., Resnick, M.D. & Blum, R.W. (1994). Weight perceptions and weight control practices in American Indian and Alaska Native adolescents. A national survey. *Archives of Pediatric and Adolescent Medicine, 148(6)*, 567-71.

Story, M., Rosenwinkel, K., Himes, J.H., Resnick, M., Harris, L.J. & Blum, R.W. (1991). Demographic and risk factors associated with chronic dieting in adolescents. *American Journal of Diseases in Children, 145*, 994-998.

Strauss C.G., Smith, K., Frame, C., & Forehand, R. (1985) Personal and interpersonal charactersitics associated with childhood obesity. *Journal of Pediatric Psychiatry, 10*, 337-343.

Strauss, R. S. (2000). Childhood Obesity And Self-Esteem. *Pediatrics, 105*(1) e15.

Suman, H. (1990). Attraction behaviour of young women in relation to their perceived physical attractiveness and self concept characteristics. *Journal of the Indian Academy of Applied Psychology, 16(1)*, 21-25.

Svobodny, L.A. (1979). Increasing self concept through outward bound. *Paper presented at the Annual International Convention*, The Council for Exceptional Children. Dallas.

Swarr, A.E. & Richards, M.H. (1996). Longitudinal effects of adolescent girls' pubertal development, perceptions of pubertal timing and parental relations on eating problems. *Developmental Psychology, 32(4)*, 636-646.

Taylor, M. & Cooper, P. (1992). An experimental study of the effect of mood on body size perception. *Behavioural Research and Therapy, 30(1)*, 53-58.

Teri, L. (1982). Depression in adolescence: Its relationship to assertion and various aspects of self image. *Journal of Clinical Child Psychology, 11(2)*, 101-106.

Theron, W., Nel, E. & Lubbe, A. (1991). Relationships between body image and self consciousness. *Perceptual Motor Skills, 73(3:1)*, 979-983.

Thompson, J.K. (1990). *Body Image Disturbance: Assessment and treatment.* New York: Pergamon Press.

Thompson, K. (1986). Larger than life. *Psychology Today, 20(4)*, 38-44.

Thompson, K. & Thompson, C., (1986). Body size distortion and self esteem in asymptomatic, normal weight males and females. *International Journal of Eating Disorders, 5(6)*, 1061-1068.

Thornton, B. Ryckman, R. (1991). Relationship between physical attractiveness, physical effectiveness and self esteem: A cross sectional analysis among adolescents. *Journal of Adolescence, 14(1)*, 85-98.

Tiggemann, M. & Pennington, B. (1990). The development of gender differences in body size dissatisfaction. Special Section: Women and psychology. *Australian Psychology, 25(3)*, 306-313.

Toro, J., Castro, J., Gracia, M. & Perez, P. (1989). Eating attitudes, socio demographic factors and body shape evaluation in adolescence. *British Journal of Medical Psychology, 62(1)*, 61-70.

Tucker, L. (1983). Effect of weight training on self concept: A profile of those influenced most. *Research Quarterly for Exercise & Sport, 54(4)*, 389-397.

Tucker, L. (1983). Muscular strength and mental health. *Journal of Personality and Social Psychology, 45(6)*, 1355-1360.

Tucker, L. (1984). Physical attractiveness, somatotype and the male personality: A dynamic interactional perspective. *Journal of Clinical Psychology, 40(5)*, 1226-1234.

Ventura, M.R. & Dundon, M. (1974). A challenging experience in canoeing and camping as a tool in approaching the drug problem. *Journal of Drug Education, 4(1)*, 123-127.

Wadden, T.A., Foster, G.D., Stunkard, A.J. & Linowitz, J.R. (1989). Dissatisfaction with weight and figure in obese girls: discontent but not depression. *International Journal of Obesity, 13*, 89-97.

Wallace, J.R., Cunningham, R.F. & Del Monte, V. (1984). Change and stability in self esteem between late childhood and early adolescence. *Journal of Early Adolescence, 4*, 253-257.

Wardle, J. & Beales, S. (1988). Restraint, body image and food attitudes in children from 12 to 18 years. *Appetite, 7*, 209-217.

Wardle, J. & Marsland, L. (1990). Adolescent concerns about weight and eating: a social-developmental perspective. *Journal of Psychosomatic Research, 34*, 377-391.

Wertheim, E.H., Paxton, S.J., Maude, D., Szmukler, G., Gibbons, K. & Hillier, L. (1992). Psychosocial predictors of weight loss behaviours and binge eating in adolescent girls and boys. *International Journal of Eating Disorders, 12*, 151-160.

Whitaker, A., Davies, M., Shaffer, D., Johnson, J., Abrams, S. & Walsh, T. (1989). The struggle to be thin: a survey of anorexic and bulimic symptoms in a non-referred adolescent population. *Psycological Medicine, 19*, 193-163.

Wichstrom, L. (1995). Social, psychological and physical correlates of eating problems. A study of the general adolescent population in Norway. *Psychological Medicine, 25(3)*, 567-79.

Wilkinson, L.C. (1988-1989). Grouping children for learning. Implications for kindergarten education. *Review of Research in Education, 15*, 203-50.

Williams, R.L., Schaefer, C.A., Shisslak, C.M., Gronwaldt, V.H., & Comerci, G.D. (1986). Eating attitudes and behaviours in adolescent women: discrimination of normals, dieters and suspected bulimics using the Eating Attitudes Test and Eating Disorders Inventory. *International Journal of Eating Disorders, 5*, 879-894.

Worsley, A. (1981). In the eye of the beholder: Social and personal characteristics of teenagers and their impressions of themselves and fat and slim people. *British Journal of Medical Psychology, 54(3)*, 231-242.

Wylie, R.C. (1979). *The Self Concept*. (Vol 2, Editor), Lincoln, Nebraska: University of Nebraska Press.

Zaharopoulos, E., & hodge., KP. (1991) Self-concept and sport participation. *New Zealand Journal of Psychology, 20* (1), 12-16.

Chapter 6

THE STABILITY AND CORRELATES OF A NEGATIVE COPING SELF AMONG ADOLESCENTS

Eila Laukkanen
Department of Psychiatry, Kuopio University Hospital,
P.O. Box 1777, FI-70211 Kuopio, Finland, Fax +358-17-172 966

Aija Koivu
Department of Psychiatry,
Kuopio University Hospital, P.O. Box 1777, FI-70211 Kuopio, Finland

Kirsi Honkalampi
Department of Psychology,
University of Joensuu, P.O. Box 111, FI-80101 Joensuu, Finland and
Department of Psychiatry, Kuopio University Hospital,
P.O. Box 1777, FI-70211 Kuopio, Finland

Anneli Aivio
Department of Psychiatry,
Kuopio University Hospital, P.O. Box 1777, FI-70211 Kuopio, Finland

Johannes Lehtonen
Department of Psychiatry, Kuopio University and
Kuopio University Hospital, P.O. Box 1777, FI-70211 Kuopio, Finland

ABSTRACT

The aim of this follow-up study was to investigate the stability of the coping self among pupils at 13 and 15 years of age as assessed by the Offer Self-Image Questionnaire. In addition, we sought to identify the factors that are associated with a negative coping self. The sample consisted of 215 secondary school pupils, representing 26% of the same-aged pupils in a middle-sized Finnish city. Information was collected on parent and peer attachment (inventory), psychosomatic symptoms (questionnaire), social skills and problem behavior in school (rating scale for teachers), academic achievements, and smoking and alcohol use. The stability of the coping self in this study group was moderate (kappa 0.53). Eighty–two percent of study subjects (177/215) were in the same class on follow up as in the initial assessment. Sixty-eight percent (38/55) of those who had a negative coping self (score ≥75th percentile) were in the same group on follow-up, while 10% (21/160) of the pupils with an originally positive coping self shifted in a negative direction. The factors associated with remaining in the negative group compared with remaining in the positive group were mental symptoms (OR 17.0, 95% CI 4.5 – 64.2, p<0.001), problems with teachers not reported by pupils (OR 13.9, 95% CI 1.5 – 126.9, p=0.02) and the grade achieved in the native language (negatively associated) (OR 0.25, 95% CI 0.11 – 0.55, p=0.001). The shift to a negative coping self was associated with a lack of cooperation with parents (OR 1.2, 95% CI 1.0 – 1.4, p=0.016) and mental symptoms (OR 4.4, 95% CI 1.1 – 17.8, p= 0.04). The development of a negative coping self should be recognized and taken in account at the age of 13 years, because it is a moderately stable condition and associated with mental symptoms, poor cooperation with parents and a lower level of school achievement at the age of 15 years.

Adolescence (from 12 to 22 years of age) is a time of many physiological, psychological, and social changes in the process of growing from a child into an adult. Many adolescents have temporary mental and psychosomatic symptoms associated with normal developmental difficulties, but during adolescence the prevalence of true psychiatric disorders is 15-20% (Roberts, Attkisson, & Rosenblatt, 1998). Previous studies have shown that recognition of these problems is not easy (Cantwell, Lewinsohn, Rohde, & Seeley, 1997). Internalizing problems in particular go undetected in adolescents, even by their parents. However, early recognition of developmental difficulties or of the possible prodromal phase of mental disease and prompt initiation of counseling, support and adequate treatment are often of great importance in supporting healthy psychic growth and the attainment of adult mental health.

Earlier studies have shown that social relationships, particularly with parents, are important for the healthy development of adolescents (Shulman, 1993; Forehand et al., 1991). Parental availability combined with respect and support for the striving of adolescents for autonomy constitute a facilitating environment for maturation and contribute to the development a young person's competence at coping with his or her environment. Giordano, Cernkovich, Groat, Pugh and Swinford (1998) showed in a ten-year follow-up study that family intimacy during adolescence - not intimacy with peers - is positively related to good self-esteem, marital satisfaction and a low level of psychological stress in adulthood. On the other hand, it has been found that popularity among peers is positively correlated with good school achievement, the pursuit of further education, social activity and good self-esteem (Boivin, Hymel, & Bukowski, 1995).

The onset of mental disease is probably an endpoint of the accumulation of biological, social, and environmental risk factors and a chain of maladaptive solutions to different intrapsychic and environmental developmental challenges (Sroufe, 1997). On this basis it can be concluded that signs of maladaptive development are possible to detect. One way to improve the early detection of developmental problems is to use self-assessment by adolescents of their coping self. This approach, focusing on an adolescent's own perception of his/her ability to cope, may be a more fruitful strategy than describing negative aspects of the adolescent such as mental symptoms, deviant behavior etc. In addition, previous reports have shown that adolescents themselves are the best informants about their mental state and their means of coping with different developmental and life-stresses (Feehan, McGee, Nada Raja, & Williams, 1994; Offer, Ostrov, Howard, & Dolan, 1992) .

The Offer Self-Image Questionnaire (OSIQ) is a self-descriptive personality test that assesses the psychological adjustment of teenagers between the ages of 13-19 years (Offer, Ostrov, Howard, & Dolan, 1992). It is based on the psychodynamic growth and developmental theory, the behavioral sciences, and observations of the behavior of normal young people and evaluates multiple areas of an adolescent's functioning. The 130 six-class items are divided into 12 scales that cover 5 major psychosocial areas or 'selves': the psychological self, social self, sexual self, familial self and coping self.

A positive coping self relates to normal healthy adolescents, while the opposite characteristics represents a negative coping self and indicate problems with psychological development (Offer, Ostrov, Howard, & Attkinson,1990). Normal adolescents are hopeful and secure about their ability to cope and only a minority, about one in five normal adolescents, feel emotionally empty and experience their life as an endless series of problems. These findings have also been supported by other studies; OSIQ scores can differentiate between normal and emotionally disturbed adolescents (Koenig, 1988; Kapfhammer, Mayer, Neumeier, & Scherer, 1994) and predict future psychological functioning (Offer, Ostrov, Howard, & Dolan, 1992). Although many studies have been conducted using the OSIQ, we are not aware of any previous longitudinal studies related to the development of an adolescent's coping self or the factors that are associated with having a negative coping self.

In this study we were especially interested in the following questions:

- How stable is the coping self of adolescents from the age of 13 years (7th grade in Finnish secondary school) to 15 years (9th grade)?
- Does the timing of puberty have any effect on the coping self?
- Are there any associations between the coping self of adolescents and their relationships with parents at 15 years of age?
- Is a negative coping self associated with mental/psychosomatic symptoms or with problems detected by teachers at 15 years of age?
- Is a negative coping self associated with poor academic success at school?

SUBJECTS AND METHODS

The study subjects consisted of a cohort of pupils in two Finnish secondary schools (n=256) who were initially studied at 13 years of age (mean 13.8 years, SD 3.6 months) in the 7th grade and then again at 15 years of age (mean 15.7 years, SD 3.6 months) in the 9th grade. The pupils represented the normal, unselected youth in Finnish comprehensive schools. The two study schools were situated in separate areas with similar socio-demographic backgrounds. The study group comprised 26% of all similar-aged children in the secondary schools of a medium-sized Finnish city. Written informed consent to participate had been obtained in advance from the parents and adolescents. Approval for the study was obtained from the Ethics Committee of Kuopio University Hospital and the University of Kuopio. On follow-up 215 (84%) pupils participated to the study. Twenty-three (9%) were excluded because of having changed the school, nine questionnaires were rejected because of missing data and eight pupils were not at school at the time of the study.

Study data were obtained via questionnaires completed by the pupils and their teachers, from school records provided by the teachers and data recorded by the school nurse concerning the commencement of menstruation/ejaculations and the spurt in growth.

Coping Self

The coping self of the OSIQ is formed from three scales: Emotional Health, describing psychopathology (14 items); Superior Adjustment describing how the adolescent copes with himself/herself, other people, and his/her environment (14 items), and Mastery, which assesses how well an adolescent adapts to his/her immediate environment (10 items). The internal reliability and discriminant validity of the questionnaire have been shown to be quite good (Offer, Ostrov, Howard, & Dolan, 1992; Laukkanen, Halonen, & Viinamäki, 1999; Laukkanen, Peiponen, Halonen, Aivio, & Viinamäki, 1999). Among our study subjects Cronbach's α for the coping self, formed from the items in the scales Emotional Health, Superior Adjustment, and Mastery, was 0.87.

Relationships with Parents

Relationships with parents and the amount of social support received from parents were investigated using a modified from of the structured inventory of parent and peer attachment (IPPA) (Armsden, & Greenberg, 1987) employing four instead of five classes of response (1=always true...4=never true). The section relating to the relationship with parents (28 items) was used in this study. The data were analyzed by principal factor analysis. Two factors, confidence in and cooperation with parents (15 items) and mistrust of and disappointment with parents (13 items), were formed and subscale scores were obtained by summing the scores for items relating to each factor. A low sum score indicates a positive relationship in the confidence subscale and a lack of mistrust in the disappointment subscale. The Cronbach's α of the subscales was high: 0.88 for confidence in parents and 0.84 for disappointment with parents.

Mental and Psychosomatic Symptoms

The frequency of mental and psychosomatic symptoms was determined with a 14-item questionnaire providing a five-item scale of responses to each question (1 = <once/month, 2 = once/month, 3 = once/week, 4 = many times/week, 5 = almost daily) (Välimaa, Kepler, & Yeganegi, 1995). Two separate sum scores were obtained by factor analysis that related to mental symptoms (feelings of depression, melancholy, irritability, nervousness, strain, fatigue, sleeping difficulties and waking up at night, $\alpha=0.84$) and to psychosomatic symptoms (dizziness, lack of appetite, stomach ache, neck ache, back ache, $\alpha=0.75$).

Academic Achievements, Problem Behavior and Social Skills

Academic school achievements of pupils were assessed on the basis of final grades at the end of the comprehensive school period (scores range from 4 = failed to 10 = excellent). The mean grade for all subjects and the grades for the native language (Finnish) and mathematics were used in the analysis.

Class teachers completed a 3-point Social Skills Rating Scale System questionnaire (1 = never, 2 = sometimes, 3 = often or very often) reflecting problem behavior (concentration problems, internalizing problems and externalizing problems of their pupils) (Gresham, & Elliot, 1990). Scores relating to the various scales were analyzed. Internal consistency of the scales was good: 0.92 for concentration problems, 0.90 for externalizing problems, 0.86 for internalizing problems. Social skills were assessed using a six-item scale. The items were cooperation which teachers, cooperation with fellow pupils, empathy, assertiveness, self-control and responsibility (1 = poor, 2 = rather poor, 3 = good, 4 = excellent). Cronbach's α for the scale was 0.87.

The pupils were also asked whether they had had problems with their teachers (no/yes), and what future educational plans they had after completing secondary school.

Family Structure and Socioeconomic Background

Information about family structure was obtained from the adolescents and checked against school records. Data on family socioeconomic background were obtained from school records and by asking pupils or parents. Parents were classified as: 1 = self-employed, 2 = higher-level salaried employees, 3 = lower-level salaried employees, 4 = manual workers and 5 = others that did not fall into the categories mentioned (Classification of the socio-economic groups, 1989).

Forming the Groups from the Coping Self Scores

In the analysis a low raw score indicates a positive and a high score a negative coping self. The pupils completed the OSIQ in both the 7th and 9th grade. Using the 75th percentile as a cut-off score (7th grade: 107, range 43-147; 9th grade: 116, range 65-148), where a raw score ≥ 75th percentile indicates a negative coping self and a score < 75th percentile indicates a positive coping self, the pupils were divided according to their scores into four groups:

Group 1, the 'positive' group, consisting of those pupils whose coping self score in both assessments was below the 75th percentile (n=139);

Group 2, the 'positive development' group, consisting of pupils whose coping self score had declined from ≥ 75th percentile in the 7th grade to < 75th percentile in the 9th grade (n=17);

Group 3, the 'negative development' group, consisting of adolescents whose score had changed in a negative direction (n=21); and

Group 4, the 'repeatedly negative' group, consisting of those pupils whose coping self score had been ≥ 75th percentile in both assessments (n=38) (Table 1).

Table 1. The coping self of pupils at the age of 13 years (7th grade in secondary school) and 15 years (9th grade), using the 75th percentile as a cut-off score for grouping (score > 75 percentile = negative and score < 75 percentile score = positive)

Coping self in 7th grade (13 years of age)	Coping self in 9th grade (15 years of age)		
	Positive	Negative	Total
Positive	139	21	160
Negative	17	38	55
Total	156	59	215

Kappa = 0.53

STATISTICAL METHODS

Differences between the coping self groups were tested by one-way ANOVA for continuous variables. The normality of the variable distributions was tested by the Shapiro-Wilk test. The chi-squared test was used for categorical variables. Multinomial logistic regression analyses were used secondarily with coping self groups as the outcome variables.

RESULTS

The stability of the scores for the coping self from the 7th to the 9th grade was moderate (kappa value 0.53) (Table 1). Eighty-two percent of study subjects were in the same class on follow up as in the initial assessment. Of the pupils with a negative coping self in the 7th grade, 68% remained in this category in the 9th grade and thus had a repeatedly negative coping self.

There were no statistically significant differences in the variables studied between the 'positive development in coping self' and the 'positive coping self' groups which were therefore combined in the following analyses into a 'positive' group (boys 49%). The other groups were the negative development group (boys 73%) and repeatedly negative group (boys 54%) (chi-squared test for gender, p = ns).

Social Background and Pubertal Status

There were no significant differences between the groups in family socioeconomic background or family structure (Table 2). In all groups the most common family structure was living with both biological parents (72% in positive group, 73% in the negative development and repeatedly negative groups). Most subjects had reached puberty before the age of 14 years (69% of the positive group, 67% of the repeatedly negative group and 50% of the negative development group, chi-squared test ns.).

Table 2. Sociodemographic background, school achievements (mean, SD), future educational plans and reported problems with teachers of the study pupils in the 9th grade of secondary school

| | Positive (n = 156) | Coping self groups | | Statistical significance |
		Negative development (n = 21)	Repeatedly negative (n = 38)	
Socioeconomic status (%)[a]				
Self-employed	7	4	11	ns.
Higher-level salaried empl.	24	9	22	
Lower-level salaried empl.	27	23	13	
Manual workers	42	64	54	
Academic achievements				
All subjects	8.0 (0.9)	7.4 (0.7)	7.4 (0.8)	$p^1 < 0.001^b$, $p^2 < 0.05^b$
Native language	7.8 (1.3)	6.9 (1.1)	6.7 (1.2)	$p^1 < 0.001^b$, $p^2 < 0.05^b$
Mathematics	7.6 (1.4)	6.9 (1.4)	6.9 (1.4)	$p^1 < 0.05^b$
Future educational plans (%)[a]				
High school	63	47	43	ns.
Vocational school	23	48	40	
No plans	14	5	17	
Pupils reported problems with teachers (%)[a]	23	10	29	ns.

a = Chi-squared test
b = One-way ANOVA with Scheffe Post Hoc Test
p^1 = repeatedly negative vs. positive
p^2 = negative development vs. positive

Academic Achievements and Social Competence at School

Academic achievements of pupils who had a repeatedly negative coping self or negative development in their coping self were poorer than those of the positive group (Table 2). There were no differences in problems with teachers reported by the pupils. Most pupils had made educational plans for the future, 63% of pupils in the positive group compared with 47% in the negative development group and 43% in the repeatedly negative group planned to go to high school.

According to assessments by teachers, the pupils of the repeatedly negative group had poorer social skills and had more internalizing problems than those in the positive group. Pupils in the negative development group also had poorer social skills and more externalizing problems than those in the positive group (Table 3).

Table 3. Social competence of the study pupils as assessed by their teachers (mean, SD), mental and psychosomatic symptoms (mean, SD) and relationships with parents (mean, SD) in the 9th grade of secondary school

| | Coping self groups | | | |
	Positive (n = 156)	Negative development (n = 21)	Repeatedly negative (n = 38)	Statistical significance
Social competence				
Social skills	17.4 (3.7)	14.3 (3.4)	15.4 (3.5)	$p^1 < 0.05^a$, $p^2 < 0.001^a$
Concentration problems	9.1 (3.6)	11.2 (3.8)	10.6 (4.3)	
Externalizing problems	6.8 (2.7)	8.8 (3.3)	7.8 (3.4)	$p^2 < 0.05^a$
Internalizing problems	9.1 (2.9)	9.9 (2.2)	10.9 (3.9)	$p^1 < 0.05^a$
Mental symptoms score	1.9 (0.6)	2.2 (0.6)	2.8 (0.8)	$p^1 < 0.001^a$, $p^3 < 0.05^a$
Psychosomatic symptoms score	1.7 (0.5)	2.0 (0.6)	2.2 (0.8)	$p^1 < 0.001^a$
Relationships with parents				
Confidence in parents score	24.1 (7.1)	30.3 (5.5)	26.5 (7.1)	$p^2 < 0.01^a$
Disappointment with parents score	21.2 (5.4)	27.7	24.7 (6.6)	$p^1 < 0.01^a$, $p^2 < 0.001^a$

a = One-way ANOVA with Scheffe Post Hoc Test p^2 = negative development vs. positive
p^1 = repeatedly negative vs. positive p^3 = repeatedly negative vs. negative development

Mental/Psychosomatic Symptoms and Relationships with Parents

Mental symptoms were more common among pupils of the repeatedly negative coping self group than among the others (Table 3). The pupils in this group had also more psychosomatic symptoms than those in the positive group. In addition cooperation with parents were poorest among pupils in the negative development group. Pupils in both the repeatedly negative group and the negative development group were more often disappointed with their parents than pupils in the positive group.

In multinomial regression the two negative groups were compared with the positive group. The background variables gender, socioeconomic background (employees = 0, workers or others = 1), family status (both parents in the family = 0, no = 1) were included in the model. Other variables were included on the basis of univariate analysis. Thus the model included the following variables: scores related to social skills, externalizing and internalizing problems, mental and psychosomatic symptoms, cooperation with parents, disappointment with parents, the grade for the native language and no problems with teachers reported by the pupils (no problems = 0, problems = 1). The Nagelkerke value for the model was 0.57.

The factors associated with a repeatedly negative coping self were mental symptoms (OR 17.0, 95% CI 4.5 to 64.2, p=0.000) and an absence of reported problems with teachers (OR 13.9 95% CI 1.5 to 126.9, p=0.02). A poor grade for the native language was associated with repeatedly negative coping (OR 0.25, 95% CI 0.11 to 0.55, p=0.001) while a low level of cooperation with parents (OR 1.2, 95% CI 1.0 to 1.4, p=0.016) and mental symptoms (OR 4.4, 95% CI 1.1 to 17.8, p= 0.04) were associated with negative development of the coping self.

DISCUSSION

The main results of our study were, firstly, that the coping self of adolescents is moderately stable from the age of 13 years to the age of 15 years and, secondly, that a negative coping self is associated with factors that reflect psychosocial dysfunction at 15 years of age.

We are aware of no comparable studies on the stability of the coping self measured by the OSIQ. However, there have been many other studies showing that psychic problems in preadolescents predict mental health problems during adolescence and adulthood (Rutter, 1995), and that discontinuity detected in the prevalence of mental diseases at the age of 15 to 16 years is perhaps a function of the sharp rise in new self-reported disorders among adolescents (McGee, Feehan, & Williams, 1995).

Our result that the timing of puberty did not have any effect on the coping self is in accordance with the study of Sinkkonen, Anttila and Siimes (1998), who have shown that pubertal events among boys are related to the Impulse Control and Emotional Tone scales but not to other aspects of the self-image.

Adolescents who repeatedly assessed their coping self as being negative displayed many signs of maladaptive development which can result in subsequent mental problems. These pupils had more mental and somatic symptoms than others. Teachers assessed them as having internalizing problems, e.g. anxiety and poor social skills. Their school achievements were also poorer than those of adolescents with a positive coping self. Interestingly, a poor grade in the native language was especially associated with a negative coping self. McGee, Feehan and Williams (1995) found in a longitudinal study of a birth cohort that a low level of language skills (e.g. reading skills) continues to be disadvantage throughout schooling and correlates with problems in psychological development. Seiffge-Krenke (1989) found that adolescents who had a passive, withdrawing coping style also had a high problem intensity, a negative self-concept, and problems with parents, peers, the opposite sex and themselves. Our study is not wholly comparable with those cited above because of the different methods used.

In addition, adolescents whose coping self had developed in a negative direction were less academically successful and had more mental symptoms than adolescents with a positive coping self. They were also somewhat different from pupils in the repeatedly negative group. The most significant characteristic of these pupils was their lack of confidence and disappointment with their parents. They also had more externalizing problems than pupils in the normal coping self group, e.g. disturbing the class during teaching. Teachers rated the social skills of this group as poorer than those of pupils in the normal group. Although poor social competence has been shown to be independently and strongly associated with mental disorders in earlier studies (Feehan, McGee, Nada Raja, & Williams, 1994), one interpretation of our results might be the turbulence of this developmental period. Many studies have shown that adolescents may have temporary mental, psychosomatic and behavioral problems, and perhaps also negative feelings about themselves, which are related more to this developmental phase than to stability problems.

In this study we found a clear association between an adolescent's perception of his/her coping self as positive and that of the parents as being supportive, confidential and respectful, and vise versa. Earlier studies have also verified the significance of parents to healthy adolescent development (Shulman, 1993; Forehand et al., 1991).

When evaluating our study, it must be noted that we used the 75th percentile as a cut-off point in placing pupils into groups with either a negative or a normal coping self. In so doing it is possible that some adolescents were wrongly classified because their OSIQ score did not reflect their true coping self. Furthermore, a score that is extremely positive may indicate psychological dysfunction, for example a poor capacity for introspection. In addition, there were relatively few subjects in the repeatedly negative and negative coping self groups, reducing the statistical power of this study and increasing the possibility of type 2 errors.

Our study subjects were representative of a medium-sized city in Finland and comprised 26% of pupils in the same grade at normal secondary schools. Eighty-four percent of pupils who took part in the initial study participated in the follow-up. Both the adolescents and their teachers were used as informants. Furthermore, the assessments of teachers and pupils were undertaken independently. The results of the teachers' assessments are noteworthy because observations of teachers are good predictors of future mental and social problems (see Boyle, Offord, Racine, Fleming, Szatmari, & Links, 1993). Pupils in our study were assessed by teachers who had known them since they were 13 years old and the methods used were previously tested and structured, which increases the reliability of our results.

It is not possible on the basis of this study design to make any conclusions about associations between a negative coping self and the possible development of mental disturbance. However, our results support those of earlier studies showing that an adolescent's negative perception of himself/herself and his/her abilities are associated with psychosocial and mental problems (Kapfhammer, Mayer, Neumeier, & Scherer, 1994; Seiffge-Krenke, 1989; Koenig, 1988). Furthermore, our study shows that a positive relationship with parents is important for good adaptation during adolescence.

In addition, the finding that 68% of adolescents with the most negative coping self at 13 years of age rated themselves in the same way at 15 years of age emphasizes the importance of recognizing how adolescents perceive themselves during early adolescence, because it can be one sign of the beginning of maladaptive development and of the later onset of psychosocial or mental problems.

REFERENCES

Armsden, G. C., & Greenberg, M. T. (1987). The inventory of parent and peer attachment: individual differences and their relationship to psychological wellbeing in adolescence. *Journal of Youth and Adolescence, 16,* 427-454.

Boivin, M., Hymel, S., & Bukowski, W. M. (1995). The roles of social withdrawal, peer rejection, and victimization by peers in predicting loneliness and depressed mood in childhood. *Development and Psychopathology, 7,* 765-785.

Boyle, M. H., Offord, D. R., Racine, Y. A., Fleming, J. E., Szatmari, P., & Links, P. S. (1993). Predicting substance use in early adolescence based on parent and teacher assessment of childhood psychiatric disorder: result from the Ontario Child Health Study follow-up. *Journal of Child Psychology and Psychiatry, 43,* 535-544.

Cantwell, D. P., Lewinsohn, P. M., Rohde, P., & Seeley, J. R. (1997). Correspondence between adolescent report and parent report of psychiatric diagnostic data. *Journal of American Academy of Child and Adolescent Psychiatry, 36,* 610-619.

Classification of the socio-economic groups. (1989). Helsinki: Tilastokeskus, käsikirja 17.

Feehan, M., McGee, R., Nada Raja, S., & Williams, S. M. (1994). DSM-III-R disorders in New Zealand 18-years-olds. *Australian and New Zealand Journal of Psychiatry, 28, 87-99*.

Forehand, R., Wierson, M., McCombs, T. A., Armistead, L., Kempton, T., & Neighbors, B. (1991). The role of family stressors and parent relationships on adolescent functioning. *Journal of American Academy of Child and Adolescent Psychiatry, 30*, 316-322.

Giordano, P. C., Cernkovich, S. A., Groat, H. T., Pugh, M. D., & Swinford, S. P. (1998). The quality of adolescent friendships: Long term effect. *Journal of Health and Social Behavior, 39*, 55-71.

Gresham, F. M., & Elliott, S. N. (1990). *Social Skills Rating System*. Manual. American Guidance Service, Circle Pines.

Kapfhammer, H. P., Mayer, C., Neumeier, R., & Scherer, J. (1994). Im ubergang von der adoleszenz zum jungen erwachsenenalte. Empirische vergleichsstudien zur psychosozialen entwicklung und problematic von psychiatrischen patienten und gesunden kontrollprobanden. (The passage from adolescence to early adulthood: Psychosocial development and the complex of problems in psychiatric inpatients and healthy volunteers). *Psychotherapie, Psychosomatik, Medizinische Psychologie, 44*, 7-14.

Koenig, L. J. (1988). Self-image of emotionally disturbed adolescents. *Journal of Abnormal Child Psychology, 16*, 111-126.

Laukkanen, E., Halonen, P., & Viinamäki, H. (1999). Stability and internal consistency of the Offer Self-Image Questionnaire: a study of Finnish adolescents. *Journal of Youth and Adolescence, 28,*71-77.

Laukkanen, E., Peiponen, S., Halonen, P., Aivio, A., & Viinamäki, H. (1999). Discriminant validity of the Offer Self-Image Questionnaire in Finnish 13-year-old adolescents. *Nordic Journal of Psychiatry, 53,*197-201.

McGee, R., Feehan, M., & Williams, S. (1995). Long-term follow-up of a birth cohort. In F. C. Verhulst, & H. M. Koot (Eds.), *The epidemiology of child and adolescent psychopathology (pp. 366-384)*. Oxford, New York, Tokyo: Oxford University Press.

Offer, D., Ostrov, E., Howard, K. I., & Atkinson, R. (1990). Normality and adolescence. *Psychiatric Clinics of North America, 13*, 377-388.

Offer, D., Ostrov, E., Howard, K. I., & Dolan, S. (1992*). Offer Self-Image Questionnaire Revised*. Los Angeles, California: Western Psychological Services.

Roberts, R. E., Attkisson, C. C., & Rosenblatt, A. (1998). Prevalence of psychopathology among children and adolescents. *American Journal of Psychiatry, 155*, 715-725.

Rutter, M. (1995). Relationships between mental disorder in childhood and adulthood. *Acta Psychiatrica Scandinavica, 91*, 73-95.

Seiffge-Krenke, I. (1989). Problem intensity and the disposition of adolescents to take therapeutic advice. In M. Brambring, F. Lösel, & H. Skowronek (Eds*.), Children at risk: Assessment, longitudinal research, and intervention* (pp. 457-477). Berlin, New-York: Walter de Gruyter.

Shulman, S. (1993). Close relationships and coping behavior in adolescence. *Journal of Adolescence, 16*, 267-283.

Sinkkonen, J., Anttila, R., & Siimes, M. A. (1998). Pubertal maturation and changes in self-image in early adolescent Finnish boys. *Journal of Youth and Adolescence, 27*, 209-218.

Sroufe, L. A. (1997). Psychopathology as an outcome of development. *Development and Psychopathology, 9*, 251-268.

Välimaa, R., Kepler, K., & Yeganegi, N. (1995). Koettu terveys ja onnelisuus sekä sairaudet koululaisten arjessa (Self-rated health, happiness and disease in the everyday life of pupils). In L. Kannas (Ed.), *Koululaisten kokema terveys, hyvinvointi ja kouluviihtyvyys (Self-rated health, well-being and experiences of school among pupils)* (pp. 31-43). Helsinki: Opetushallitus.

Chapter 7

AUTONOMIC SUBSTRATES OF HEART RATE REACTIVITY IN ADOLESCENT MALES WITH CONDUCT DISORDER AND/OR ATTENTION-DEFICIT/HYPERACTIVITY DISORDER

Theodore P. Beauchaine[*]

University of Washington

ABSTRACT

Heart rate (HR) reactivity was assessed in adolescents with attention-deficit/hyperactivity disorder (ADHD), conduct disorder and ADHD (CD/ADHD), and controls during an incentive-motivation task that included trials of reward and extinction. Contrary to predictions derived from models postulating excessive approach motivation in aggression, no differences in HR reactivity were observed between the CD/ADHD participants and either of the other groups. However, analyses of cardiac pre-ejection period and respiratory sinus arrhythmia revealed that HR changes among CD/ADHD probands were mediated primarily by the parasympathetic nervous system. In contrast, HR changes among ADHD and control participants were mediated by both autonomic nervous system branches. Findings are interpreted as more consistent with sensation seeking than with reward dominance models of aggression.

Key Words: conduct disorder, attention-deficit/hyperactivity disorder, pre-ejection period, respiratory sinus arrhythmia, heart rate reactivity

[*] Department of Psychology, University of Washington, Box 351525, Seattle, WA 98195-1525. E-mail: tbeaucha@u.washington.edu. Phone: (206) 685-2734.

This work was supported by National Research Service Award 1F31MH12209 from the National Institute of Mental Health. The author expresses thanks to William Guethlein, Edward Katkin, Robert Kelsey, Brett Martin, Elizabeth Mezzacappa, Lindsay Reinhardt, and Richard Sloan for their helpful contributions.

Much has been written in the past two decades about the motivational substrates of hyperactivity and aggression (e.g., Beauchaine, 2001; Beauchaine, Katkin, Strassberg, & Snarr, 2001; Fowles, 1980, 1988; Haenlein & Caul, 1987; Iaboni, Douglas, & Ditto, 1997; Quay, 1988, 1993, 1997). The bulk of these writings have focused on the roles of two psychobiological systems in regulating behavior, one governing approach responses, and the other governing avoidance responses. The crux of motivational accounts of externalizing disorders is that deficientcies in either or both of these systems result in hyperactivity and/or instrumental aggression. Such outcomes can result from excessive approach motivation, deficient avoidance motivation, or both.

The theoretical bases from which this literature emerged were advanced initially by Jeffrey Gray (1982a, 1982b, 1987a, 1987b; see also Gray & McNaughton, 2000). Gray elaborated most extensively on the avoidance motivational system, often referred to as the behavioral inhibition system (BIS). Through the production of aversive motivational states including fear and anxiety, the BIS inhibits appetitive behaviors in the presence of cues for punishment. Theoretically, children with a relatively unresponsive BIS, including those who are hyperactive and/or aggressive, are likely to persist in reward-seeking behaviors longer than typically developing children, especially in the face negative consequences. As specified by Gray, the BIS is mediated centrally by the septo-hippocampal system, including the serotonergic projections of the raphe nucleus and the noradrenergic projections of the locus ceruleus. I have reviewed elsewhere a corpus of neurotransmitter and psychophysiological evidence supporting the underactive BIS hypothesis in both conduct disorder (CD) and attention-deficit/hyperactivity disorder (ADHD) (Beauchaine, 2001).

In contrast to avoidance motivation, appetitive motivation falls under control of the behavioral approach system (BAS; Gray & McNaughton, 1996). Through the production of pleasurable motivational states, the BAS encourages approach behaviors in the presence of cues for reward. Although Gray elaborated less on the neurobiology of approach, he did suggest that incentive motivation is likely governed by the dopaminergic projections of the tegmentostriatal pathway, including the ventral tegmental area, the nucleus accumbens, and the ventral striatum. This is consistent with a voluminous literature on approach motivation in both animals and humans (for reviews see Ashby, Isen, & Turken, 1999; Nadir, Bechara, & van der Kooy, 1997).

There are two somewhat opposing views regarding the role of the approach motivational system in hyperactivity and aggression. One school of thought is that aggressive CD and it's adult sequelae result from reward dominance, or excessive BAS activity (Quay, 1988, 1993, 1997; Fowles, 1980, 1988). According to this view, when deficiencies in BIS functioning are coupled with an overactive BAS, impulsive aggression results. By this reasoning, hyperactivity is tied to deficient BIS functioning alone, whereas impulsive aggression results from deficient BIS functioning *and* excessive BAS activity.

Both behavioral and psychophysiological evidence have been offered in support of the overactive BAS hypothesis. Behavioral evidence comes from response perseveration tasks in which children play into a decreasing schedule of reward. When faced with contingencies in which the probability of monetary incentives at the beginning of a game is high but gradually decreases to zero (e.g., Newman, Patterson, & Kosson, 1987), children with CD play longer and lose more money than controls (Matthys, van Goozen, de Vries, Cohen-Kettenis, & van Engeland, 1998; Shapiro, Quay, Hogan, & Schwartz, 1988). As we have noted elsewhere, however, these results do not provide strong support for the overactive BAS hypothesis in aggressive CD (Beauchaine et al., 2001), both because similar findings are observed with ADHD children (Daugherty & Quay, 1991; Milich, Hartung, Martin, & Haigler, 1994), and because reward and punishment cues are mixed within trials, thereby eliciting both BAS and BIS reactivity. It therefore cannot be determined whether the perseverative responding observed in ADHD and CD participants is due to excessive BAS activation, deficient BIS activation, or both.

At the psychophysiological level, Fowles (1980, 1988) has suggested that BAS activity is reflected in heart rate (HR) changes during reward. This conjecture is based on the finding that during incentive motivation tasks, changes in heart rate are observed that are proportional to the amount of money at stake (see Fowles, 1988). Moreover, such heart rate changes are not observed when incorrect responses are punished, and are therefore specific to reward. According to Fowles, aggressive probands should exhibit greater HR reactivity to reward than controls, following the hypothesis that their aggression results from excessive appetitive motivation. Unfortunately, no studies have compared aggressive and non-aggressive samples on HR reactivity during reward. This is somewhat surprising given the theoretical literature linking cardiac reactivity to appetitive motivational states.

In contrast to the reward dominance or overactive BAS hypothesis, stimulation seeking accounts of aggression (e.g., Eysenck & Gudjonsson, 1989) suggest that CD and related disorders are marked by diminished rather than enhanced reward system activity, and that probands engage in instrumental aggression to attain satisfactory reward states (see Beauchaine, 2001; Beauchaine et al., 2001). This conjecture follows from two observations. First, individual differences in tonic BAS activity are likely to affect the degree of positive affect one experiences (Davidson, 1994, 2000). Second, increased activity in the dopaminergic pathway and associated positive affect do not *elicit* appetitive behaviors. Rather, they are *elicited by* appetitive behaviors (see Ashby, Isen, & Turken, 1999; Davidson, 1994). Thus, instrumental aggression may be the product of low tonic BAS activity, resulting in an anhedonic motivational state that promotes reward-seeking behaviors, coupled with relative BAS insensitivity, so that larger incentives are required to achieve satisfying levels of positive affect. Note that stimulation seeking and reward dominance accounts make opposite predictions regarding heart rate reactivity in aggressive participants compared with controls. The stimulation-seeking hypothesis predicts less HR reactivity given equivalent rewards, whereas the reward dominance hypothesis predicts greater HR reactivity.

We have argued elsewhere, however, that HR is a contaminated measure of BAS functioning. This is because BAS activity should be indexed more accurately by sympathetic nervous system (SNS) linked cardiac activity (Beauchaine, 2001; Beauchaine et al., 2001), yet HR is determined by both the sympathetic and parasympathetic autonomic branches. The assertion that BAS activity is marked specifically by SNS-linked cardiac activity is based on both evolutionary and functional considerations. Appetitive behaviors require increased metabolic output, and the primary function of the SNS is often viewed as one of mobilizing resources to meet metabolic demands. In turn, increased metabolic demands require increased cardiac output, which is facilitated by SNS-mediated changes in the contractile force of the left ventricle (see Brownley, Hurwitz, & Schneiderman, 2000; Sherwood, Allen, Obrist, & Langer, 1986; Sherwood et al., 1990). Moreover, the reticular nuclei that control parasympathetic nervous system (PNS) influences on HR are evolutionarily recent developments, with maximum differentiation in the brainstems of mammals (Porges, 1995).

These nuclei therefore evolved after systems supporting appetitive motivation. Thus, BAS activity is likely to be reflected more specifically by SNS-linked cardiac activity than by HR.

With this discussion in mind, the primary objectives of this investigation were to (a) compare HR reactivity during reward among aggressive CD, ADHD, and control groups of adolescents, and (b) explore the autonomic substrates (i.e., SNS vs. PNS) of HR reactivity in these groups. Following from sensation-seeking accounts of aggression, it was hypothesized that SNS mediation of HR reactivity would be absent or attenuated in CD participants, reflecting insensitivity to reward. It was further hypothesized that SNS-linked cardiac reactivity would be more effective than HR reactivity in differentiating CD participants from the other groups. A pure ADHD group was included because the vast majority of CD probands exhibit comorbid ADHD in clinical samples (e.g., Klein et al., 1997). Thus, effects that have been attributed to CD could be associated with ADHD. Including a pure ADHD group provided for disentanglement of this confound.

METHOD

Participants

Participants included 22 control, 17 ADHD, and 20 aggressive CD adolescent males between the ages of 12 and 17. Diagnoses were derived from interviews with parents, who completed the CD, ADHD, and major depressive disorder (MDD) scales of the Adolescent Symptom Inventory (ASI; Gadow & Sprafkin, 1997), and the Aggression, Hyperactivity, Delinquent Behavior, and Anxious/Depressed scales of the Child Behavior Checklist (CBCL; Achenbach, 1991). The ASI yields diagnostic cut-offs based on *Diagnostic and Statistical Manual of Mental Disorders* (DSM-IV; American Psychiatric Association, 1994) criteria. Sensitivity, specificity, and reliability of the scales used are adequate (Gadow & Sprafkin, 1997). The CBCL yields percentile rankings of target syndromes based on national norms. Reliabilities of the scales used are excellent (CBCL; Achenbach, 1991). Participants in the CD group were required to meet DSM-IV criteria for CD, and to score above the 95th percentile on both the Delinquent Behavior and Aggressive Behavior scales of the CBCL. Although not recruited on this basis, all participants in the CD group also met criteria for hyperactive-impulsive ADHD, and will thus be referred to as the CD/ADHD group. Participants in the pure ADHD group were required to meet DSM-IV criteria for hyperactive-impulsive ADHD, and to score above the 95th percentile on the Attention Problems scale of the CBCL. Potential ADHD participants were excluded if they endorsed any CD criteria, or if they scored above the 70th percentile on the CBCL Aggressive or Delinquent Behavior scales. Potential ADHD and CD participants who met criteria for MDD or scored above the 70th percentile on the Anxious/Depressed subscale of the CBCL ($n = 4$) were rejected from the study. This procedure was necessary given evidence that psychophysiology-behavior relations may differ in children with pure CD versus those with comorbid symptoms of anxiety and depression (Beauchaine, Gartner, & Hagen, 2000). Potential control group participants were rejected if they met DSM-IV criteria for any disorder, or if they scored above the 60th percentile on any CBCL scale. In total, 256 parents were interviewed. Parents whose sons qualified for the study were invited for a lab visit that included the procedure outlined below. Each family was paid $40 for participating. To eliminate possible medication effects on the psychophysiological variables, parents were asked to discontinue administering stimulants to their children 48 hours prior to their visit. Mean ages of participants were 13.1 ($SD = 1.2$) for the ADHD group, 14.0 ($SD = 1.6$) for the CD/ADHD group, and 13.2 ($SD = 1.3$) for the control group. These age differences were not significant. Descriptive statistics outlining CBCL and ASI scores by group are reported in Beauchaine et al. (2001).

Task

During the lab visit, patterns of cardiac activity were monitored at baseline and during conditions of reward for and extinction of repetitive responding. The task employed was nearly identical to that described by Iaboni, Douglas, and Ditto (1997). After psychophysiological measures were collected during the last 2 min of a 5-min baseline, participants were presented with large, single digit odd numbers (i.e., 1, 3, 5, 7, or 9) on a video monitor mounted at eye level. Numbers were presented in random order, and participants were required to depress the matching digit on a 10-key pad mounted on a platform in front of them. Thus, only hand movement was required to depress digits. Participants then depressed the enter key located on the 10-key pad to initiate presentation of the next stimulus. After a 2-min practice epoch, the task was performed across six 2-min blocks, each separated by a 2.5-min rest period. As outlined by Iaboni et al. (1997), four of these blocks were 2-min reward trials in which signal tones and three-cent incentives accompanied correct responses. The remaining two blocks included 30-s of reward and 90-s of extinction during which monetary incentives and signal tones were omitted. Throughout the task, a running total of money earned was presented in the upper right corner of the computer monitor. For purposes of this study, only the pure 2-min. reward blocks (4) and the 90-s extinction portions of the mixed reward and extinction blocks (2) were analyzed. The 30-s reward portions of the mixed blocks were omitted because this epoch length is too short for assessment of stimulus-induced changes in SNS-linked cardiac activity. Such changes are characterized by a slower onset, longer delay to peak, and slower recovery than PNS-linked changes, which are nearly instantaneous (see Berntson et al., 1997). Analyzing the 30-s epochs could therefore work against finding SNS-linked changes in cardiac activity. Thus, data reported here are averaged across the four 2-min reward trials, and across the two 90-s extinction trials.

The Iaboni et al. (1997) task was chosen because it separates reward and extinction trials. As noted above, other tasks represented in the literature mix cues for reward and extinction within trials (e.g., Newman, Patterson, & Kosson, 1987), and therefore do not provide for disentanglement of incentive- and extinction-specific patterns of psychophysiological responding. In addition, in previous research the Iaboni et al. task has elicited group differences in psychophysiological responding, but not in response speed. This is important because differences in metabolic activity associated with variations in response speed could influence the criterion measures systematically, producing spurious effects.

Measures

Pre-Ejection Period (PEP)

Sympathetic influences on HR were assessed using impedance cardiography. This technique allows for extraction of PEP, or the time interval between the onset of left ventricular depolarization and ejection of blood into the aorta. The specificity of PEP as an index of beta-adrenergic (sympathetic) activity has been established via pharmacologic blockade, with shorter intervals representing greater SNS influence (see Sherwood et al., 1986). Electrocardiographic (ECG) and impedancecardiographic (ICG) signals were obtained using a Minnesota Impedance Cardiograph, model 304B. Pre-ejection period was defined as the time interval between the ECG Q-wave and the dZ/dt B-wave. The ECG and ICG waveforms were sampled at 1kHz using tetrapolar aluminum/mylar tape electrodes, which were placed around the upper neck and abdomen according to established guidelines (Sherwood et al., 1990). Transthoracic impedance (Z_0) and the first derivative of changes in transthoracic impedance (dZ/dt) were recorded and saved for later scoring. Digitized ECG and ICG signals were ensemble-averaged in 30 s epochs (see Kelsey et al., 1997). PEP and RSA values were then averaged across epochs within each trial. Artifactual cardiac cycles were edited by the author and excluded from ensemble averaging.

Respiratory Sinus Arrhythmia (RSA)

Parasympathetic influences on cardiac activity were assessed using spectral analysis (see Berntson et al., 1997). This involves the use of fast-Fourier transformations to decompose the ECG R-wave time series into component HR variability frequencies. Results are expressed in a spectral density function, which specifies the amount of spectral power within given frequency bands. Parasympathetic influences on HR were estimated by the amount of spectral power above 0.15 Hz (Berntson et al., 1997). These high frequency spectral densities were calculated from the ECG within each trial, using a software package developed by Richard Sloan and colleagues at Columbia University. All RSA values were normalized through log transformations. Heart rates were also extracted from the ECG signal.

RESULTS

Task Responding

Correct and incorrect responses during reward and extinction are presented in Table 1, averaged across trials. No group differences were observed in response speed, amount of money earned, correct responses, or incorrect responses. Thus, differences in psychophysiological responding during the task cannot be attributed to differences in metabolic demands.

Table 1. Task Performance Averaged Across Reward and Extinction Trials

	Correct responses per minute			Incorrect responses per minute		
	CD	ADHD	Control	CD	ADHD	Control
Condition	M(SD)	M(SD)	M(SD)	M(SD)	M(SD)	M(SD)
Reward	57.5 (9.6)	53.8 (9.2)	59.1 (10.8)	9.0 (9.3)	4.1 (3.5)	8.7 (8.2)
Extinction	60.0 (12.4)	54.7 (10.5)	61.4 (13.6)	8.7 (9.1)	6.6 (6.9)	11.9 (13.6)

Note. All figures are averaged across the 2-min reward trials (4) and the 90-s extinction trials (2). ADHD = attention-deficit/hyperactivity disorder; CD = conduct disorder.

Heart Rate

Heart rate during the last two minutes of the 5-min baseline is reported by group in the leftmost column of Table 2. A one-way ANOVA yielded no group differences in resting HR, $F_{(2,56)} = .92$, $p = .40$, $\eta^2 = .03$. Heart rate reactivity in response to reward was assessed with a 3 (group) × 4 (reward trials) repeated measures ANOVA in which change scores from baseline were entered. The trials and group × trials interaction effects, which were computed using Greenhouse-Geisser-adjusted degrees of freedom to correct for departures from sphericity, were both non-significant. Mean HRs during reward are thus collapsed across trials in the middle column of Table 2. A significant group effect was uncovered, $F_{(2,56)} = 3.41$, $p = .04$, $\eta^2 = .11$. Post hoc comparisons using the Tukey HSD test indicated greater HR reactivity among control participants than among ADHD participants ($p = .03$). Although HR reactivity among controls also exceeded that among CD/ADHD participants, the group difference was not significant. However, single degree of freedom contrasts indicated that all groups exhibited HR accelerations that were significantly greater than zero during reward, all $Fs > 16.29$, all $ps < .001$.

**Table 2. Heart Rate Values by Group at
Baseline, During Reward, and During Extinction**

	Heart Rate (bpm)		
Group	Baseline	Reward	Extinction
CD/ADHD	80.5 (12.5)	90.3 (11.1)	87.7 (11.0)
ADHD	80.9 (7.9)	87.1 (8.4)	85.1 (8.0)
Control	76.9 (9.6)	88.6 (11.7)	85.3 (10.8)

Note. ADHD = attention deficit/hyperactivity disorder; CD/ADHD = conduct disorder and ADHD. All values are expressed in the form M(SD). Entries in the reward and extinction columns are averaged across trials.

Heart rate reactivity during extinction was assessed with a 3 (group) × 2 (reward trials) repeated measures ANOVA in which change scores from baseline were entered. The group, trials, and group × trials interaction effects were all non-significant. Thus, mean HRs during extinction are collapsed across trials in the rightmost column of Table 2. Single degree of freedom contrasts indicated that all groups exhibited significant HR accelerations during extinction, all $Fs > 8.94$, all $ps < .005$. To compare heart rate reactivity during reward vs. extinction, a 3 (group) × 6 (4 reward, 2 extinction) repeated measures ANOVA was conducted. A significant trials effect was uncovered, $F_{(5,280)} = 14.79$, $p < .001$, $\epsilon = 0.59$). A follow-up contrast analysis indicated that HR accelerations during reward were significantly greater than HR accelerations during extinction, $F_{(1,56)} = 36.83$, $p < .001$.

Autonomic Origins of Heart Rate Reactivity

Mean PEP and RSA values are reported at baseline, and collapsed across reward and extinction trials in Table 3. The significance of group differences at rest and during extinction has been reported in detail elsewhere (Beauchaine et al., 2001). In summary, CD/ADHD participants exhibited longer PEPs at baseline and during task responding, suggesting reduced SNS-linked cardiac activity. In addition, CD/ADHD participants exhibited significantly less PEP reactivity (i.e., PEP shortening) during reward than control participants. No other group differences were significant.

Table 3. Pre-Ejection Period and Respiratory Sinus Arrhythmia at Baseline, During Reward, and During Extinction

| | PEP (ms) | | | RSA ($\log[\text{beats/min}^2/\text{Hz}]$) | | |
	Baseline	Reward	Extinction	Baseline	Reward	Extinction
CD/ADHD	97.2 (8.9)	98.2 (12.1)	99.5 (11.2)	6.4 (1.5)	4.9 (1.2)	5.1 (1.2)
ADHD	88.9 (10.9)	86.9 (11.9)	90.2 (10.8)	6.7 (1.0)	5.6 (1.0)	5.8 (.97)
Control	90.7 (14.9)	86.2 (16.1)	89.5 (15.2)	7.3 (1.1)	5.8 (1.2)	6.1 (1.2)

Note. ADHD = attention deficit/hyperactivity disorder; CD/ADHD = conduct disorder and ADHD; PEP = pre-ejection period; RSA = respiratory sinus arrhythmia. All values are expressed in the form *M(SD)*. Entries in the reward and extinction columns are averaged across trials.

To assess the autonomic origins of HR reactivity to reward and extinction, which have not been reported previously, partial correlation coefficients were computed between changes in HR from baseline to reward and concurrent changes in both RSA and PEP. For example, independent SNS influences on HR reactivity were assessed by calculating the correlation between HR change and PEP change, controlling for changes in spectral power. These correlations are reported in Table 4, averaged across reward and extinction trials. Correlations were calculated using both raw and residualized change scores. Because the chronotropic effects of SNS and PNS activation are known to be positive and negative, respectively, all reported *p*-values are one-tailed. Heart rate increases during both reward and extinction were related inversely to RSA for all groups, and were thus mediated in large part by vagal withdrawal. None of the HR-RSA partial correlations differed significantly across groups.

Findings regarding PEP change were more complex. During reward, changes in PEP were related to HR accelerations for the ADHD and control groups. As expected, these correlations were negative, indicating that HR accelerations for ADHD and control participants were driven in part by shortened PEP, marking increased SNS activity. Thus, both autonomic branches contributed independently to heart accelerations for the ADHD and control groups during reward. For CD/ADHD participants, small and positive partial correlations were observed between HR change and PEP change during reward. Thus, HR reactivity to reward in this group was mediated by vagal withdrawal, with no independent contribution from the SNS. Moreover, group differences between the CD/ADHD group and both the ADHD and control groups in HR-PEP partial correlations were significant ($ps < .05$).

Table 4. Partial Correlations between Changes in Heart Rate and Changes in PEP and RSA During Repetitive Responding for Reward

Condition	ΔPEP controlling for ΔRSA			ΔRSA controlling for ΔPEP		
	ADHD	CD/ADHD	Control	ADHD	CD/ADHD	Control
Reward	-.48*$_a$	.13$_b$	-.41*$_a$	-.65**	-.55**	-.60**
	(-.58**)$_a$	(.14)$_b$	(-.39*)$_a$	(-.70**)	(-.55**)	(-.61**)
Extinction	-.40*$_a$	.31$_b$	-.09$_{a,b}$	-.60**	-.61**	-.66**
	(-.42*)$_a$	(.31)$_b$	(-.08)$_{a,b}$	(-.59**)	(-.59**)	(-.64**)

Note. ADHD = attention deficit/hyperactivity disorder; CD/ADHD = conduct disorder and ADHD; PEP = pre-ejection period; RSA = respiratory sinus arrhythmia. All entries represent averaged correlations calculated across reward and extinction trials. Entries in the PEP change columns represent partial correlations with heart rate change, controlling for changes in RSA. Entries in the RSA change columns represent partial correlations with heart rate change, controlling for changes in PEP. Parenthesized entries were calculated using residualized change scores. Reported significance levels are one-tailed. Correlations with different subscripts differ significantly at $p < .05$.
*$p \le .05$. ** $p \le .01$.

During extinction, heart rate changes among ADHD participants were mediated by both autonomic nervous system branches, which was not the case for either the CD/ADHD or the control groups. Although not significant, the partial correlation between PEP change and HR change was again positive for CD/ADHD participants. Group comparisons of HR-PEP partial correlations during extinction indicated significant differences only between the CD/ADHD and the ADHD groups ($p < .05$).

DISCUSSION

The first hypothesis outlined in the introduction of this article was that SNS mediation of HR reactivity would be absent or attenuated in CD participants, reflecting insensitivity to reward. The second was that SNS-linked cardiac reactivity during reward would be more effective than HR reactivity in differentiating CD/ADHD participants from the other groups. Both of these hypotheses were supported. Contrary to predictions derived from reward dominance hypotheses of aggression (Fowles, 1980, 1988; Quay, 1993), differences in HR reactivity were not observed between the CD and ADHD groups, or between the CD and control groups. In contrast, independent SNS mediation of HR reactivity, which was observed in both the ADHD and control groups, was absent in the CD/ADHD group. These findings are more consistent with sensation seeking models of aggression than with models suggesting excessive reward system activity. Thus, CD/ADHD participants were characterized by SNS insensitivity to reward. Future research might examine whether independent PEP reactivity can be elicited in CD probands using larger incentives, as the stimulation seeking hypothesis predicts.

Because a pure ADHD group was included, findings of reduced PEP reactivity cannot be attributed to disinhibition, which characterizes both CD and ADHD samples (see Beauchaine, 2001). Rather, reduced PEP reactivity during reward was restricted to the CD/ADHD group, marking their aggressive tendencies. Such findings suggest that a lack of PEP reactivity may be a more specific indicator of aggression than are other psychophysiological markers. Attenuated electrodermal responding, for example, is observed among both CD and ADHD groups (Beauchaine et al., 2001).

This is the first study in which the autonomic origins of HR reactivity have been examined in aggressive and/or ADHD probands. Strengths of the study include carefully selected diagnostic groups, both ADHD and normal control groups, and the use of PEP, which has not been used previously with these populations. Given this, and given the modest sample sizes, future replications should be pursued.

One finding that deserves elaboration is the lack of baseline differences in HR between aggressive CD/ADHD participants and controls, which runs contrary to other findings reported in the literature (e.g., Mezzacappa et al., 1997; Raine, Venables, & Mednick, 1997; Raine, Venables, Williams, 1990). This is especially noteworthy given that the CD/ADHD group was selected for characteristics that mark significant risk for future psychopathy (Lynam, 1996). However, while it is often suggested that reduced resting HR is a robust marker of psychopathy and aggression, such findings are not as consistent as is often supposed. In a recent meta analysis of 41 studies in which HR was compared between aggressive participants and controls, Lorber (2002) noted that the aggregated effect size is small by Cohen's (1988) standards. Moreover, results from 18 (44%) of the studies suggested either no difference across groups, or resting HRs in aggressive participants that *exceeded* resting HRs among controls. These findings were not accounted for by diagnostic heterogeneity, as similar effect sizes were obtained when the studies were grouped according antisocial, conduct problem, and psychopathic characteristics of participants. We have reported elsewhere that reduced resting PEP differentiates aggressive CD participants from controls (Beauchaine et al., 2001), even in the absence of differences in HR. Thus, resting PEP may be a more sensitive marker of aggression than resting HR, although replications will be required to verify this supposition.

It should also be noted that partialling out the effect of one autonomic nervous system branch to isolate the independent effects of the other is not without interpretive caveats. It has been known for some time, for example, that the effects of sympathetic activation on HR are reduced at high levels of parasympathetic activation (e.g., Levy & Zieske, 1969). Thus, group differences in PNS-linked cardiac activity could result in spurious effects of SNS-linked HR changes. This is unlikely to be a problem in the present study, however, since the CD/ADHD group was characterized by less PNS activity than controls, both at baseline and during task responding. Thus, the finding of less SNS-linked HR reactivity cannot be attributed to higher PNS activation among CD/ADHD participants.

Finally, factors other than those assessed in this study contribute to HR regulation. These include baroreceptor reflexes, ventricular receptor reflexes, and hormonal influences, among others. While group differences in these factors cannot be ruled out, any such effects do not diminish the absence of SNS-mediated HR acceleration in response to reward among aggressive CD adolescents. It is hoped that future research will further elucidate the motivational and autonomic substrates of disinhibition and aggression.

REFERENCES

Achenbach, T. M. (1991). *Manual for the Child Behavior Checklist/4-18 and 1991 Profile.* Burlington VT: University of Vermont Department of Psychiatry.

American Psychiatric Association. (1994). *Diagnostic and statistical manual of mental disorders* (4th ed.). Washington, DC: Author.

Ashby, F. G., Isen, A. M., & Turken, A. U. (1999). A neuropsychological theory of positive affect and its influence on cognition. *Psychological Review, 106*, 529-550.

Beauchaine, T. P. (2001). Vagal tone, development, and Gray's motivational theory: Toward an integrated model of autonomic nervous system functioning in psychopathology. *Development and Psychopathology, 13*, 183-214.

Beauchaine, T. P., Gartner, J. G., & Hagen, B. (2000). Comorbid depression and heart rate variability as predictors of aggressive and hyperactive symptom responsiveness during inpatient treatment of conduct-disordered, ADHD boys. *Aggressive Behavior, 26*, 425-441.

Beauchaine, T. P., Katkin, E. S., Strassberg, Z., & Snarr, J. (2001). Disinhibitory psychopathology in male adolescents: Discriminating conduct disorder from attention-deficit/hyperactivity disorder through concurrent assessment of multiple autonomic states. *Journal of Abnormal Psychology, 110*, 610-624.

Brownley, K. A., Hurwitz, B. E., & Schneiderman, N. (2000). Cardiovascular psychophysiology. In J. T. Cacioppo, L. G. Tassinary, & G. G. Berntson (Eds.), *Handbook of psychophysiology* (2nd ed., pp. 224-264). Cambridge: Cambridge University Press.

Berntson, G. G., Bigger, T. J., Eckberg, D. L., Grossman, P., Kaufmann, P. G., Malik, M., Nagaraja, H. N., Porges, S. W., Saul, J. P., Stone, P. H., & van der Molen, M. W. (1997). Heart rate variability: Origins, methods, and interpretive caveats. *Psychophysiology, 34*, 623-648.

Cohen, J. (1988). *Statistical power analysis for the behavioral sciences* (2nd ed.). New York: Academic Press.

Daughtery, T. K., & Quay, H. C. (1991). Response perseveration and delayed responding in childhood behavior disorders. *Journal of Child Psychiatry and Psychology, 32*, 453-461.

Davidson, R. J. (1994). Asymmetric brain function, affective style, and psychopathology: The role of early experience and plasticity. *Development and Psychopathology, 6*, 741-758.

Davidson, R. J. (2000). Affective style, mood, and anxiety disorders. In R. J. Davidson (Ed.), *Anxiety, depression, and emotion.* New York: Oxford University Press.

Eysenck, H. J., & Gudjonsson, G. H. (1989). *The causes and cures of criminality.* New York: Plenum.

Fowles, D. C. (1980). The three arousal model: Implications of Gray's two-factor learning theory for heart rate, electrodermal activity, and psychopathy. *Psychophysiology, 17*, 87-104.

Fowles, D. C. (1988). Psychophysiology and psychopathology: A motivational approach. *Psychophysiology, 25*, 373-391.

Gadow, K. D., & Sprafkin, J. (1997). Adolescent symptom inventory 4 screening manual. Stony Brook, New York: Checkmate Plus.

Gray, J. A. (1982a). The neuropsychology of anxiety: An enquiry into the function of the septo-hippocampal system. New York: Oxford University Press.

Gray, J. A. (1982b). Precis of the neuropsychology of anxiety: An enquiry into the functions of the septo-hippocamplal system. *The Behavioral and Brain Sciences, 5*, 469-534.

Gray, J. A. (1987a). Perspectives on anxiety and impulsivity: A commentary. *Journal of Research in Personality, 21*, 493-509.

Gray, J. A. (1987b). *The psychology of fear and stress*. New York: Cambridge University Press.

Gray, J. A., & McNaughton, N. (1996). The neuropsychology of anxiety: Reprise. In D. A. Hope (Ed.), *Nebraska Symposium on Motivation, 1995: Perspectives on anxiety, panic,*

Gray, J. A., & McNaughton, N. (2000). The neuropsychology of anxiety (2nd ed.). New York: Oxford University Press.

Haenlein, M., & Caul, W. F. (1987). Attention deficit disorder with hyperactivity: A specific Hypothesis of Reward Dysfunction. *Journal of The American Academy of Child and Adolescent Psychiatry, 26*, 356-362.

Iaboni, F., Douglas, V. I., & Ditto, B. (1997). Psychophysiological response of ADHD children to reward and extinction. *Psychophysiology, 34*, 1997.

Kelsey, R. M., Reiff, S., Wiens, S., Schneider, T. R., Mezzacappa, E. S., & Guethlein, W. (1997). The ensemble-averaged impedance cardiogram: An evaluation of scoring methods and interrater reliability. *Psychophysiology, 35*, 1-4.

Klein, R. G., Abikoff, H., Klass, E., Ganeles, D., Seese, L. M., & Pollack, S. (1997). Clinical efficacy of methylphenidate in conduct disorder with and without attention deficit hyperactivity disorder. *Archives of General Psychiatry, 54*, 1073-1080.

Lorber, M. (2002). The psychophysiology of aggression, psychopathy, antisocial personality characteristics, and conduct problems: A meta-analysis. Manuscript submitted for publication.

Levy, M. N., & Zieske, H. (1969). Autonomic control of cardiac pacemaker activity and atrioventricular transmission. *Journal of Applied Physiology*, 27, 465-470.

Lynam, D. R. (1996). The early identification of chronic offenders: Who is the fledgling psychopath? *Psychological Bulletin, 120*, 209-234.

Matthys, W., van Goozen, S. H. M., de Vries, H., Cohen-Kettenis, P. T., & van Engeland, H. (1998). The dominance of behavioral activation over behavioral inhibition in conduct disordered boys with or without attention deficit hyperactivity disorder. *Journal of Child Psychology and Psychiatry, 39*, 643-651.

Mezzacappa, E., Tremblay, R. E., Kindlon, D., Saul, J. P., Arseneault, L., Seguin, J., Pihl, R. O., & Earls, F. (1997). Anxiety, antisocial behavior, and heart rate regulation in adolescent males. *Journal of Child Psychology and Psychiatry, 38*, 457-469.

Milich, R., Hartung, C. M., Martin, C. A., & Haigler, E. D. (1994). Behavioral disinhibition and underlying processes in adolescents with disruptive behavior disorders, In D. K. Routh (Ed.), *Disruptive behavior disorders in childhood*. New York: Plenum.

Nadir, K., Bechara, A., & van der Kooy, D. (1997). Neurobiological constraints on behavioral models of motivation. *Annual Review of Psychology, 48*, 85-114.

Newman J. P., Patterson, C. M., & Kosson, D. S. (1987). Response perseveration in psychopaths. *Journal of Abnormal Psychology, 96*, 145-148.

Quay, H. C. (1988). Attention deficit disorder and the behavioral inhibition system: The relevance of the neuropsychological theory of Jeffrey A. Gray. In L. Bloomingdale & J.

Sergeant (Eds.) *Attention deficit disorders: Criteria, cognition, and intervention* (pp. 117-125). New York: Pergamon.

Quay, H. C. (1993). The psychobiology of undersocialized aggressive conduct disorder: A theoretical perspective. *Development and Psychopathology, 5,* 165-180.

Quay, H. C. (1997). Inhibition and attention deficit hyperactivity disorder. *Journal of Abnormal Child Psychology, 25,* 7-13.

Porges, S. W. (1995). Orienting in a defensive world: Mammalian modifications of our evolutionary heritage. A polyvagal theory. *Psychophysiology, 32,* 301-318.

Raine, A., Venables, P. H., & Mednick, S. A. (1997). Low resting heart rate at age 3 years predisposes to aggression at age 11 years: Evidence from the Mauritius Child Health Project. *Journal of the American Academy of Child and Adolescent Psychiatry, 36,* 1457-1464.

Raine, A., Venables, P. H., & Williams, M. (1990). Relationships between central and autonomic measures of arousal at age 15 and criminality at age 24 years. *Archives of General Psychiatry, 47,* 1003-1007.

Shapiro, S. K., Quay H. C., Hogan, A. E., & Schwartz, K. P. (1988). Response perseveration and delayed responding in undersocialized aggressive conduct disorder. *Journal of Abnormal Psychology, 97,* 371-373.

Sherwood, A., Allen, M. T., Obrist, P. A., & Langer, A. W. (1986). Evaluation of beta-adrenergic influences on cardiovascular and metabolic adjustments to physical and psychological stress. *Psychophysiology, 23,* 89-104.

Sherwood, A., Allen, M. T., Fahrenberg, J., Kelsey, R. M., Lovallo, W. R., & van Doornen, L. J. P. (1990). Committee report: Methodological guidelines for impedance cardiography. *Psychophysiology, 27,* 1-23.

Chapter 8

COUNTING IN MENTALLY RETARDED ADOLESCENTS

V. Camos[*] and F. Freeman

Université René Descartes – Paris V

ABSTRACT

Counting is an important everyday skill, especially because it is the root of all arithmetic activities. Indeed, the first addition problems are solved by counting. Every few studies were dedicated to the early arithmetic skills of children with severe intellectual disabilities. Moreover, they usually focused on the conceptual understanding underlying the arithmetic activities with few considerations on the performances and their variations across tasks. In this study, we examined the counting ability of small arrays (1 to 7 objects) in mentally retarded adolescents through 4 different tasks (i.e., counting of dots, counting up to n, counting of objects and choice of cards). We compared adolescents to a group of nursery school pupils of similar mental age. The results obtained in the various counting situations show a higher rate of errors and also a greater use of manual pointing in mentally retarded subjects. These observations lead us to examine the effective subitizing ability of mentally retarded subjects. Moreover, because the role of gesture was recently re-examined in the development of counting in preschoolers (Alibali & DiRusso, 1999; Graham, 1999), we will discuss the importance of manual pointing for the mentally retarded population.

Key words: Mental Retardation, Counting, Subitizing, Manual Pointing

According to Halford (1993), it is inconceivable to develop the concept of number in a meaningful way in the absence of the quantification processes because it is impossible without them to assign numeric values to collections, investigate the size relations between collections or determine any of the complex relations that exist between numbers. The quantification processes are therefore fundamental. They consist of determining the

[*] Correspondence concerning this article should be addressed to: Valérie Camos, Laboratoire Cognition et Développement – CNRS, Université René Descartes - Paris 5, Institut de Psychologie, 71, avenue Edouard Vaillant, 92774 Boulogne-Billancourt Cedex, France, *Email*: camos@psycho.univ-paris5.fr

numerosity of a set of objects. We distinguish between three quantification processes: counting, subitizing and estimation (Klahr, 1973; Klahr & Wallace, 1976; for a summary of the literature, see Dehaene, 1992, 1997; Fayol, 1985, 1990; Geary, 1994; Nunes & Bryant, 1996).

COUNTING

Counting is the quantification process that has been the most thoroughly studied. It is often considered to underpin all other arithmetical learning. Indeed, as Grégoire and van Nieuwenhoven (1995) pointed out, counting produces the evidence that permits the empirical verification of the validity of reasoning, for example in a conservation task (Mc Evoy & O'Moore, 1991) or in arithmetic problem solving (Groen & Parkman, 1972; Svenson, 1975).

Even though most researchers agree that there is a certain sensitivity to discrete quantities from birth on (Briars & Siegler, 1984; Fuson, 1988; Gallistel & Gelman, 1992; Gelman & Gallistel, 1978; Resnick, 1986; Wynn, 1990), they do not all accord the same level of importance to innate capacities when compared to the effect of practice. Indeed, when we consider the emergence of counting during childhood, we find two opposing theoretical viewpoints, namely the so-called "principles-first" and "principles-after" theories.

The principles-first theory (Gelman & Gallistel, 1978) holds that the principles guiding counting are innate (Starkey, Spelke & Gelman, 1991), a view that seems to find confirmation in studies that use the habituation paradigm (Cooper, 1984). Such principles are considered to exist in children even before they have any experience of counting. They would allow children to identify counting activities as what they are rather than of activities that are devoid of meaning, as well as to acquire and control their own counting procedures. Gelman and Gallistel (1978) identified five principles: the one-to-one principle according to which each element in the collection that is to be counted is associated with a single label; the stable-order principle in which the successive labels constitute an ordered list, a fixed sequence; the cardinal principle that holds that the last label used represents the cardinal value of the collection; the abstraction principle whereby the heterogeneity (vs homogeneity) of the elements in the collection has no effect on the way they are counted; and the order-irrelevance principle according to which the order in which the elements in the collection are counted has no effect on the cardinality of the collection.

According to this model, children have an implicit knowledge of the, similar to their implicit knowledge of the grammar of a language (Chomsky, 1957). This knowledge constrains their action and enables them to recognise legitimate procedures in the same way that knowledge of a grammar makes it possible to recognise legitimate sentences in a language even if you have never heard them before (Gelman & Greeno, 1989). Gelman and Gallistel (1978) saw a second parallel between linguistic and mathematical knowledge. In the same way that grammar makes it possible to produce an infinite number of new sentences (generative grammar), a knowledge of the principles permits the generation of counting strategies that are adapted to different types of task.

In counting as defined by Gelman and Gallistel (1978), the labels must - if they are to be useable - simply constitute an ordered list (stable order principle). Thus, given this definition, counting using an idiosyncratic list such as "one, two, six, three, eight" can be considered perfectly successful. It should also be noted that this success does not necessitate the use of number-words since the labels can be non-verbal. Counting can be based on the use of the hand or different parts of the body to represent numerosity as is observed in certain tribes in Papua-New Guinea (Saxe, 1981; Saxe & Posner, 1983).

For Gallistel & Gelman (1992), counting skill is not linguistic. This numerical skill is therefore thought to be accessible to animals and very young children. Indeed, many studies have shown that animals are capable of some numerical processing (Boysen & Berntson, 1989; Davis & Pérusse, 1988; Gallistel, 1990; Gallistel & Gelman, 1992; Matsuzawa, 1985; Meck & Church, 1983). For example, a chimpanzee was trained to choose the Arabic numeral corresponding to the cardinal value of a collection of 1 to 6 objects (Matsuzawa, 1985). Meck and Church (1983) conditioned a rat to press one lever in response to a sequence of 2 beeps and another in response to a sequence of 8 beeps. By varying the interval separating the beeps, the authors were able to show that the rats relied exclusively on numerosity to perform the task. However, the variability in the representation of numerosity increased with the size of the presented collection, thus suggesting that an imprecise quantification procedure is used. In their model of animal counting, Meck and Church (1983) postulated that numbers are represented by the continuous states of an accumulator. Thus, the end state of the accumulator is correlated with the numerosity but the representation is not very precise because the added quantity is not fixed. Unlike the slow, verbal counting practised by human beings, this model endows animals with a fast, mechanical procedure. (Dehaene, 1997). Gallistel and Gelman (1992) suggested that young children might possess a similar pre-verbal mechanism before acquisition of the verbal number system.

Beyond performance itself, a very large number of studies have attempted to identify the skills involved, thus re-igniting the competence/performance opposition. Attention has focused not so much on what children do but on what they might be able to do. Indeed, as Gelman & Gallistel (1978) have stated, if counting were merely a simple skill then would not be able to adapt it to situations other than those in which it was acquired. In contrast, if children have a knowledge of the underlying principles they will be able to apply counting to new situations.

In contrast to this principles-first theory, the principles-after theory postulates that principles are gradually abstracted through the repeated practice of counting procedures that are acquired through imitation (Briars & Siegler, 1984; Fuson, 1988; Fuson & Hall, 1983). In this view, counting is initially a purposeless activity or routine, with children only gradually learning how it is related to cardinality (Fuson, 1988; Wynn, 1990). This conception does not deny that children are sensitive to number as of birth. It is this sensitivity on which their arithmetical learning is constructed, but it does not serve as the structure for it as is the case in the principles-first theory. Here, the link between counting and cardinality is thought to have its origins in subitizing. Studies using the habituation paradigm showed that young children can detect differences between two numerosities that fall within the subitizing range (1 to 4 objects) but not between numerosities outside of this range (Starkey & Cooper, 1980; Starkey, Spelke & Gelman, 1990; Strauss & Curtis, 1984). Very young children would therefore seem to have a certain sensitivity to number which allows them to succeed in this type of task. They would even appear able to "subitize" (i.e. globally perceive) the cardinal value of small collections even before they can count (Shipley & Shepperson, 1990; Wagner & Walters, 1982). Klahr and Wallace (1976) have suggested that by applying a counting routine (which is not initially meaningful) to collections that can be subitized, children might associate the last spoken number-word with the cardinal value obtained by subitizing and in this way acquire the principle of cardinality. The conceptual knowledge of counting would derive from the regularities that children might be able to extract from their counting activity (Briars & Siegler, 1984).

Subitizing would therefore play an important role in the acquisition of arithmetic concepts (i.e., the acquisition of cardinality) and would be linked to counting. However, its status is still a matter of debate and some authors go as far as to deny its existence (Gallistel, 1988) while it is affirmed by others (Davis & Pérusse, 1988).

SUBITIZING

In some experiments investigating judgements of numerosity, adults have to determine the number of presented objects as quickly and accurately as possible. If the adults are counting then the response time should increase as a linear function of the size of the collection. However, this linear relation between response time and numerosity has only been evidenced for certain numerosities. Mandler and Shebo (1982) have observed a linear increase in time of approximately 300 ms per object when collections exceed 4-6 objects. For numerosities of 1-3, the times were short and increased only slightly with the number of objects. For numerosities greater than 7, the response times were approximately constant but the accuracy of the responses fell sharply. These results suggest that counting is only used for numerosities from 4 to 6 (Chi & Klahr, 1975; Mandler & Shebo, 1982). The term "subitizing" designates the process responsible for the rapid responses on small numerosities (Kaufman, Lord, Reese & Volkmann, 1949), and the term "estimation" the process that is preferentially used for large collections. Within this perspective, subitizing is a rapid and reliable perceptual process for the immediate apprehension of numerosity (Kaufman et al., 1949).

Gallistel and Gelman (1991, 1992) adopted a radical point of view according to which subitizing is nothing other than very fast counting using non-verbal labels. Subitizing is therefore considered to be only a primitive form of counting (Gelman & Gallistel, 1978). If we again consider Meck and Church's model (1983), these authors suggested that human beings also possess a counting method similar to that of animals and that is very fast but imprecise (see also Wynn, 1992b). Because response variability increases with numerosity, the response will only be accurate for small numerosities (from 1 to 4). Moreover, the fact that the response times are not constant across the range 1-4 but increase from 1 to 2 and from 2 to 3 (Chi & Klahr, 1975; Mandler & Shebo, 1982; Folk, Egeth & Kwak, 1988) suggests that we are indeed in the presence of a counting procedure.

Mandler and Shebo (1982) proposed an alternative model of subitizing based on the recognition of canonical configurations or perceptual patterns (Von Glaserfeld, 1982; Wolters, Kempen & Wijhuisen, 1987). In the case of small collections, the arrangement of the objects is unvarying or forms canonical spatial configurations that can be recognized in parallel: 1 = a dot, 2 = a line, 3 = a triangle. The visual system might, for example, recognize ternary values on the basis of a triangular configuration irrespectively of the nature of the objects forming it. In the case of 4, the numerosity might again be determined on the basis of the configuration since four objects can only form two canonical configurations (a quadrilateral or a triangle with a dot inside). Since the number of possible configurations increases with numerosity, this model predicts the moderate increase habitually observed in the response times. Mandler and Shebo (1982) have also shown that the response times for canonical configurations from 1 to 3 do not differ significantly from the times for random arrangements. They concluded that the recognition of canonical configurations is a tool that is usually employed when determining the cardinal value of small collections.

Other results confirmed that subitizing is a pre-attentional visual recognition process. Firstly, it appears only when the target objects are distinguished without effort ("pop-out" phenomenon). When an attentional, serial process is necessary to isolate the targets, for example in feature-conjunction task, subitizing becomes inoperative (Treisman, 1991; Treisman & Gelade, 1980; Treisman & Gormican, 1988; Treisman & Sato, 1990; Trick, 1992; Trick & Pylyshyn, 1993, 1994). Secondly, it only appears to operate if the objects are sufficiently distanced from one another (Atkinson, Campbell and Francis, 1976). Finally, the objects to be subitized must occupy distinct, rapidly identifiable positions within the space. Rectangles or concentric circles cannot be subitized (Trick, 1992; Trick & Pylyshyn, 1993, 1994).

This view, which confers a fundamental role on canonical configurations, can nevertheless be challenged. Subitizing can be observed even when the existence of geometrical configurations is doubtful, for example when the objects are aligned (Atkinson, Francis & Campbell, 1976). Some authors have suggested that the information that is accessible during subitizing is not geometrical but more abstract in nature. According to Trick and Pylyshyn (1993, 1994), subitizing and counting are two effects of the construction of our visual system: they assume there is a parallel (pre-attentional) stage that controls subitizing and a serial (attentional) stage that guides counting. Trick and Pylyshyn (1993, 1994; Trick, 1988) postulated that a limited number of spatial indices, known as FINSTs (i.e., "FINgers of INSTantiation") automatically attach to each object and make it accessible to the visual routines that require attention. In subitizing, individuals simply report the number of FINSTs associated with the objects. However, as Dehaene (1992) pointed out, if the stage involving the assignment of one and only one FINST to each object is accomplished by means of a rapid serial mechanism, then the model becomes equivalent to the model of pre-verbal counting presented by Gallistel and Gelman (1991, 1992).

Other authors have suggested that subitizing is not an independent procedure. Unlike Gelman and Gallistel (1991, 1992), who believe that subitizing involves the use of pre-verbal counting, others hold that it is based on the application of a general estimation process. In one or two seconds, adults can estimate the numerosity of a collection consisting of up to several hundred dots, provided that they have received training (Ginsburg, 1976, 1978; Kaufman et al., 1949; Krueger, 1972, 1982; Mandler & Shebo, 1982; Taves, 1941). The variability of estimation increases with the numerosity (Krueger, 1982). The detection of a difference of 1 between two numerosities is easier with small collections (e.g., 5 vs. 6) than with larger ones (e.g., 8 vs. 9, van Oeffelen & Vos, 1982). The subitizing range is therefore simply the range within which estimation is sufficiently precise to produce only a single candidate. This range is not necessarily constant but may vary with the type and discriminability of the objects involved, thus explaining the differences observed in the subitizing limit.

The existence of subitizing and estimation as distinct counting processes therefore remains a matter of debate.

ESTIMATION

Even if the authors whom we have cited above tend to merge subitizing and estimation, they nevertheless do not explain the process that supports estimation. Mathematical models have been proposed to explain this process (Allik & Tuulmets, 1991; van Oeffelen & Vos, 1982; Vos, van Oeffelen, Tibosch & Allik, 1988). Numerosity is thought to be evaluated on the basis of simple relations between physical quantities: the product of the area of vision multiplied by the object density. Mistakes in the estimation of numerosity might be explained by an incorrect perception of the area occupied by the objects (Allik & Tuulmets, 1991; Frith & Frith, 1972; Vos et al., 1988). Thus, Cuneo (1982) has suggested that children, and even adults, use an erroneous rule (i.e. area + density) rather than the correct one (area x density) to estimate numerosities. This would explain the frequently observed overestimates (Ginsburg, 1976, 1978; Indow & Ida, 1977; Kaufman et al., 1949; Krueger, 1972, 1982; Mandler & Shebo, 1982; Taves, 1941).

Among the various processes of quantification that we have described above, one - counting - would appear to stand out from the others in terms of the volume of research devoted to it and the theoretical importance attributed to it. The two other quantification processes, subitizing and estimation, can apply only to a limited number of phenomena. In addition, they might also themselves be dependent on counting. We shall concentrate more specifically on this latter aspect by studying the counting abilities of mentally deficient adolescents.

THE PRESENT STUDY

Our research was intended to study the numerical abilities of mentally deficient adolescents and, more specifically, their ability to count small collections (from 1 to 7 objects). We used a comparative study with a sample of children with an equivalent mental age (evaluated using the EDEI category analysis scale) to attempt to answer the following questions: when confronted with small collections do mentally deficient subjects count equally well as children of the same mental age? Does the discontinuity in the processes observed in normal children (i.e. subitizing for collections smaller than 4 and counting beyond 4) also appear in mentally deficient subjects?

To answer these questions, we studied the quantification processes in the spontaneous use of numbers during the course of a game that we had created. Four different counting tasks were presented during this game. The first task consisted of counting the dots on a card. The subjects had to memorize the cardinal value in order to subsequently reproduce it when counting squares. This requirement to count to n constituted our second task. The subjects' third task consisted of counting objects. Finally, the subjects had to identify the numerical pattern corresponding to the number of counted objects. We named this final task the "card selection task". These four tasks were designed to allow us to compare the performances of deficient subjects when confronted with various counting situations

The empirical results reported in the literature concerning normal children seem to indicate a distinction between the numerosities from 1 to 4 in which quantification is based on the perception of groups that can be apprehended simultaneously by means of subitizing and other quantities which are determined by counting (Camos, 1999; Chi & Klahr, 1975; Pesenti,

2001). According to Mandler and Shebo (1982), subitizing is the recognition of canonical perceptual patterns, thus making it a highly effective quantification process with an error rate of practically zero. In order to test the effect of canonicity on the subitizing abilities of deficient subjects, we presented them, in our first and fourth tasks, with collections of 1 to 7 objects arranged either in a canonical configuration (i.e., configuration similar to that used on a dice), or a random configuration. We expected to observe the same discontinuity in the use of the procedures in the deficient subjects (subitizing up to 4 and counting beyond 4). This discontinuity should be observable through a change in the error rates, with counting giving rise to more errors than subitizing. Finally, according to Mandler and Shebo (1982), canonical configurations should result in better performances than random configurations. In the latter case, the necessary distinction between the "already-counted" and the "still-to-be-counted" objects should become increasingly difficult as the size of the collection grows (Camos, Barrouillet & Fayol, 2001; Tuholski & Engle, 2001).

Participants

We formed two groups of subjects: an experimental group and a control group. To match our subjects, we used the category activity tasks of the Echelles Différentielles d'Efficiences Intellectuelles (EDEI = Differential Scales of Intellectual Efficiency). This battery of tests is particularly well suited to mentally deficient subjects. It permits a fine discrimination in profound and medium ranges of mental deficiency. It also has the advantage of being suitable for use with normal children and is calibrated for them (from 3 to 11 years).

The experimental group consisted of nine adolescents (three girls and six boys) who were attending a Medical Institution offering manual vocational training. They were aged between 16 and 22 years, but had a mean mental age of 5 years 5 months according to the E.D.E.I. category analysis tests. They were situated either in the lower range of the severe intellectual deficiency or at the upper range of the average intellectual deficiency. They suffered from a variety of pathologies: three subjects suffered from Down's syndrome, three subjects suffered from a mental deficiency due to an impaired X chromosome, one subject exhibited a developmental disharmony associated with psychotic behavioural difficulties, one subject suffered from a global psychological retardation while the final subject exhibited an infantile psychosis.

The control group consisted of 9 children in their final year of nursery school. They had a mean age of 5 years and 5 months with a mental age equivalent to their physical age in the same EDEI tests as were used for the experimental group.

Material and Procedure

The experiment took place over eight sessions at the rate of one session per week. The subjects played in groups of three during either the morning or the afternoon. By alternating the time of the sessions, no group was advantaged by morning learning. The game comprised four phases corresponding to the four tasks defined above. The instructions were formulated clearly and precisely:

"Everyone choose an otter (a counter) and place it on a square where there's a drawing of a little black otter. You take turns. When it's your go, you take a card and move forward the number written on the card. Don't forget, you always start counting at the next square, the one that comes after your otter, not the one that your otter is on (this instruction was accompanied by a demonstration). Next you choose a box that is the same colour as the square you've landed on. The boxes have got fish in them. You have to count them and then point in the board at the card corresponding to the number of fish that you've won. Do you understand? When there are no boxes left, the person with the most fish has won. The first person to go is the one who draws the card with the highest number".

For dot counting, we used uniform white cards of size 10 x 15 cm, on which we had stuck red stickers of diameter 18 mm. We preferred cards to dice because these allowed us to present quantities of up to 7. In this first task, the subject took a card (presented in the middle of the game board) and counted the dots. The cards had been arranged in such a way that the numerosities did not follow the numberline and that the same card was not picked up by two players in succession or twice in succession by the same player.

For counting to n, we used a modified form of snakes and ladders. The path was made up of different coloured boxes and five colours were used in total. To advance along the path, each player had a different coloured counter in the form of an otter. The subjects moved their otters forward the same number squares as the number represented on the card taken in the first task.

For object counting, we made 3-dimensional, blue fish that were one and a half centimetres in length. These fish were placed in white matchboxes each of which had a coloured sticker on it. These boxes were arranged in columns corresponding to the different colours. The subjects had to choose a box that was the same colour as the square they had landed on and then count the fish in the box. Each subject had a container to hold the fish they had.

For card selection, we used cards of the same size as for dot counting (first task) but the stickers were blue like the fish in order to minimize confusion between the number of squares moved (determined by the card chosen in the first task) and the number of fish won. In this final task, the subjects had to turn round to indicate the card representing the number of fish they had just won. The subjects were seated in such a way that they turned their backs on the board so that they could not keep comparing the number of fish won with the cards fixed to the board. In addition, the order of the cards on the board was frequently changed. Seven different orders were displayed on the table during any given session. This was done to prevent subjects from choosing a card by matching a number with a particular location. Furthermore, the orders were designed in such a way that the numbers did not follow the numberline and similar configurations were not located next to one another.

For each of the two tasks that involved cards (i.e., the first and fourth tasks), we formed two different configurations, namely a canonical and a random configuration, for each numerosity. For half of the sessions, each subject played with the cards in their canonical configuration and for half the sessions with randomly configured cards.

Results

We analysed the percentage of errors made on all four counting tasks. In addition to these analyses, we used another criterion for evaluating performance in the dot counting and card selection tasks, i.e. the percentage use of manual pointing. This indicator provides an easy way of evaluating the attentional demands of the task. In effect, the more attentional control the task requires, the more frequently subjects resort to manual pointing (Alibali & Dirusso, 1999; Graham, 1999). Moreover, the use of manual pointing clearly testifies to the application of a counting procedure (Camos, 1999).

1 - Counting Dots on A Card

a/ Error Percentages
The mentally deficient subjects made slightly more errors (5%) than the children of equivalent mental age (3%). Furthermore, there were more errors on random configurations (5%) than canonical configurations (3%). However, these two effects were not significant. In contrast, the error percentage increases with the number of dots presented on the card, $p <$ .001. We should also note that while the result pattern for canonical configurations was very similar in the two groups (i.e., no error up to 4), the mentally deficient subjects started making errors as of size 3 on the random configurations whereas no error appeared until size 6 in the nursery school children.

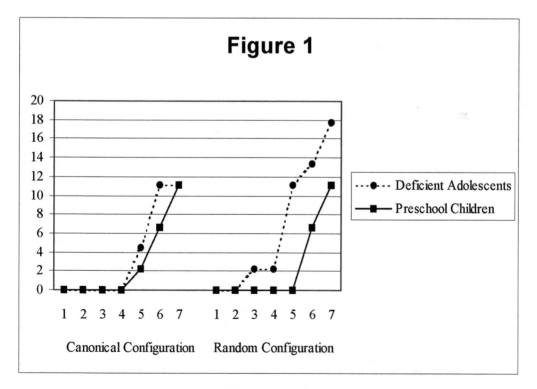

Figure 1: Percentage of errors according to the size and configuration of the collection in mentally deficient adolescents and preschool children when counting dots.

b/ Percentage Use of Manual Pointing

The mentally deficient subjects used manual pointing more frequently (78%) than the nursery school children (41%, $p<.001$). The nursery school children were more sensitive to the configuration of the cards (50% manual pointing for the random configurations vs 33% for the canonical configurations, $p < .05$) than the mentally deficient subjects who made considerable use of manual pointing in both cases (80% vs 75% respectively, $p > .05$). Finally, the effect of collection size on the frequency of manual pointing differed significantly depending on the group and configuration ($p < .001$). Indeed, the percentage of manual pointing in the nursery school children did not differ significantly from 1 to 4 dots in the canonical configuration, whereas it increased significantly between 4 and 7 ($p = .05$). In contrast, in the mentally deficient subjects recourse to manual pointing increased significantly for collections of 1 to 4 in the canonical configuration ($p < .01$). Beyond 4, we observed a ceiling effect with practically 100% manual pointing. In the case of the random configuration, we observed the same result pattern in the mentally deficient subjects with a ceiling effect appearing at 3. For the nursery school children, the result pattern was also very similar to that observed for the canonical configurations. The percentage of manual pointing differed for collections of 3 to 7 in the random configuration ($p < .05$), whereas there was no significant difference for the three other sizes.

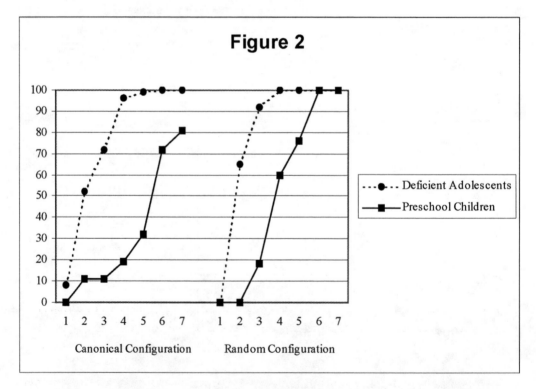

Figure 2: Percentage of manual pointing according to the size and configuration of the collection in mentally deficient adolescents and preschool children when counting dots.

2 - Counting to n

In this second task, the mean percentage of trials containing at least one error includes misrememberings of the cardinal value represented by the card previously taken during the first task, errors in saying the numberline, path errors taking the form of counting the same square twice or skipping a square, incorrect correspondences between recitation of the number-words and the squares, and cases where subjects started to count from the square in which the counter was currently located.

On average, the mentally deficient subjects made twice as many errors (22 %) as the children in the last year of nursery school (11%, $p = .08$). The percentage of trials affected by an error increased significantly with the size of the collection ($p < .001$). The interaction between group and collection size was not significant. However, it should be noted that the nursery school children made almost no errors for collections smaller than 4 whereas errors were observed in the mentally deficient subjects above size 2.

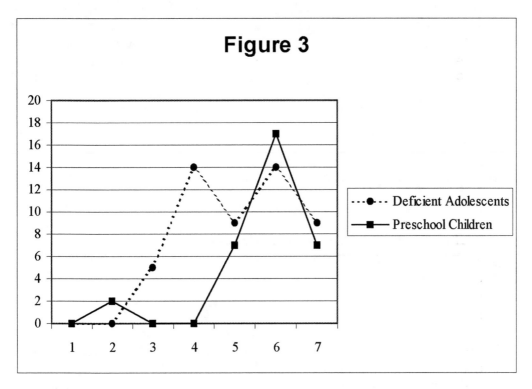

Figure 3: Percentage of errors according to the size of the collection in mentally deficient adolescents and preschool children when counting up to n.

3 - Object Counting

In this third task, errors took the form of a poor correspondence between number-words and objects, omission or double-counting.

On average, the mentally deficient subjects committed more errors (7%) than the nursery school children (6%), $p = .09$. The mean percentage of trials on which an error was observed increased significantly with collection size ($p < .001$). This percentage was larger for quantities between 4 and 7 (9%) than for the first three numbers (0.2%, $p < .001$). This difference between the first three numerosities and the following four was greater in the mentally deficient subjects (1% vs 49%, $p < .001$) than in the normal children (0% vs 32%, $p = .052$). We also observed that errors appeared as of size 3 in the mentally deficient subjects and only as of 4 in the nursery school children.

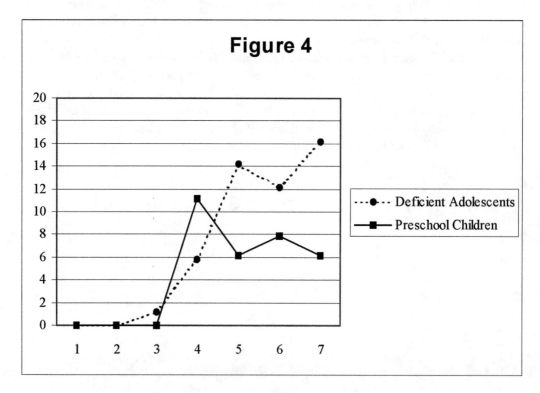

Figure 4: Percentage of errors according to the size of the collection in mentally deficient adolescents and preschool children when counting objects.

4 - Card Selection

We conducted two analyses based on this final task. The first related to the percentage of errors made on the first attempt to choose a card. When the correct card was chosen, the correct response could be the result of subitizing (i.e. when subjects immediately pointed to the correct card without counting and with great confidence in their choice), or of counting with or without manual pointing. In the second analysis, we examined the percentage of counting operations involving manual pointing.

a/ Error Percentages

The nursery school children identified numerosity better (25% errors) than the mentally deficient subjects (34%, $p = .09$). The error percentage increased with the size of the collection ($p < .001$). It was significantly lower for the first three numbers (5%) than for numerosities between 4 and 7 (49%, $p < .001$). The error percentages associated with the three smallest sizes did not differ from each other. In contrast, above 3, these percentages increased significantly ($p < .01$). The collection size effect did not differ significantly as a function of group ($p = .72$). Finally, the effect of configuration differed significantly as a function of collection size ($p < .01$). The error percentages for the two types of configuration differed only for sizes 4 and 5 ($p < .05$), with the canonical configuration resulting in a higher success level.

It should be noted that the error percentage in this card selection task (30%) was much higher than that observed in the three preceding tasks (7%). This difference is due to the specificity of the requested task. In the card selection task, and unlike in the three preceding tasks, the subjects were not explicitly instructed to count the dots. In order to perform this task, they could simply guess which card was right and thus give a random response, thus explaining the increased number of errors.

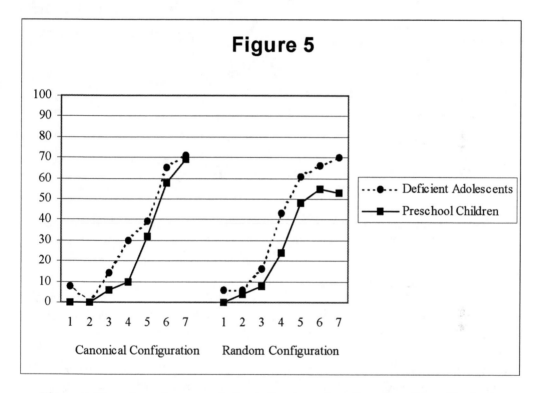

Figure 5: Percentage of errors according to the size and configuration of the collection in mentally deficient adolescents and preschool children when selecting cards.

b/Percentage Use of Manual Pointing

Where the correct card is identified, the mentally deficient subjects made greater use of manual pointing than did the nursery school children (20% vs 11% respectively, $p < .01$), when confronted both with the canonical configurations and the random configurations. However, the effect of the canonicity of the configurations was at its greatest for the nursery school children, $p = .07$. These children were able to correctly identify numerosity without recourse to manual pointing in collections up to size 5 for canonical configurations and 3 for random configurations. In the case of the mentally deficient subjects, we find similar curves for the canonical and random configurations with both peaking at sizes 4-5.

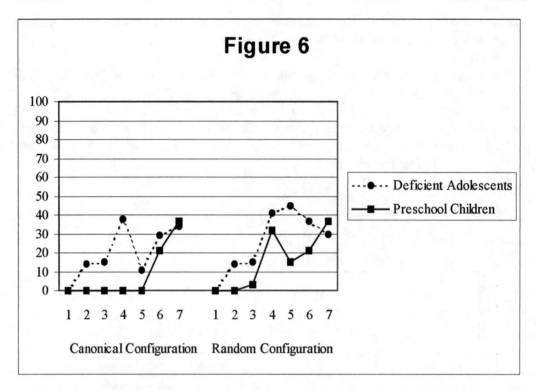

Figure 6: Percentage of manual pointing according to the size and configuration of the collection in mentally deficient adolescents and preschool children when selecting cards.

4- Comparison of the Different Tasks

We shall now perform a comparative analysis of the different tasks. First of all, we shall compare the error rates obtained by the two groups in the three counting tasks, i.e. counting dots, counting to n and counting objects. Since the dot counting task involved different configurations, we have decided to use the data obtained for the random configurations in the following analysis since these were obtained under conditions closer to those used in the counting to n and object counting tasks. We shall then compare the percentage use of manual pointing in the dot counting and card selection tasks.

a/ Comparison of the Error Percentages

Over all three tasks, the mentally deficient subjects committed more errors on average than the nursery school children (8 vs 5% respectively), even though this effect was not significant, $p > .10$. Unlike the nursery school children, who exhibited equivalent error rates whatever the task, the mentally deficient subjects made, on average, more mistakes in the counting to n and object counting tasks (10%) than in the dot counting task (5%), $p < .03$. The statistical analysis also reveals no significant effect of collection size, $p < .001$. There was no significant difference between the first four sizes (5%) taken individually although they did differ from the larger sizes (9%) ($p < .03$). The latter also did not differ significantly among themselves, $ps > .10$. These effects were observed in both groups. Finally, it is important to note that the first counting errors in the mentally deficient subjects appeared as of size 3 for counting to n and object counting whereas, for dot counting, it was observed as of size 5 just as for the nursery school children.

b/ Comparison of the Percentage Use of Manual Pointing

Overall, the mentally deficient subjects (50%) used manual pointing more frequently than the nursery school children (27%, $p<.01$). The nursery school children were more sensitive to the effect of the canonicity of configurations (20 vs 33% for canonical and random configurations respectively) than the mentally deficient subjects (48 vs 53%). Both groups made more use of manual pointing as collection size increased but this increase was more marked in the mentally deficient subjects. As of size 2, the mentally deficient subjects used manual pointing much more (36%) than did the nursery school children (3%). Finally, manual pointing was used more often in the dot counting task (59%) in which counting was explicitly requested of the subjects than in the card selection task (16%) in which guessing strategies could have been used.

CONCLUSION

During this research, we studied the ability of mentally deficient adolescents to count small collections. We also compared their performances in four different tasks to those of children of a similar mental age in their last year of nursery school. We expected to observe a subitizing ability up to collections of size 4 as well as the errors that characterize this ability in both the mentally deficient adolescents and the preschool children. We postulated that if subitizing is based on the recognition of the canonical configuration of small collections as Mandler and Shebo (1982) suggested, then the canonical nature of the presented collections should be observed for numerosities smaller than 4. Thus the use of pointing-based counting and the number of errors should increase for random configurations as well as with the size of the collection. We also postulated that the performances of nursery school children would be better than those of the mentally deficient subjects and this would be all the more prominent the more complex the task was. In general, the results that we obtained confirm these hypotheses. However, the main hypothesis of the existence of subitizing in the mentally deficient subjects remains controversial.

Over the four tasks that made up the game, we observed major differences in the counting procedures used by our two groups. Whatever the task and card configuration, the mentally deficient subjects preferred to count by pointing manually at each element. In the dot counting task, since the quantity 3, this procedure was used in 75% of all trials. Contrary to our hypotheses, no discontinuity in the percentage of manual pointing appeared from 4 onwards except in so far as this percentage did not stop increasing. In the case of object counting, this manual pointing of each element was also observed in two-thirds of the trials. This procedure did not attain the same level of predominance in the card selection task. When the mentally deficient subjects identified the card correctly at the first attempt (66% of cases), manual pointing was used in only 20% of the trials. In this card selection task, the mentally deficient adolescents used pointing-based counting twice as often as the nursery school children (11%). Contrary to our hypothesis, the effect of pattern canonicity had no significant effect either on the percentage of manual pointing or on the error rates irrespectively of the task in question. These counting errors increased with the size of the collection: they were rare, indeed practically non-existent, for the first three numbers. However, they were twice as frequent in counting to n and object counting as they were in the first task. The mentally deficient subjects made twice as many errors as the nursery school children on these second and third tasks but these errors were not significant due to the great variability between the mentally deficient subjects.

As far as subitizing abilities are concerned, we observed subitizing in the nursery school children up to 3 or 4 in three counting tasks presented via our game. This result is similar to those already described in the literature concerning 5 to 6-year-old children (Cueno, 1982; Chi & Klahr, 1975; Svenson & Sjoberg, 1978). This discontinuity in the quantification procedure appears after size 4 for the canonical configurations and after 3 for the random configurations in our group of nursery school children. It appears that nursery school children are well aware of the canonical configurations up to sizes 4 and 5 since they were always quick to choose the right card without having recourse to manual pointing. It should be noted that canonical representations of numerosities up to 7 were displayed in the children's classroom. It appears that these regular arrangements are memorized and that for some of these children they act as a reference for the choice of card. Indeed, a certain number of errors confusing very similar configurations were produced in the fourth task, for example 5 instead of 7 and 6 instead of 8. This type of error was very rare in the mentally deficient subjects. This data concerning nursery school children is consistent with Mandler and Shebo's data (1982), according to which subitizing is nothing more than the recognition of canonical, perceptual patterns relating to a small range of numerical quantities. This recognition could be extended to any quantity provided that it is associated with elementary configurations (Wolters Van Kempen & Wijilhuisen, 1987).

If we suppose that subitizing is an associative process between a name and a numerical pattern, then this process seems to be lacking in mentally deficient subjects. Indeed, whatever the task, we do not find an effect of the canonicity of the patterns on the percentage of manual pointing and the error rate. However, the mean percentage of manual pointing is smaller in dot counting when 3 is represented in the canonical configuration than in a random configuration. This difference on 3 also appears for the error percentage in the card selection task. According to the hypothesis that it is canonical patterns that are recognized, subitizing seems to be limited to the numerosity 2 in the case of mentally deficient adolescents. However, on average these mentally deficient adolescents identify regular collections of 3 more often than regular collections of 4 in the card selection task. Similarly, the level of manual pointing for the first three numerosities is less than that for other numerosities in this task and does not differ as a function of the configuration type. Manual pointing was used in 15% of the correct identifications of 3 irrespectively of the configuration and in 40% of cases for 4. This discontinuity also appears in the counting errors. It appears that there is a change of procedure as of 4. These analyses seem to indicate the existence of more efficient processing of the first three numbers rather than a genuine subitizing process.

However, we can question the aptness of the selection task as a task for the evaluation of subitizing abilities. This task differs from classic subitizing tasks in which subjects are asked to determine the number of presented elements as quickly and as accurately as possible. This task is more complex. On the one hand, it requires subjects to maintain the number of fish they have won in working memory and, on the other, to perform a systematic comparison of the set of cards. This comparison can lead subjects to perform a global estimation or mental counting. If we adopt Gallistel and Gelman's hypothesis (1991), then we can conceive that very fast, precise counting occurs when subjects choose cards corresponding to small numerosities. In this task, subjects might use very fast mental counting to select the cards representing the first three numerosities. This internal counting would then be applied to larger numerosities when subjects can control their counting better. In the card selection task, two of the young mentally deficient subjects identified the canonical configurations up to 5 and the random configurations up to 4, whereas they used manual pointing as of 3 or even 2 in the first task. The immediate estimation of the first three numbers could also be the result of a general estimation process (Van Oeffelen & Vos, 1982). The subitizing range would then simply be the range in which estimation is sufficiently precise to produce a single candidate for selection.

To conclude, the limit and nature of the subitizing process seem difficult to establish on the basis of these different data. The procedures used by the mentally deficient subjects differ from one task to another and even from one trial to another. Despite this variability in their performance, we can imagine that subitizing is possible as of 2 and could extend to 3 in the least deficient subjects. This hypothesis is based on a qualitative analysis of the procedures used by each subject in the range 1- 4. Finally, it is clear that more wide-ranging studies are necessary to explore the subitizing and counting abilities of mentally deficient subjects.

REFERENCES

Alibali, M.W., & DiRusso, A.A. (1999). The function of gesture in learning to count: more than keeping track, *Cognitive Development*, 14, 37-56.

Allik, J., & Tuulmets, T. (1991). Occupancy model of perceived numerosity, *Perception & Psychophysics, 49* (4), 303-314.

Atkinson, J., Campbell, F.W., & Francis, M.R (1976). The magic number 4 +/- 0: a new look at visual numerosity judgements, *Perception, 5,* 327-334.

Boysen, S.T., & Berntson, G.G., (1989). Numerical competence in a chimpanzee, *Journal of Comparative Psychology, 103* (1), 23-31.

Briars, D., & Siegler, R.S. (1984). A feature analysis of preschoolers' counting knowledge. *Developmental Psychology, 20,* 607-618.

Camos, V. (1999). Le dénombrement: une activité complexe à deux composantes, *Rééducation Orthophonique, 199,* 21-31.

Camos, V., Barrouillet, P., & Fayol, M. (2001). Does the coordination of verbal and motor information explain the development of counting in children ?, *Journal of Experimental Child Psychology, 78,* 240-262.

Chi, M.T.H., & Klahr, D. (1975). Span and rate of apprehension children and adults, *Journal of Experimental Child Psychology, 19,* 434-439.

Chomsky, N. (1957). *Syntactic structures,* The Hague: Mouton.

Cooper, R.G. (1984). Early number development: Discovering number space with addition and subtraction. In C. Sophian (Ed.), *The origins of cognitive skills,* Hillsdale (NJ): LEA.

Cuneo, D.O. (1982). Children's judgments of numerical quantity: A new view of early quantification, *Cognitive Psychology, 14,* 13-44.

Davis, H., & Pérusse, R., (1988). Numerical competence in animals: Definitional issues, current evidence and a new research agenda, *Behavioral and Brain Sciences, 11,* 561-615.

Dehaene, S. (1992). Varieties of numerical abilities, *Cognition, 44*, 1-42.

Dehaene, S. (1997). *La bosse des maths*, Paris: O. Jacob.

Fayol, M. (1985). Nombre, numération et dénombrement: Que sait-on de leur acquisition?, *Revue Française de Pédagogie, 70*, 59-77.

Fayol, M. (1990). *L'enfant et le nombre: Du comptage à la résolution de problèmes*, Neuchâtel: Delachaux et Niestlé.

Folk, C.L., Egeth, H., & Kwak, H.W. (1988). Subitizing: Direct apprehension or serial processing?, *Perception & Psychophysics, 44* (4), 313-320.

Frith, C.D., & Frith, U. (1972). The solitaire illusion: An illusion of numerosity, *Perception & Psychophysics, 11*, 409-410.

Fuson, K. C. (1988). *Children's counting and concepts of number*, New-York: Springer-Verlag.

Fuson, K. C. & Hall, J.W. (1983). The acquisition of early number word meanings. In H. Ginsburg (Ed.), *The development of children's mathematical thinking* (pp. 49-107), New-York: Academic Press.

Gallistel, C.R. (1988). Counting versus subitizing versus the sense of number, *Behavioral and Brain Science, 11* (4), 585-586.

Gallistel, C.R. (1990). Representations in animal cognition: An introduction. In C.R. Gallistel (Ed.), *Animal cognition*, Cambridge (MA): MIT Press.

Gallistel, C.R., & Gelman, R. (1991). Subitizing: The preverbal counting process. In W. Kessen & A. Ortony (Eds.), *Memories, thoughts, and emotions: Essays in honor of George Mandler*, Hillsdale (NJ): LEA.

Gallistel, C.R. & Gelman, R. (1992). Preverbal and verbal counting and computation, *Cognition, 44*, 43-74.

Geary, D.C. (1994). *Children's mathematical development: Research and practical applications*, Washington: A.P.A.

Gelman, R., & Gallistel, C.R. (1978). *The child's understanding of number*, Cambridge (MA): Harvard University Press.

Gelman, R., & Greeno, J.G. (1989). On the nature of competence: Principles for understanding in a domain. In L.B. Resnick (Ed.), *Knowing and learning: Issues for a cognitive science of instruction* (pp. 125-186), Hillsdale (NJ): LEA.

Ginsburg, N. (1976). Effect of item arrangement on perceived numerosity: randomness vs. regularity, *Perceptual and Motor Skills, 43*, 663-668

Ginsburg, N. (1978). Perceived numerosity, item arrangement, and expectancy, *American Journal of Psychology, 91*, 267-273.

Graham, T.A. (1999). The role of gesture in children's learning to count, *Journal of Experimental Child Psychology, 74*, 333-355.

Grégoire, J., & Van Nieuwenhoven, C. (1995). Counting at nursery school and at primary school: Toward an instrument for diagnostic assessment, *European Journal of Psychology of Education, 10* (1), 61-75.

Groen, G.J., & Parkman, J.M. (1972). A chronometric analysis of simple addition, *Psychological Review, 79*, 329-343.

Halford, G.S. (1993). *Children's understanding: The development of mental models*, Hillsdale (NJ): LEA.

Indow, T., & Ida, M. (1977). Scaling of dot numerosity, *Perception & Psychophysics, 22*, 265-276.

Kaufman, E.L., Lord, M.W., Reese, T.W., & Volkmann, J. (1949). The discrimination of visual number, *American Journal of Psychology, 62*, 498-525.

Klahr, D. (1973). Quantification processes. In W.G. Chase (Ed.), *Visual information processing, 8th Annual Carnegie Symposium Cognition*, New-York: Academic Press.

Klahr, D., & Wallace, J.G. (1976). *Cognitive development*, Hillsdale (NJ): LEA.

Krueger, L.E. (1972). Perceived numerosity, *Perception & Psychophysics, 11*, 5-9.

Krueger, L.E. (1982). Single judgments of numerosity, *Perception & Psychophysics, 31*, 175-182.

Mandler, G., & Shebo, B.J. (1982). Subitizing: An analysis of its component processes, *Journal of Experimental Psychology: General, 111*, 1-22.

Matsuzawa, T. (1985). Use of numbers by a chimpanzee, *Nature, 315*, 57-59.

Mc Evoy, J., & O'Moore, A.M. (1991). Number conservation: A fair assessment of numerical understanding, *The Irish Journal of Psychology, 12* (3), 325-337.

Meck, W.H., & Church, R.M. (1983). A mode control model of counting and timing processes, *Journal of Experimental Psychology: Animal Behavior Processes, 9*, 320-334.

Nunes, T. & Bryant, P. (1996). *Children doing mathematics*. Oxford: Blackwell.

Pesenti, M. (2001). Les procédures de quantification chez l'enfant. In C. Meljac & A. Van Hout (Eds.), *Troubles du calcul et dyscalculies chez l'enfant*, Paris: Masson.

Resnick, L.B. (1986). The development of mathematical intuition. In M. Perimutter (Ed.), *Perspectives on intellectual: The Minnesota symposia on Child Psychology*, Hillsdale (NJ): LEA.

Saxe, G.B. (1981). Body parts as numerals: A developmental analysis of numeration among the Oksapmin in Papua New Guinea, *Child Development, 52*, 306-316.

Saxe, G., & Posner, J. (1983). The development of numerical cognition: Cross-cultural perspective. In H.P. Ginsburg (Ed.), *The development of mathematical thinking*, New-York: Academic Press.

Shipley, E.F., & Shepperson, B. (1990). The what-if of counting, *Cognition, 36*, 285-289.

Starkey, P., & Cooper, R.G. (1980). Perception of numbers by human infants, *Science, 210*, 1033-1035.

Starkey, P., Spelke, E.S., & Gelman, R. (1990). Numerical abstraction by human infants, *Cognition, 36*, 97-127.

Starkey, P., Spelke, E.S. & Gelman, R. (1991). Toward a comparative psychology of number, *Cognition, 39*, 171-172.

Strauss, M.S., & Curtis, L.E. (1984). Development of numerical concepts in infancy. In C. Sophian (Ed.), *Origins of cognitive skills*, Hillsdale (NJ): LEA.

Svenson, O. (1975). Analysis of time required by children for simple addition, *Acta Psychologica, 39*, 289-302.

Svenson, O., & Sjoberg, K. (1978). Subitizing and counting in young children, *Scandinavian Journal of Psychology, 19*, 247-250.

Taves, E.H. (1941). Two mechanisms for the perception of visual numerousness, *Archives of Psychology, 37*, n°265.

Treisman, A. (1991). Search, similarity, and integration of features between and within dimensions, *Journal of Experimental Psychology: Human Perception and Performance, 17* (3), 652-676.

Treisman, A., & Gelade, G. (1980). A feature-integration theory of attention, *Cognitive Psychology, 12*, 97-136.

Treisman, A., & Gormican, S. (1988). Feature analysis in early vision: Evidence from search asymmetries, *Psychological Review, 95* (1), 15-48.

Treisman, A., & Sato, S. (1990). Conjunction search revisited, *Journal of Experimental Psychology: Human Perception and Performance, 16* (3), 459-478.

Trick, L., & Pylyshyn, Z. (1993). What enumeration studies can show us about spatial attention: Evidence for limited capacity preattentive processing, *Journal of Experimental Psychology: Human Perception and Performance, 19*, 331-351.

Trick, L.M., & Pylyshyn, Z.W. (1994). Why are small and large numbers enumerated differently? A limited-capacity preattentive stage in vision, *Psychological Review, 101* (1), 80-102.

Tuholski, S., & Engle, R.W. (2001). Individual differences in working memory capacity and enumeration, *Memory and Cognition, 29*, 484-492.

Van Oeffelen, M.P., & Vos, P.G. (1982). A probabilistic model for the discrimination of visual number, *Perception & Psychophysics, 32* (2), 163-170.

Von Glaserfeld, E. (1982). Subitizing: The role of figural patterns in the development of numerical concepts, *Archives de Psychologie, 50*, 191-218.

Vos, P.G., Van Oeffelen, M.P., Tibosch, H.J., & Allik, J. (1988). Interactions between area and numerosity, *Psychological Research, 50*, 148-154.

Wagner, S.H., & Walters, J. (1982). A longitudinal analysis of early number concepts: From numbers to number. In G.E. Foreman (Ed.), *From sensorimotor schemas to symbolic operations*, New-York: Academic Press.

Wolters, G., Kempen, H., & Wijhuisen, G. (1987). Quantification of small numbers of dots: Subitizing or pattern recognition, *American Journal of Psychology, 100* (2), 225-237.

Wynn, K. (1990). Children's understanding of counting, *Cognition, 36*, 155-193.

Wynn, K. (1992b). Addition and subtraction by human infants, *Nature, 358*, 749-750.

Chapter 9

MEANING OF LIFE AND ADJUSTMENT AMONG CHINESE ADOLESCENTS WITH AND WITHOUT ECONOMIC DISADVANTAGE[*]

Daniel T.L. Shek, M.C. Lam, C.M. Lam, Vera Tang, K.W. Tsoi
Department of Social Work
The Chinese University of Hong Kong
and Sandra Tsang
Department of Social Work and Social Administration
The University of Hong Kong

ABSTRACT

Meaning in life in adolescents with and without economic disadvantage was examined in two studies. In Study 1, the relationship between meaning in life indexed by the Existential Well-Being Scale and adjustment of adolescents with and without economic disadvantage was examined in 1,519 Chinese adolescents. Results showed that adolescents with higher scores in the Existential Well-Being Scale had better psychological well-being and school adjustment and less problem behavior (including substance abuse and delinquency), and the relationship was stronger in adolescents with economic disadvantage than in adolescents without economic disadvantage. In Study 2, life meaning in 12 Chinese adolescents with economic disadvantage was explored via qualitative interviews. Results showed that poor adolescents derived life meaning from different sources and money was not an important factor in the origin of life meaning in poor adolescents. Adolescents who placed greater emphasis on the importance on money tended to have poorer psychosocial adjustment. Adolescents who felt their lives to be controlled by fate rather by themselves generally showed poorer adjustment.

[*] This work was financially supported by the Research Grants Council of the UGC, Government of the Hong Kong Special Administrative Region (Grant CUHK4087/99H). Address all correspondence to Daniel T.L. Shek, Department of Social Work, The Chinese University of Hong Kong, Shatin, Hong Kong (E-Mail: DANIELSHEK@CUHK.EDU.HK).

Stressful life events such as experience of adversity are detrimental to the development of children and adolescents (e.g., Compas, Orosan & Grant, 1993; Dulmus & Rapp-Paglicci, 2000). Nevertheless, the impact of stressful life events is not overwhelming and adolescents experiencing adversity such as socio-economic disadvantage do not necessarily end up in failures. Research findings show that adolescents may adjust well despite the presence of adversity (Garmezy, 1991, 1993; Rutter, 1987; Werner, 1989). Because of this observation, researchers have suggested that certain factors may protect the adjustment of children and adolescents experiencing stressful life events. According to Rutter (1985), protective factors are "influences that modify, ameliorate or alter a person's response to some environmental hazard that predisposes to a maladaptive outcome" (p.600).

Based on a review of the resilience literature, Hauser (1999) outlined several categories of protective factors, including individual (e.g., healthy attribution style, self-efficacy, hope, faith), relational (e.g., supportive home environment), community (e.g., good schools and other community assets) and general (e.g., good fortune) protective factors. In a review of stress, coping and resilience in children and youth, Smith and Carlson (1997) similarly suggested that individual factors (e.g., optimism and faith), family factors (e.g., parental support and guidance), and external support systems (e.g., supportive non-parent adults) are important protective factors in children and adolescents experiencing environmental hazards. In short, as Lerner and Galambos (1998) suggested, "there are both person- and context-protective factors that promote developmental resilience" (p.431).

With reference to protective factors on the individual level, there are studies suggesting that personal beliefs are important protective factors. Werner (1989) showed that optimism and beliefs about control in lives were related to the adjustment of high-risk children. Rutter (1985) pointed out the importance of self-efficacy in adversity. Werner and Smith (1992) also suggested that faith and religious beliefs were important protective factors. However, while there are studies demonstrating that personal beliefs, such as beliefs about control, are related to resilience, there is limited empirical exploration of how meaning of life is related to resilience.

The hypothesis that life meaning plays an important role in human behavior is exemplified by the existential theory by Frankl. Frankl's conceptualization about human nature is based on the premise of "will to meaning" - human behavior is neither motivated by the "will to pleasure" as Freudian psychoanalysts hypothesized nor the "will to power" as Adlerian emphasized, but by the inborn urge of human beings to search for meaning (Frankl, 1955, 1958, 1959, 1966). When a person fails to find meaning in life and a state of vacuum of perceived meaning in personal existence (i.e. existential vacuum) is present, he or she is confronted by "existential frustration", which is characterized by the feeling of boredom (Crumbaugh, 1968; Crumbaugh & Maholick, 1964). Although the occurrence of existential vacuum does not necessarily lead to noogenic neuroses, it was contended that existential vacuum is an etiological factor of psychopathology - that when there is a vacuum in existence, mental problems come in to "fill the vacuum" (Dyck, 1987; Frankl, 1967).

Although the proposal that the absence of meaning in life (existential vacuum) is intimately linked to psychopathology is an attractive one, particularly with respect to its treatment implications, Shek (1992a) pointed out that there are two areas of ambiguities associated with the hypothesis. First, based on a review of the available conceptual frameworks (e.g., Paloutzian, 1981; Reker, Peacock & Wong, 1987; Shapiro, 1988) and empirical research findings, Shek (1992a) argued that the concept of meaning of life should be understood in terms of two dimensions - meaning in life may refer to the presence of beliefs and related goals of life (cognitive aspect) or the presence of feeling and subjective experiences that life is meaningful (affective aspect), or both.

The second source of ambiguity concerns the relationship between meaning in life and the so-called "conventional psychiatric syndromes" (Crumbaugh, 1968). While Frankl (1960) maintained that emptiness in purpose in life (existential vacuum) might lead to noogenic neuroses, a pathological condition which is distinct from other "conventional" forms of psychopathology, there are conflicting research findings supporting this conjecture (e.g., Crumbaugh, 1968; Dyck, 1987).

A survey of PSYCINFO shows that very few studies have been carried out to examine life meaning and adolescent adjustment. In particular, very few studies have been conducted to examine the relationship between meaning of life and adjustment in adolescents experiencing economic disadvantage. As commented by Orthner (1996), the study of poverty "has not been accorded the level of research attention as families in middle class" (p.589) and Luthar (1997) similarly remarked "there is a need for greater attention to theoretical conceptualizations regarding 'normative development' in the context of poverty" (p.579). Furthermore, available scientific studies on the relationship between life meaning and adjustment among Chinese adolescents experiencing economic disadvantage are almost non-existent in the Chinese context.

Against the above background, two studies on meaning of life and adolescent adjustment are reported in this paper. In Study 1, research findings on the relationship between meaning in life as indexed by the Existential Well-Being Scale and adolescent psychological well-being, school adjustment, and problem behavior of Chinese adolescents with and without economic disadvantage are presented. In Study 2, meaning in life perceived by Chinese adolescents experiencing economic disadvantage was examined via a qualitative study. Specifically, the following four aspects related to meaning in life were examined: 1) What are the views of Chinese adolescents with economic disadvantage on meaning of life? 2) Does money occupy an important role in the origin of meaning of life among poor Chinese adolescents? 3) How do poor Chinese adolescents look at fate when they consider the issue of meaning in life? 4) Is meaning in life related to the psychosocial adjustment of poor adolescents experiencing economic disadvantage?

STUDY 1

Method

Participants

The study was based upon the responses of 1,519 secondary school students aged between 11 to 18 years (733 males and 762 females). They were all Secondary 1 to Secondary 3 students recruited from four schools in Hong Kong. Regarding the economic status of the participants, the respondents were asked to indicate whether their families were receiving Comprehensive Social Security Assistance (CSSA) or full Textbook Allowance (TBA). In Hong Kong, families receiving CSSA or full TBA can be regarded as families with financial difficulty. A total of 44 participants did not indicate the financial situation of the family. For the rest of the participants, 80 adolescents responded that their families were receiving Comprehensive Social Security Assistance (CSSA) and 88 adolescents were receiving full Textbook Allowance (TBA). These participants formed the Poor Group (N=168). For participants who did not receive CSSA or TBA, they formed the Non-Poor Group (N=1,307). There were no differences between the two groups in terms of mean age (13.5 and 13.5 in the Poor Group and Non-Poor Group, respectively), gender ratio (47.6% and 49.2 of the participants were boys in the Poor Group and Non-Poor Group, respectively), and mean number of persons in the family (4.4 and 4.4 in the Poor Group and Non-Poor Group, respectively).

Instruments

Assessment of Meaning of Life
The Existential Well-Being Scale (EWB), which formed a part of the Spiritual Well-Being Scale, was constructed by Paloutzian and Ellison (1982) to assess life purpose and satisfaction apart from any religious reference (i.e., horizontal dimension of spiritual well-being). There are ten items in this scale. In line with Shek's (1992a) argument that there are two basic aspects of life meaning, Paloutzian and Ellison (1982) reported that the Existential Well-Being Scale measures life direction (i.e., purpose of life) and life satisfaction (i.e., whether life is meaningful). It was also reported that the EWB Scale was significantly correlated with the Purpose in Life Test (Crumbaugh & Maholick, 1964). The Existential Well-Being Scale was found to be reliable in this study (alpha=.85)

Assessment of Psychological Well-Being
- *Life Satisfaction Scale (LIFE)*. The Satisfaction with Life Scale was designed by Diener, Emmons, Larsen, and Griffin (1985) to assess an individual's own global judgment of his or her quality of life. The Chinese version of this scale was translated by the author (Shek, 1992b) and adequate reliability of this scale was found in this study (alpha=.76).
- *Chinese Self-Esteem Scale (ESTEEM)*. The Rosenberg Self-Esteem Scale was designed to assess the self-esteem of high school students (Rosenberg, 1979). The Chinese Rosenberg Self-Esteem Scale was developed by the author and acceptable reliability of this scale has been reported (Shek, 1992b). Based on factor analysis, 5 items were retained. A higher ESTEEM scale score indicates a higher level of self-esteem in this study (alpha=.77).
- *Mastery Scale (MAS)*. Modelled after the Mastery Scale of Pearlin and Schooler (1978), the 7-item Chinese Mastery Scale was constructed by the author that attempts to measure a person's sense of control of his or her life. This scale was found to be reliable in this study (alpha=.78).
- *The Chinese version of the 30-items General Health Questionnaire (GHQ)*. The General Health Questionnaire was developed to measure current non-psychotic disturbances (Goldberg, 1972). Chan (1985) found that the Chinese GHQ compared favorably with the English version at the scale level and there is evidence suggesting that the GHQ possesses acceptable psychometric properties (Shek, 1989, 1993b). Based on the findings of Shek (1993b), 15 items based on Factor 1 (Anxiety) and Factor 2 (Depression) of the GHQ were used. The scale was found to be internally consistent in this study (alpha=.93).

While the GHQ can be treated as an instrument assessing manifested psychiatric symptoms, the other scales can be regarded as tools assessing coping resources (i.e., personal attributes that assist an individual to cope with stress; Folkman et al., 1979) or positive mental health characteristics (Diener, 1984).

Assessment of School Adjustment

One item was constructed to assess a respondent's perception of his or her academic performance when compared with schoolmates in the same grade (APC). The respondents were asked to rate "Best", "Better than usual", "Ordinary", "Worse than usual", or "Worst" in this item. Besides, another item was constructed to assess the respondent's satisfaction of his or her academic performance (APS). The respondents were asked to rate "Very satisfied", "Satisfied", "Average", "Dissatisfied", or "Very dissatisfied" in this item. Finally, one item was constructed to assess the respondent's perception of his or her conduct (CONDUCT). The respondents were asked to rate "Very good", "Good", "Average", "Poor", or "Very poor" in this item. Shek (1997) showed that these three items were temporally stable.

Assessment of Problem Behavior

- *Substance Abuse (DRUG1 and DRUG2)*: Based on a review of the foreign and local literature, eight items were developed to examine the respondents' frequency of using alcohol, tobacco, ice (methylamphetamine), cannabis, cough mixture, organic solvent, tranquilizers and narcotics. Reliability findings showed that the items assessing consumption of alcohol and cigarettes (i.e., gateway drugs: DRUG1) and other drugs (DRUG2) are reliable (alpha= .56 and .84, respectively).
- *Delinquency (DELIN)*: Based on a review of the literature (e.g., Shek & Ma, 1997), twelve items were developed to examine the respondents' frequency of engaging in antisocial behavior. The related behavior includes stealing, cheating, truancy, running away from home, damaging others' properties, assault, having sexual relationship with others, gang fighting, speaking foul language, staying away from home without parental consent, strong-arm others, and breaking in others' places. Reliability showed that this scale was reliable (alpha=.75).

On the basis of the above discussion, it was predicted that, if there were a relationship between meaning in life and adolescent adjustment, higher EWB scores would be related with better psychological well-being (higher LIFE, MAS and ESTEEM scores and lower GHQ scores) and school adjustment (lower APC, APS and CONDUCT) and less problem behavior (lower DRUG1, DRUG2 and DELIN scores).

Procedures

The purpose of the study was mentioned and the confidentiality of the data collected was repeatedly emphasized to all of the students in attendance on the day of testing. The students were asked to indicate their wish if they did not want to participate in the study (i.e., "passive" informed consent was obtained from the students). All participants responded en masse to all the instrument scales in the questionnaire in a self-administration format. Adequate time was provided for the subjects to complete the questionnaire. The questionnaire took roughly 45 to 60 minutes to complete.

Results

Correlation coefficients on the linkage between the EWB scores and different measures of adolescent adjustment are presented in Table 1. Because several correlation analyses were carried out in different samples, the multistage Bonferroni procedure (Larzelere & Mulaik, 1977) was carried out to determine those significant correlations that were not attributable to Type 1 error. The data generally showed that those who had a high level of meaningful life displayed less mental health problems and problem behaviors and they had better school adjustment, and this observation was found in both Poor Group and Non-Poor Group. However, in terms of the relative strength of association between existential well-being and the outcome measures in both groups, the magnitude of the correlation coefficients was generally higher in the Poor Group than in the Non-Poor Group. In addition, there was no significant difference between the Poor Group and the Non-Poor Group in their EWB scores (M=39.84, SD=9.45 and M=40.33, SD=8.41 for the Poor Group and Non-Poor Group, respectively).

Because there were many developmental outcome variables, factor analyses were performed to reduce the data volume. A principal components analysis was performed for the developmental outcome variables, yielding three factors with eigenvalues exceeding unity that was rotated to a varimax criterion for interpretation. The first factor, which could be labeled Mental Health, included variables related to mental health characteristics (LIFE, ESTEEM, MAS and GHQ). Because items that were concerned with school adjustment (APC, APS and CONDUCT) were loaded strongly on Factor II, this factor could hence be labeled School Adjustment. Finally, Factor III was labeled Problem Behavior because measures of adolescent problem behavior (DRUG1, DRUG2 and DELIN) were strongly loaded on this factor. To further understand the stability of the factors extracted, the total sample was randomly split into two subsamples and identical factor analytic procedures were then carried out to assess the stability of the factor structure. Results showed that the factors extracted from the two random subsamples were highly stable (coefficients of congruence=.99, .98 and .98 for Mental Health, School Adjustment, and Problem Behavior, respectively).

Based on the composite scores of the child developmental outcome variables, two observations can be highlighted. First, the EWB scores were significantly related to all composite measures in the Poor Group and Non-Poor Group. Second, the correlation between the School Adjustment factor and the EWB scores in the Poor Group was significantly stronger than that in the Non-Poor Group.

Table 1: Correlation Coefficients on the Linkage between the Scores of the Existential Well-Being Scale and Measures of Adolescent Psychological Well-Being, School Adjustment and Problem Behavior

Variables	Total (N=1,519)	Poor (P) (N=168)	Non-Poor (NP) (N=1307)	P vs. NP on related correlation coefficients
LIFE	.55*	.68*	.54*	P > NP #
ESTEEM	.56*	.66*	.52*	P > NP #
MAS	.65*	.72*	.64*	P > NP
GHQ	-.56*	-.66*	-.54*	P > NP @
APS	-.26*	-.35*	-.27*	P > NP
APC	-.28*	-.35*	-.24*	P > NP
CONDUCT	-.24*	-.34*	-.21*	P > NP
DELIN	-.26*	-.34*	-.24*	P > NP
DRUG1	-.18*	-.19*	-.17*	P > NP
DRUG2	-.06	-.06	-.05	P > NP
MH	.83*	.88*	.81*	P > NP
SA	-.13*	-.28*	-.11*	P > NP @
PB	-.14*	-.19*	-.13*	P > NP

Note: LIFE: Life Satisfaction Scale. ESTEEM: Self-Esteem Scale. MAS: Mastery Scale. GHQ: General Health Questionnaire. APS: Perceived academic performance. APC: Academic performance compared with others. CONDUCT: School conduct. DELIN: Delinquent behavior. DRUG1: Smoking and alcohol consumption. DRUG2: Use of narcotics and psychotropic substances. MH: Mental Health factor. SA: School Adjustment factor. PB: Problem Behavior factor.

A two-tailed multistage Bonferroni procedure was used to obtain the data. *pFW* is based on the familywise Type 1 error rate; *pT* is based on the Type 1 error rate per test.

* *pFW* < .05, *pT* < .025 in the total sample, non-poor sample, and the poor sample

\# Significant difference between the Non-Poor Group and Poor Group on the related correlation coefficients at the 1% level (one-tailed test)

@ Significant difference between the Non-Poor Group and Poor Group on the related correlation coefficients at the 5% level (one-tailed test)

Discussion

The present study showed that meaning of life indexed by the Existential Well-Being Scale was associated with adolescent psychological symptoms, positive mental health (including life satisfaction, self-esteem and sense of mastery), academic performance, substance abuse and delinquency. Because no studies have been conducted to examine the linkage between meaning in life and adjustment in poor Chinese adolescents, the present findings can be regarded as pioneering. The present findings are consistent with the previous findings that meaning in life is related to adolescent adjustment (Shek, 1992a, 1993a) and they can be interpreted in terms of the theoretical framework of Frankl (1958, 1959, 1967).

The present findings also suggest that a lower level of life meaning is related to a higher level of conventional psychiatric symptoms.

Another interesting finding of the present study is that life meaning was found to have a stronger relationship with adolescent adjustment in poor adolescents than in non-poor adolescents. In other words, the relationship between life meaning and adjustment is stronger in poor adolescents than in non-poor adolescents. This finding is consistent with the findings in the resilience literature that positive life outlook is associated with better adolescent adjustment in high-risk adolescents (e.g., Hauser, 1999). Because there are limited research findings in this area, the present findings are interesting additions to the literature.

Given the correlational nature of the data, one cannot make a causal link between life meaning and adolescent adjustment. Those with mental health problems might perceive their life meaning in a more negative manner (i.e., perceptual distortion hypothesis). In addition, poor adolescent adjustment (e.g., psychological distress) may be a precursor of negative meaning of life rather than vice versa. Longitudinal research, consequently, is sorely needed to assess the direction of effect between meaning in life and adolescent adjustment.

STUDY 2

As mentioned in the introduction of this paper, empirical studies on meaning of life amongst adolescents are few, particularly in Chinese adolescents experiencing economic disadvantage. Because of the paucity of empirical research findings in this area, a qualitative study was conducted to examine poor adolescents' meaning of life via in-depth interviews.

The use of qualitative methods to explore meaning in life in Chinese adolescents experiencing economic disadvantage is justified for two reasons. First, because existing studies in the area of developmental psychopathology are primarily quantitative in nature, the use of qualitative research methods would offer a fresh perspective on the problem area. By looking at the worldviews, language and context-specific experiences of adolescents with economic disadvantage (Denzin & Lincoln, 2000), the related phenomena could be more fully understood. Actually, there are increasing voices arguing for the adoption of qualitative methods in the study of resilience (Gilgun, 1999), family stress (Boss, 1987) and human development (Jessor, Colby & Shweder, 1996). In addition, the use of qualitative findings would offer new insight to established theories on the adjustment of poor adolescents to adversity. For example, in a study of the lives of poor adolescents, Figueira-McDonough (1998) reported that their findings did not fully support the cultural and structural theories.

Second, according to Tashakkori and Teddlie (1998), there is a growing interest in combining quantitative and qualitative methods. Greene, Caracelli and Graham (1989) outlined five arguments for the combination of quantitative and qualitative methods. These include: triangulation (i.e., seeking convergence of results via different data types), complementary usage, developmental utilization (e.g., the first method is used sequentially to help inform the second method), initiation (emergence of fresh perspective), and expansion (broadening of scope and breadth of a study by combining different methods).

Method

The present study attempted to provide detailed examination of the personal accounts of Chinese adolescents experiencing economic disadvantage. Although there are many strands of qualitative research (Denzin & Lincoln, 2000), a general qualitative research orientation was adopted in which in-depth interviews without preset responses, close encounter with the informants, analyses of the findings without predetermined codes and categories, and critical discussion among the researchers on the interpretations of the data were emphasized.

A total of twelve adolescents experiencing economic disadvantage participated in this study. Their ages were 12 to 16 (M=13.9). In terms of the nature of economic disadvantage, nine participants were from families receiving Comprehensive Social Security Assistance and the families of three participants were receiving full Textbook Allowance, both of which could be considered as poor families in Hong Kong. Based on their responses to several assessment tools on their psychological well-being, family health and interpersonal relationships (see Shek, 2002 for a detailed description of the scales), the participants were categorized into "high-risk" or "low risk" status in terms of their psychosocial adjustment. While six "high-risk" participants generally scored in the unhealthy direction in most of the measures of psychosocial adjustment, another six "low-risk" participants generally scored in the healthy direction in the related scales.

Data were collected through intensive interviews that collected information on different areas, including family life, school life, peer relations, mentors, community life, meaning in life, significant life events, and views on poverty. The detail of the interview guide is available from the first author. To ensure the quality of the interviews, four university professors (three social workers and one clinical psychologist) carried out the interviews. A total of 35 interviews involving 51.5 hours were conducted. While the participants were encouraged to answer the questions in the interview guide, they could stop conversing about any topic if they did not feel comfortable.

The interviews were tape-recorded and the narratives were fully transcribed by research assistants via Chinese word processing. After the narratives were typed, a trained research assistant checked the transcripts. The transcripts were then content analyzed to reveal the themes in the different areas. The procedures involving in qualitative data analyses were utilized (Miles and Huberman, 1984; Patton, 1990; Taylor & Bodgan, 1998). Consistent with the spirit of qualitative research, the first author and the fourth author discussed the narratives and the related codes and interpretations. In case of discrepancies in views amongst the two researchers, critical discussion and negotiations were carried out until a consensus was reached.

Because there is a vast amount of data pertinent to the qualitative data collected, the present discussion would focus on the following questions. 1) What are the views of Chinese adolescents with economic disadvantage on meaning of life? 2) Does money occupy an important role in the meaning of life among poor Chinese adolescents? 3) How do poor Chinese adolescents look at fate when they consider the issue of meaning in life? 4) Is meaning in life related to the psychosocial adjustment of poor adolescents experiencing economic disadvantage?

Results

Regarding the views of the informants on meaning in life, the responses from 10 adolescents revealed that the views of the informants on meaning of life were quite diversified and the life meanings expressed appeared to anchor on a wide range of activities and people. Further analyses of the data showed that the narratives could be divided into two categories. In the first category of narratives, life meaning was related to the significant-others. These include: to have friends (N=2), to concern other people (N=1), to find parents who love me (N=1), to live for one's family (N=4). The second category of narratives on life meaning were related to the self, which include: to be happy (N=3), to do some memorable things (N=1), to do something that can satisfied oneself (N=2), to accept new things (N=1), to continue life (N=2), to live for oneself (N=1), to study (N=3) and to dream (N=1). The narratives of a "high-risk" case and a "low risk" case would be presented for illustrations.

Informant CWC was "low-risk" in terms of psychosocial adjustment. The father of the informant died when she was aged three. She enjoyed good relationships with her mother, elder sister and friends. Probably because of the support of the relatives of the mother, her perception of financial strain was not high. When asked about her view on meaning of life, her narratives were as follows:

> *"Actually much of the purpose of existence is to study and to increase one's knowledge. ... Actually, I feel that if a person does not have any interest and dreams, then there is not much point in existing".*

Informant SKM was "high-risk" in terms of psychosocial adjustment. Because of extra-marital affair, his parents divorced when he was young. While he had very poor perception about his father, his relationship with the mother was very close and he regarded filial behavior toward the mother (not the father) was very important. When asked about his view of meaning of life, he could not described *his* life meaning and he responded in the following way:

> *"The purpose of my existence is intrinsic to my mother".*

Two observations could be highlighted from the above findings. First, similar to other Western studies, different purposes and life goals were identified in Chinese adolescents with economic disadvantage. In particular, significant-others, such as parents, family members and friends, are important sources of life meaning. This finding is consistent with the findings of the resilience literature that significant-others play an important role in the lives of adolescents experiencing economic disadvantage (Hauser, 1999; Shek, 2002; Smith & Carlson, 1997).

The second observation was that money did not play an important role in the narratives of the adolescents when the question of life meaning was posed. This observation is consistent with the findings in the literature that few adolescents place strong emphases on making money and getting rich. For example, using the "What Kids Admire" Scale and the Childs Priority Sort, Cohen and Cohen (1996) showed that children and adolescents did not place a high priority in money and material possession. Unfortunately, whether the role of money differed in adolescents with different socio-economic backgrounds was not examined in the study.

In the Chinese context, because Chinese parents tend not to reveal the financial situation to their children and not to discuss financial problem with their children (Shek, 2001), the children might not really feel the pain associated with economic disadvantage. As a result of this protective attitude, life goals such as "to earn more money" or "to live a materially abundant life" might not play an important role in the life meanings of adolescents with economic disadvantage. The present findings demystify the common myth that money may occupy an important role in the life purpose of poor people.

Although adolescents under study did not mention any materialistic goals as their life meanings, there was some variation in their views of the importance of money. When asked about whether they perceived money to be important, the narratives based on 10 adolescents showed that only four of them regarded money as important and three of them were from the "high-risk" group. Actually, money did not seem to occupy an important role in the informants of the "low-risk" group.

Although the father of Informant SYY (informant in the "low-risk" group) was unemployed, the informant was satisfied with the family relations. Because of financial constrains, the informant gave up the idea of joining an art club. When asked about her view about money, her narratives were as follows:

> "Although people perceive money to be important, but you can't use money to buy everything. Money can't buy health. Money can't buy happiness. Most important of all, you can't use money to buy your life".

Informant HWY was an informant in the "high-risk" condition. The parents of the informant did not work because of their poor health. She was very sensitive about the fact that the family had to rely on welfare. When asked about whether money was important, she said the following:

> "Money is very important. You can't live without money and the society is money-oriented. Perhaps I am too pessimistic. But I really think this is very important, everybody looks at money".

The relationship between materialism and well-being has been addressed on both philosophical (e.g., Belk, 1985) and empirical (e.g., Wright & Larsen, 1993) levels. While there are research findings showing a negative relationship between materialism and overall life satisfaction (Diener & Oishi, 2000; Sirgy, 1998), the relationship between these two domains in adolescents with economic disadvantage has not been adequately addressed. The present findings suggest that there is a need to examine the relationship between perception of money and adjustment in poor adolescents in future.

Finally, because fate has been regarded as an important dimension of meaning in life (Crumbaugh & Maholick, 1964), the informants were asked whether they believed in fate. The narratives based on 9 adolescents showed that among the 4 informants in the "low-risk" group, all of them did not believe in fate. In contrast, among the five adolescents in the "high-risk" group, three strongly believed in fate and one moderately believed in fate.

When Informant CWC, an informant in the "low-risk" group, was asked the view of fate in life, she narrated *"Fate – of course it is 'man who determines fate'. I can change my fate"*. When asked how fate had affected her way of coping with economic strain, she believed that the belief in self-control made her more optimistic and self-contended.

As mentioned above, Informant HWY was in the "high-risk" group. When asked about her view of fate in life, her narrative was:

> *"Life is somewhat determined. It does not mean the happenings can't be changed. But I think when you make a decision, it somewhat has determined the consequences of your decisions. That is there is a model or something that predestinates your path".*

The present findings are consistent with the resilience literature that a sense of control over life is a protective factor for adolescents facing adversity. While the four informants in the "low-risk" group did not believe in fate in their life, most of the informants in the "high-risk" group did. In a review of protective factors for poor adolescents, Lerner and Galambos (1998) concluded that individual factors such as self-competence, aspirations and future perception are protective factors. In their qualitative findings based on disadvantaged youth, Smokowski, Reynolds and Bezrucko (1999) also concluded that "a mixture of optimistic future expectations, realistic appraisal of one's strengths, having personal goals or a mastery experience, and avoiding the initial excitement and subsequent danger inherent in risk situations seemed to be the recipe for many students to 'keep on track'" (p.438). Similarly, Conger, Conger, Matthews and Elder (1999) also found that a lower sense of mastery was related to more emotional stress.

Although fatalistic beliefs may constitute a form of emotion-focused coping and they may be beneficial to those who are facing adversity, prolonged fatalistic beliefs would lead to motivational deficit that inhibits the willingness of poor people to change (Kane, 1987). In addition, it is noteworthy that people with fatalistic religious beliefs would still be discontented about their conditions (Sadeque, 1986).

DISCUSSION

The primary aim of this paper was to report research findings on life meaning and psychosocial adjustment in Chinese adolescents with and without economic disadvantage. In Study 1, the relationship between life meaning and adolescent psychological well-being, school adjustment, and problem behavior in Hong Kong Chinese adolescents with and without economic disadvantage was examined. It was expected that adolescents with a higher level of life meaning would have better adjustment. In Study 2, life meaning in Chinese adolescents experiencing economic disadvantage was examined via in-depth interviews. The role of money and fate in relation to life meaning was also explored.

Results of Study 1 showed that those who had a higher level of life meaning displayed a lower level of psychological symptoms indexed by the GHQ scores. Furthermore, positive life meaning was related to higher levels of adolescent positive mental health (including life satisfaction, self-esteem and sense of mastery), better school adjustment as well as less problem behavior. These findings are generally consistent with the studies in the literature that life meaning is related to adolescent adjustment (e.g., Shek, 1992a, 1993a) and substance abuse (Lecci, MacLean & Croteau, 2002).

While there were no significant differences between the Poor Group and Non-Poor Group in terms of their levels of existential well-being, life meaning was found to have a stronger relationship with adjustment in poor adolescents than in non-poor adolescents. Assuming that life meaning influences individual adjustment, the present findings showed that life meaning is an important protective factor for adolescents with economic disadvantage in Hong Kong.

From a stress and coping framework, there are at least two ways how meaning in life may influence the impact of adversity on adolescents experiencing adversity. First, meaning in life can influence how adversity is defined and conceptualized. If adversity were seen as a chance for growth and challenge, tolerance of the threat would be easier. On the other hand, if adversity were seen as punishment from God, retribution or transmigration, it would be more difficult for the person concerned to accept it. This point is illustrated by the claim of Nietzche that "he who has a why to live for can bear with almost any how."

Second, meaning in life shapes the coping resources and behavior of a person facing adversity. A poor adolescent who perceives poverty as a result of bad fate would lack the motivation to change (Kane, 1987) and might use more emotion-focused coping methods. On the other hand, a poor adolescent who perceives poverty as a result of exploitation and injustice would adopt a "fight back" stand in coping with stress, such as engagement of delinquent behavior. In short, life meaning provides the basis upon which people experiencing adversity makes sense of their experience and develops his or her coping.

Based on the conceptual framework of Sandler (2001), meaning in life can be regarded as resilience resources that serve three functions: prevent the occurrence of stressors, protect the person by reducing the harmful effects of adversity on the person, and promote the functioning of a person by increasing satisfaction and cultivation of developmental competencies. However, it is noteworthy that the relationships between life purpose and other psychological constructs, such as optimism and other beliefs (Affleck & Tennen, 1996), are under-researched. In addition, how life meaning can be incorporated in the multicultural model of the stress process (e.g., Slavin, Rainer, McCreary & Gowda, 1991) is an exciting topic to be further explored.

There are two limitations of Study 1. First, because life meaning was measured via a self-report measure, it is possible that the relationship between the two domains may be due to common method variance. Therefore, it would be methodologically superior if multiple methods and multiple sources of data can be employed in future studies. Second, it is obvious that without longitudinal data, the causal linkages between life meaning and adolescent adjustment cannot be firmly established.

Regarding Study 2, there are several contributions of the related findings. First, the findings are consistent with the existing quantitative findings (e.g., Cohen & Cohen, 1996) that money does not occupy an important position in the life goals of adolescents. In addition, the findings demystify the common belief that money occupies an important role in the life meaning of poor adolescent. Second, the findings provide some bases for the hypothesis that perceived importance of money is negatively related to adolescent adjustment. Because the relationship between money and adjustment is still not clear (Diener & Oishi, 2000), more work should be done. Finally, the findings that those in the "high-risk condition" had a stronger belief that their lives were controlled by fate reinforce the quantitative findings of Study 1 that there is a positive relationship between life meaning and adolescent adjustment.

There are two limitations intrinsic to Study 2. First, because the sample size was small, generalizability of the findings is limited. Second, because many topics were covered in the in-depth interviews, different aspects of life meaning could not be adequately explored. It would be more illuminating if different facets of life meaning, including the antecedents and consequences of life meanings, could be explored in future. Despite these limitations, the present findings are stimulating, particularly with reference to our understanding of the nature of life meanings in adolescents experiencing economic disadvantage and the linkage between life meaning and adjustment in Chinese adolescents with economic disadvantage in Hong Kong.

REFERENCES

Affleck, G., & Tennen, H. (1996). Construing benefits from adversity: Adaptational significance and dispositional underpinnings. *Journal of Personality, 64*, 899-922.

Belk, R. W. (1985). Materialism: Trait aspects of living in the material world. *Journal of Consumer Research, 12*, 265-280.

Boss, P. G. (1987). Family stress. In M.B. Sussman and S.K. Steinmetz (Eds.), *Handbook of marriage and the family (pp.695-723)*. New York: Plenum.

Chan, D. W. (1985). The Chinese version of the General Health Questionnaire: Does language make a difference? *Psychological Medicine, 15*, 147-155.

Cohen, P., & Cohen, J. (1996). *Life values and adolescent mental health*. Mahwah, NJ: Erlbaum.

Compas, B. E., Orosan, P. G., & Grant, K. E. (1993). Adolescent stress and coping: Implications for psychopathology during adolescence. *Journal of Adolescence, 16*, 331-349.

Conger, R. D., Conger, K. J., Matthews, L. S., & Elder, G. H. (1999). Pathways of economic influence on adolescent adjustment. *American Journal of Community Psychology, 27*, 519-541.

Crumbaugh, J. C. (1968). Cross-validation of purpose in life test based on Frankl's concepts. *Journal of Individual Psychology, 24*, 74-81.

Crumbaugh, J. C., & Maholick, L. T. (1964). An experimental study in existentialism: The psychometric approach to Frankl's concept of noogenic neurosis. *Journal of Clinical Psychology, 20*, 200-207.

Denzin, K., & Lincoln, Y. S. (2000). *Handbook of qualitative research*. Thousand Oaks, CA: Sage.

Diener, E. (1984). Subjective well-being. *Psychological Bulletin, 95*, 542-575.

Diener, E., Emmons, R. A., Larsen, R. J., & Griffin, S. (1985). The Satisfaction with Life Scale. *Journal of Personality Assessment, 49*, 71-75.

Diener, E., & Oishi, S. (2000). Money and happiness: Income and subjective well-being across nations. In E. Diener and E. M. Suh (Eds.), *Culture and subjective well-being (pp.185-218)*. Cambridge, Massachusetts: MIT Press.

Dulums, C. N., & Rapp-Paglicci, L. A. (2000). The prevention of mental disorders in children and adolescents: Future research and public policy recommendations. *Families in Society, 81*, 294-303.

Dyck, M. J. (1987). Assessing logotherapeutic constructs: Conceptual and psychometric status of the Purpose in Life and Seeking of Noetic Goals Tests. *Clinical Psychology Review, 7*, 439-447.

Figueira-McDonough, J. (1998). Environment and interpretation: Voices of young people in poor inner-city neighborhood. *Youth and Society, 30*, 123-163.

Folkman, S., Schaefer, C., & Lazarus, R. S. (1979). Cognitive processes as mediators of stress and coping. In V. Hamilton and J. Warburton (Eds.), *Human stress and cognition (pp.265-298)*. New York: Wiley.

Frankl, V. E. (1955). *The doctor and the soul.* New York: Knoft.

Frankl, V. E. (1958). The will to meaning. *Journal of Pastoral Care, 12*, 82-88.

Frankl, V. E. (1959). *From death-camp to existentialism.* Boston: Beacon Press.

Frankl, V. E. (1960). Beyond self-actualization and self-expression. *Journal of Existential Psychiatry, 1*, 5-20.

Frankl, V. E. (1966). Logotherapy and existential analysis: A review. *American Journal of Psychotherapy, 20*, 252-260.

Frankl, V. E. (1967). *Psychotherapy and existentialism: Selected papers on logotherapy.* New York: Simons and Schuster.

Garmezy, N. (1991). Resiliency and vulnerability to adverse developmental outcomes associated with poverty. *American Behavioral Scientist, 34*, 416-430.

Garmezy, N. (1993). Children in poverty: Resilience despite risk. *Psychiatry, 56*, 127-136.

Gilgun, J. F. (1999). Mapping resilience as process among adults with childhood adversities. In H.I. McCubbin and E.A. Thompson (Eds.), *The dynamics of resilient families (pp.41-70)*. Thousand Oaks, CA: Sage.

Goldberg, D. P. (1972). *The detection of psychiatric illness by questionnaire.* Oxford: Oxford University Press.

Greene, J. C., Caracelli, V. J., & Graham, W. F. (1989). Toward a conceptual framework for mixed-method evaluation designs. *Educational Evaluation and Policy Analysis, 11*, 255-274.

Hauser, S. T. (1999). Understanding resilient outcomes: Adolescent lives across time and generations. *Journal of Research on Adolescence, 9*, 1-24.

Jessor, R., Colby, A., & Shweder, R. A. (1996). *Ethnography and human development: Context and meaning in social inquiry.* Chicago: University of Chicago Press.

Kane, T. J. (1987). Giving back control: Long-term poverty and motivation. *Social Service Review, 61*, 405-419.

Larzelere, R. E., & Mulaik, S. A. (1977). Single-sample tests for many correlations. *Psychological Bulletin, 84*, 557-569.

Lecci, L., MacLean, M. G., & Croteau, N. (2002). Personal goals as predictors of college student drinking motives, alcohol use and related problems. *Journal of Studies in Alcohol, 63*, 620-630.

Lerner, R. M., & Galambos, N. L. (1998). Adolescent development: Challenges and opportunities for research, programs and policies. *Annual Review of Psychology, 49*, 413-446.

Luthar, S. S. (1997). Sociodemographic disadvantage and psychological adjustment: Perspectives from developmental psychopathology. In S.S. Luthar, J.A. Burack, D. Cicchetti, and J.R. Weisz (Eds.), *Developmental psychopathology (pp.459-585)*. New York: Cambridge University Press.

Miles, M. B., & Huberman, A. M. (1984). *Qualitative data analysis*. Thousand Oaks, Calif.: Sage.

Orthner, D. K. (1996). Families in poverty: Key issues for research. *Journal of Family Issues, 17*, 588-592.

Paloutzian, R. F. (1981). Purpose in life and value changes following conversion. *Journal of Personality and Social Psychology, 41*, 1153-1160.

Paloutzian, R. F., & Ellison, C. W. (1982). Loneliness, spiritual well-being and the quality of life. In L.A. Peplau and D. Perlman (Eds.), *Loneliness: A sourcebook of current theory, research and therapy (pp.224-237)*. New York: Wiley.

Patton, M.Q. (1990). *Qualitative evaluations and research methods*. Newbury Park, CA: Sage.

Pearlin, L. I., & Schooler, C. (1978). The structure of coping. *Journal of Health and Social Behavior, 22*, 337-356.

Reker, G. T., Peacock, E. J., & Wong, P. T. P. (1987). Meaning and purpose in life and well-being: A life-span perspective. *Journal of Gerontology, 42*, 44-49.

Rosenberg, M. (1979). *Conceiving the self*. New York: Basic Books.

Rutter, M. (1985). Resilience in the face of adversity: Protective factors and resistance to psychiatric disorder. *British Journal of Psychiatry, 147*, 589-611.

Rutter, M. (1987). Psychosocial resilience and protective mechanisms. *American Journal of Orthopsychiatry, 57*, 316-331.

Sadeque, M. (1986). The survival characteristics of the poor: A case study of a village in Bangladesh. *Social Development Issues, 10*, 11-27.

Sandler, I. (2001). Quality and ecology of adversity as common mechanisms of risk and resilience. *American Journal of Community Psychology, 29*, 19-61.

Shapiro, S. B. (1988). Purpose and meaning: A two-factor theory of existence. *Psychological Reports, 63*, 287-293.

Shek, D. T. L. (1989). Validity of the Chinese version of the General Health Questionnaire. *Journal of Clinical Psychology, 45*, 890-897.

Shek, D. T. L. (1992a). Meaning in life and psychological well-being: An empirical study using the Chinese version of the Purpose in Life Questionnaire. *Journal of Genetic Psychology, 153*, 185-200.

Shek, D. T. L. (1992b). "Actual-ideal" discrepancies in the representation of self and significant-others and psychological well-being in Chinese adolescents. *International Journal of Psychology, 27*, 229.

Shek, D. T. L. (1993a). Meaning in life and psychological well-being in Chinese college students. *The International Forum for Logotherapy, 16*, 35-42.

Shek, D. T. L. (1993b). The factor structure of the Chinese version of the General Health Questionnaire (GHQ-30): A confirmatory factor analysis. *Journal of Clinical Psychology, 49*, 678-684.

Shek, D. T .L. (1997). The relation of family functioning to adolescent psychological well-being, school adjustment, and problem behavior. *Journal of Genetic Psychology, 158*, 467-479.

Shek, D. T. L. (2001). Chinese adolescents and their parents' views on a happy family: Implications for family therapy. *Family Therapy, 28*, 73-103.

Shek, D. T. L. (2002). The relation of parental qualities to psychological well-being, school adjustment and problem behavior in Chinese adolescents with economic disadvantage. *American Journal of Family Therapy, 30*, 215-230.

Shek, D. T. L., & Ma, H. K. (1997). Perceptions of parental treatment styles and adolescent antisocial and prosocial behavior in a Chinese context. *Psychologia, 40*, 233-240.

Sirgy, M. J. (1998). Materialism and quality of life. *Social Indicators Research, 43*, 227-260.

Slavin, L. A., Rainer, K. L., McCreary, M. L., & Gowda, K. K. (1991). Toward a multicultural model of the stress process. *Journal of Counseling and Development, 70*, 156-163.

Smith, C., & Carlson, B. E. (June, 1997). Stress, coping and resilience in children and youth. *Social Service Review*, 231-256.

Smokowski, P. R., Reynolds, A. J., & Bezrucko, N. (1999). Resilience and protective factors in adolescence: An autobiographical perspective from disadvantaged youth. *Journal of School Psychology, 37*, 425-448.

Tashakkori, A., & Teddlie, C. (1998). *Mixed methodology: Combining qualitative and quantitative approaches*. Thousand Oaks, CA: Sage.

Taylor, S. J., & Bodgan, R. (1998). *Introduction to qualitative research methods: A guide and resource*. New York: Wiley.

Werner, E. E. (1989). High-risk children in young adulthood: A longitudinal study from birth to 32 years. *American Journal of Orthopsychiatry, 59*, 72-81.

Werner, E. E., & Smith, R. S. (1992). *Overcoming the odds: High risk children from birth to adulthood*. Ithaca, N.Y.: Cornell University Press.

Wright, N., & Larsen, V. (1993). Materialism and life satisfaction: A meta-analysis. *Journal of Consumer Satisfaction, Dissatisfaction, and Complaining Behavior, 6*, 158-165.

INDEX